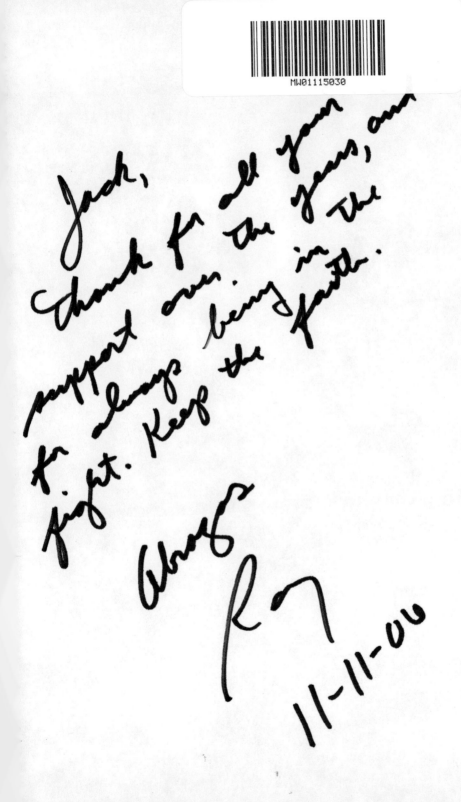

Jack,

Thank you for all your
support over the years, and
for always being in the
fight. Keep the faith.

Always

Ray

11-11-00

A LIFETIME OF DISSENT

A LIFETIME OF DISSENT

*Passionate and Powerful Articles on the
Critical Issues of our Times*

Raymond J. Gonzales, PH.D.

Library of Congress Control Number:		2006907643
ISBN 10:	Hardcover	1-4257-3133-3
	Softcover	1-4257-3132-5
ISBN 13:	Hardcover	978-1-425731-33-5
	Softcover	978-1-425731-32-8

A portion of the proceeds from this book will go to the Dolores Huerta Foundation and the Holloway-Gonzales Library.

To order additional copies of this book, contact:
Xlibris Corporation
1-888-795-4274
www.Xlibris.com
Orders@Xlibris.com
35631

CONTENTS

I. Politics and Social Movements

Summary of Articles

II. Latino Movement

Summary of Articles

III. International Issues

Summary of Articles

IV. Education Issues

Summary of Articles

For my children and grandchildren,
Paul, Emily, Austin, Alex, Gabriella.
In case anyone should ask you,
"what was your dad or granddad doing
during the wars?"

Acknowledgement

A special thanks to my daughter Emily for her assistance in editing and photo layouts and design, and to my nephew Jason Gonzales for his cover design layout. And a special thanks to Janet Banion Meulemans for her editing, advice, and continuous inspiration.

Forward

In November of 2003, Ray Gonzales was inducted to the Heritage of America's Hall of Fame, along with César Chávez and myself. On that occasion Ray took the opportunity to express his regrets at not having always enthusiastically supported the UFW efforts. He noted: "I would like to take this opportunity to publicly apologize to Dolores Huerta and the Chávez family for my failure in the early days of the union effort to fully encourage the efforts to organize and support the farmworkers of the state . . . I was naïve to think that there would not always be a need for someone to work for the rights and social justice for farmworkers . . . César understood this, but it took me awhile to understand this as well. We owe much to the vision of César and Dolores and the many who have worked tirelessly in the UFW in support of farmworkers."

Ray has more than made up for his early hesitancy. He has made up for it since those early days when we all toiled in the San Joaquin Valley for social justice for all Latinos. He published, over the years, a body of work that has addressed the many abuses suffered by the poorest and least protected members of our society. His work has addressed issues in politics, education, civil rights, foreign affairs and Latino issues. While serving as a university professor, legislator, diplomat, Peace Corps administrator, and civil rights activist, he has been in the forefront of America's battles against intolerance and injustice.

Ray was with us in Delano in May of 1993 on the occasion of César's funeral, the largest funeral for a labor leader in the history of the nation. In a touching tribute published in the *Hispanic Link News Service*, Ray commented on the fact that the Kern County Board of Supervisors had not even bothered to acknowledge César's death. Fifty thousand friends joined us in Delano on that May day, but Ray noted in his article: "Even California's Republican governor had ordered the flags on state buildings be flown at half mast. But in Kern County, home of the grapes

of wrath, and in later years *La Huelga*, the political pawns of the vested interest
of the Southern San Joaquin Valley had not even acknowledged the passing of
the great leader, while the Pope, the President, and numerous foreign leaders had
sent envoys or sent their condolences." Ray also captured in his article the words
of my eulogy when I attempted to comfort the thousands there with us: "César's
spirit is alive. It is alive. It is a million times stronger in death than in life. César,
in dying, has ensured the farmworkers' union will live on."

And indeed it has. Several years later in 1997 when Ray was teaching at
California State University, Monterey Bay, he joined us again on the occasion of
the very successful rally for the strawberry workers of Watsonville. He brought
many students from the campus to join the 30,000 who came to march with us.
Again he published a description of the march and rally in the *Hispanic Link
News Service*: "In a peaceful gathering reminiscent of the 1960s marches of
social protest and civil rights crusades, the United Farm Workers Union had
successfully organized, perhaps, the largest pro-labor rally in this country in
many years in support of the strawberry workers of California. And again,
Ray's reporting captured the spirit of the occasion: "And of course, figures who
had spoken at similar rallies in the past were as eloquent three decades later.
Jesse Jackson, 'we will not retreat because our cause is fair, our cause is just,
our cause is right.' The tireless Dolores Huerta, '*Sí se puede, César está con
nosotros.*' Arturo Rodríguez, 'we are on the march, *el pueblo es el poder*. The
people are the power."

But Ray's writing has not been limited only to farmworker issues. He has
challenged much of the negative political behavior prevalent in our country today.
He was a lonely voice in the California Legislature challenging the abuses of the
influence of lobby money as early as 1973. Susan Sward of the *Associated Press*
was one of many reporters who noticed the different approach Dr. Gonzales was
taking as an assemblyman, the first Latino elected in the San Joaquin Valley. In
an Oct. 8, 1973 syndicated article she wrote: "From the start, the 35-year-old,
Gonzales set a totally different tone for himself. The Bakersfield Democrat quickly
broke the legislators' unspoken taboo against members speaking publicly about
lobbyists and behind-the-scenes legislative dealings . . . Gonzales' behavior makes
backroom manipulators shake their heads."

Though Ray's tough lobby control legislation never made it out of the
Legislature, it was taken up by Common Cause and became a significant part
of Proposition 9, the Political Reform Initiative passed by the voters in 1974.
Ray went on to publish strong commentary on the issue in the influential
California Journal and the *Sacramento Bee*. In February of 1975, he wrote in
the Journal: "The public is concerned today about the relationship that exists
between special interests and government officials. And since the general public
and the more poorly funded grassroots consumer groups do not have the means
to carry on an extensive wining-and-dining operation of their own, they seem

to be at a disadvantage when competing for the legislator's ear." Unfortunately, the influence of lobby money is still more than significant, and especially at the national level.

Ray, in much of his writing, has also taken on what he has often referred to as "nasty politics." He was especially critical of Governor Pete Wilson who, in his 1996 presidential bid, sank as low as politicians can go. In the *Link* in March of 1996 Ray wrote: "There is no limit to how far Governor Pete Wilson will go in his quest for the Republican nomination for president. Having already championed the immigrant-bashing Proposition 187 on last year's California ballot, he most recently led the trustees of the University of California system to vote to end affirmative action programs at the nine campuses of the institution . . . It is the politicians like Wilson who seek to become leaders through demagoguery and malevolent opportunism rather than by more noble example. So much for profiles in courage." In fact, Ray saw the presidential campaign of that year, with Robert Dole as the ultimate GOP nominee, as one of the sorriest the nation has seen. "The race-bating, homophobia, xenophobia and chauvinism of some politicians and right-wing religious groups recalls the elections of one hundred years ago when the nation was being stirred-up to hate the arriving immigrants (Irish, Italians, Jews) and continue the Jim Crow laws of the South, and the denial of the vote to women."

In much of his civil rights activism, Ray has championed the cause of equality for, not only Latinos, but for Blacks, women, the physically impaired and the disadvantaged in general. In a November 28, 2004 keynote address to the Heritage of American awards banquet and carried on the *Latino Wires*, Ray noted: "Today women, minorities, immigrants refuse to be treated like second-class citizens . . . Locally, we made a little history back in 1969 when we challenged the transfer of license from Time-Life to McGraw-Hill ownership here at Channel 23. We were able to improve broadcasting, eventually at the nation level, by breaking down barriers for women and minorities . . . Today, no self-respecting local T.V. news program goes on the air without a female co-anchor."

As a Ph.D. in Latin American Studies and as a ten-year veteran of the U.S. Foreign Service of the Department of State, Dr. Gonzales has written extensively on U.S. foreign policy and its impact on Third World nations. Ray has not preached the party line, while remaining a loyal American. This ex-Marine was not hesitant to criticize the many failures of U.S. diplomacy around the world. Before joining the Foreign Service in 1980, Ray published a series of articles in the *McClatchy Bee* newspapers on issues of foreign policy. In November of 1978, while the dictator Somoza's Nicaragua was beset by civil strife, Ray wrote: "At this same time he (Anastacio Somoza) attempts to have the world believe that there is a Communist conspiracy reaching to Cuba and even Moscow behind the civil war in his country. In the past, this has been an appealing enough reason to guarantee U.S. sympathy for dictators and even intervention in Latin America."

Prophetically, in May of 1979, Ray published, in the *Sacramento Bee*, an article dealing with "The Two Big U.S.—Mexico Problems: Oil and Immigration." These issues are still with us. Ray noted: "Indeed, though the current U.S. administration (Carter) views the illegal immigration a crisis situation, the reality is that former U.S. policy is greatly responsible for the three million 'illegal' border crossing that occur each year. At one time, the migration north from Mexico was legalized under the name of the "*Bracero* Program" which was begun in 1942 primarily for the purpose of providing cheap labor in agriculture and railroad work during the war years when the U.S. was experiencing a labor shortage. The program proved so popular with U.S. agricultural interests that it was extended by Congress until 1964 when the pressure of the civil rights movement and the organization efforts of the CSO and the United Farm Workers Union caused Congress to end it." Does this sound familiar. The issue is still with us, and the current Administration would like to reactivate its own version of the *Bracero* Program.

Perhaps the most important writing Ray did on foreign affairs issues occurred during the years he served as political officer, labor attaché, and human rights officer in the Department of State at U.S. embassies abroad. While serving at the U.S. Embassy in Guatemala from 1980 to 1982, during the years of civil strife in Central America, Ray drafted a secret cable on the turmoil besetting the Church in Guatemala during those years. As it was a secret cable, Ray had to request that it be released by the Department of State under the Freedom of Information Act for publication in this book. I call the readers attention to this cable, which contains a very vivid historical analysis of the human rights abuses suffered by the clergy under the military regime of that country in the 1980s. Ray noted: "One influential general in discussion with an Embassy official echoed the attitude of President Lucas Garcia—'They had better stick to their soul-saving or we'll take care of them.' And it appears that they have, since the latest killing of a Spanish priest in El Quiche province on February 16 (1981), was attributed to the military (Guat. 1072). This could have been a symbolic warning, since there is no evidence that the priest was engaged in political activity." In a very poignant memoir, Ray recounts "The Death of Father Francisco" (Stanley Rother), a friend and American missionary assassinated in the volcano region of Guatemala by suspected right wing-government assassins. Ray negotiated the burial of Father Francisco's heart in his parish as his Mayan parishioners were refusing to let his body be taken out of the country for burial in Oklahoma. Ray's human rights reporting in 1982 resulted in Guatemala being declared, "the grossest violator of human rights in the Western Hemisphere," in the annual World Human Rights Report issued by the Department of State.

Ray also sent a significant dissent channel cable from U.S. Embassy, Barbados in which he criticized U.S. policy in Central America in the 1980s. "It should be clear to us by now that we have been part of the problem in Latin America not part of the solution. The area has been in our sphere of influence for over two hundred years. The Soviets just arrived in the 1950s. We must drastically change our perspective on Latin America if, in our own national security interest, we wish to keep these countries from falling into the Soviet/Cuban camp. We should recall here the words of General Smedly Butler, the venerable Commandant of the Marine Corps in the early years of the 20th Century, who noted in his memoirs that he had come to the conclusion after fifty years of service, that he had been nothing more than the policeman in the world for Wall Street interests." The dissent channel message system was instituted in the Department of State in the1970s so that a foreign service officer could officially dissent from U.S. policy. During 1982 there were only six dissent channel messages sent by officers from the 150 U.S. embassies around the world. Dr. Gonzales sent half of them himself from Guatemala.

Perhaps one of Ray's most significant contributions in this text is his commentary on the emerging Latino population of the country. Several of the articles in this section appeared in the *Latino Encyclopedia* and the *70s Almanac*. Of the Chicano movement, he wrote that Chicano high school and college students were courageous in their efforts to improve their own education in the 60s and early 70s: "What was to follow was a decade that would see an expansion of the Chicano's role in American society. A focus of the Chicano movement took place on college campuses with more than 50 institutions, not all of them in the Southwest, beginning Chicano/Mexican-American studies departments and initiating the celebration of *Cinco de Mayo* as a national cultural event. High schools and grade schools too were beginning to reflect more realistic curricula. Educational institutions were prodded into action by the U.S. Supreme Court's 1974 Lau v. Nichols case that mandated the establishment of bilingual education in the land. Both the introduction of Chicano studies and bilingual education resulted in a doubling of college attendance by Chicanos."

Ray also wrote extensively about the growth of the Latino population. In a December 2, 1979 article in the *Sacramento Bee*, he anticipated the phenomenal growth of the Latino community in this country. "These predictions of the growth of the Hispanic community in the nation—and most specifically in California—will have enormous effects in the 1980s and beyond. This accelerated population increase among Hispanics will result in significant movement in economic development, education, and political participation of Hispanic Americans as well." Ray has also presented much commentary on the many issues affecting Latinos in the country such as "the English Only movement," bilingual education, the immigrant issue, the effects of globalization and multiculturalism on our workforce and society in general.

Finally, let me say a word about one of the issues the Ray raises in this text, and that is that Latinos in this country, as the largest cultural group in the land, numbering well over 40 million, do not receive the attention or respect that they should as the key players that they are in the social, economic and cultural life of the country. In an article that appeared in the *Latino Journal* in October of 1996, "Latinos and the Rodney Dangerfield Syndrome," Ray noted that: "Latinos, as a group in this country, like the Dangerfield character, seem to suffer from perpetual disrespect. Presidential candidate Pat Buchanan vented his disrespect on national news referring to "José" whenever he made disparaging remarks about immigrants from the south coming into the U.S." Ray also noted that, "as a group, Latinos seem to be considered either intellectually shallow or possessed only of Latinomindedness, as if we had no knowledge or interest in other topics of concern to America. It is as if there are no Latinos to be found in this country who can make relevant comments on the issues of the day . . . Surely, a "Jose" can be found somewhere in these United States with greater knowledge and more honor and civility than a Pat Buchanan, or convicted felons Ollie North or Gordon Liddy, who make millions of dollars spouting their venom over the airwaves."

Ray's well founded concern is that the national electronic media, especially on the news-talk programs such as NBC's *Meet the Press*, CBS's *Face the Nation*, ABC's *This Week* and the CNN and FOX programs fail to have any Latinos as regular commentators, suggesting that there are no Latinos in the country able to discuss the many issues of national concern, such as the war in Iraq, the minimum wage dispute, the Bush abuse of the constitution, and the like. Ray concludes that there seems to be a "Tortilla Ceiling" hampering Latinos in broadcast commentary, and he suggest that Latinos themselves comment more frequently on non-Latino issues of importance to the country.

In a *Lifetime of Dissent*, Ray has made it clear that we, as Latinas and Latinos, have much to say about such issues as the impact of globalization, NAFTA and CAFTA on American labor, the immerging role of women in politics and the economy, on hate crimes and bigotry, on the shortcomings of U.S. foreign policy, the War in Iraq, and much more. Clearly, it is time for Latinas and Latinos to fully participate in, and comment on, the major issues facing the American public.

Sí se puede,

Dolores Huerta

Dolores Huerta, Co-founder of the UFW with Ray Gonzales

Prologue

The Articles in Lifetime of Dissent

I began my professional career teaching at Bakersfield Community College in 1965. Bakersfield, California was the city I was born and raised in, and after an education that took me to a seminary in Ann Arbor, Michigan, university studies in Barcelona, Spain, San Francisco, and Mexico City, I returned to the place of my birth to begin 40 years as a public servant.

This collection of writings, which I call *A Lifetime of Dissent,* reflects my struggle in print against the social and cultural injustices I have seen, both up close and from a distance in my lifetime, in my own country and around the world.

I have never been one to stand on the sidelines. In my own lifetime I have participated in the civil rights movements of the 60s and 70s, the farm labor struggle, which continues in the San Joaquin Valley and other parts of the country today, and the political emergence of the Latino in the political life of California. I worked in the fields of the Southern San Joaquin Valley as a young man, and later went on to serve as the first Latino elected to the California State Legislature in 1972 from this valley, an area larger than England.

As an educator in this same valley, I was the first local Ph.D. Latino to teach at the community college and subsequently, the new state university in my hometown. As a public servant, I also spent years as a California State Administrator, as a U.S. Foreign Service officer with service in Guatemala, Barbados, Brussels, and Washington, D.C. I also served as Director of Minority Recruitment for the Peace Corps, and as a lecturer and columnist.

The articles contained in this collection reflect my personal opinions, mostly dissenting views, based on academic research and practical experience on the many issues that have troubled our nation during my professional life—from César Chávez' farm labor movement to my opposition to the War in Iraq. I have commented on the emergence of the Latino community from Sleeping Giant to the dynamic force for change that it is today.

My 1971 Doctoral Dissertation in Latin American Studies from USC was focused on the phenomenon of Latin American dictatorship over the years as portrayed by various Latin writers. This background as well as my experience as a political officer in the diplomatic service of the United States led me to write, frequently, about the successes and failures, mostly failures, of U.S. Foreign policy in Latin America and Third World countries.

Also, as an educator, I have written on controversial topics such as bilingual education, school integration and funding, and the labor movement in education. Likewise, I have often focused on such Latino cultural issues as Cinco de Mayo, Hispanic Heritage Month, the impact of Spanish/Mexican influence on the culture of the American West. I have written extensively on multiculturalism and the emergence and significance of the Latino culture in America, now that Latinos have become the largest minority group in the U.S.

I have written early and often on the emergence of Chicanos, now Latinos, on the political life of the country. From the early 70s when I served as one of five Latino members in the 140 member California state legislature, to today when the last three Speakers of the California Assembly have been Latinos and the City of Los Angles, the second largest city in the nation, now boasts a Latino mayor. I have traced the emergence of Latinos as a political force in rural areas as well as major cities in the country.

Most of my writings have appeared in publications of mass circulation rather than scholarly learned journals. This has been by choice, as I have always attempted to speak to the average citizen rather than the collection of educators who generally read the academic journals.

I have appreciated over the years the McClatchy newspaper chain, (*Sacramento, Fresno, Modesto Bees*) and my hometown papers the *Bakersfield California* and the *Mexicalo* that often ran my articles. I have also been a frequent contributor to the *Hispanic Link News Service, Latino Vote and Latino Political Wires*. I especially appreciate the *California Journal* and Editor Ed Salzman who, in the 70s, first ran a series of my articles on Chicano politics. I also published during that era in *Nuestro, Somos, Caminos, Hispanic Business*, publications which were pioneers among Latino magazines in the 1970s.

Also included here are several SECRET cables that I sent from various U.S. embassies while I served as a diplomat from 1980 to 1990. I was successful in obtaining declassified copies of these cables through the Freedom of Information Act from the Department of State. Like much of my writing, these cables were dissent channel messages sent in opposition to what I considered erroneous U.S. policy in Latin America.

The reader may note some repetition of ideas and wording in the various articles. This has been intentional as I have found as a writer, that once having made a strong argument in dissent or in explanation, and having coined a strong, forceful phrase, it is perfectly reasonable to repeat the argument or phrase, as repetition often makes the point.

It is my hope that this collection of articles that spans some forty years, and often produced in the heat of America's social and political battles, may serve as a stimulus to young Americans of all social and racial backgrounds, who should be constantly vigilant in the defense of justice and civil and political rights in our Nation. It is my deepest belief, that whenever there is injustice and intolerance in our land, it should be the obligation of our citizens to **dissent, dissent, dissent.**

R.G.

Introduction

On Induction to the Heritage of America Hall of Fame
Latino Political Wires, **Nov. 21, 2003**

I would like to thank Dr. Jess Nieto and the committee members of *Heritage of America* for this great honor, especially by putting me in the company of such outstanding figures in the Latino Community who are honored here today. I am humbled by being inducted at the same time that Cesar Chavez, Dolores Huerta, Ventura Cuen, and Tomás Arciniega are being inducted. I am also pleased to be sharing this occasion with my son Paul and daughter Emily and all my family that are here with me on this day. I would like to take this opportunity to publicly apologize to Dolores Huerta and the Chávez family for my failure in the early days of the union effort to fully encourage the efforts to organize and support the farm workers of the state. When I began teaching at Bakersfield College in 1965, I had the notion that we should be getting workers out of the fields and into school. I was naive to think that there would not always be a need for someone to work for rights and social justice for farmworkers. I was naive to think that there would not always be a need in California agriculture for laborers. César understood this but it took me awhile to understand this as well. We owe much to the vision of César and Dolores and the many who have worked tirelessly in the UFW in support of farmworkers.

As I think about our present induction to this Heritage of America Hall of Fame, I am happy to say that I look back on my own life, as a lifetime of dissent. I recall the many instances where I have had to stand and dissent from the popular thought or the prevailing opinion. I recall my arrival at Bakersfield

College back in 1965. I recall that I was the only Latino faculty member among a faculty of 200.

I recall that for the five years I was there I continued to be the only Latino, along with one African American and one Asian American. Upon my departure from B. C., I submitted a resolution to the Academic Senate asking that they demand that ten minority faculty be hired for the following year. With their support and the energy of student groups, including returning Viet Nam veteran students, the Administration agreed to the demand and 10 minority faculty were hired for the following year. This group included Jess Nieto and Jessie Bradford among others. Things have never been the same at Bakersfield College, which now has a Latina as college president.

I recall also dissenting from the prevailing attitude in the 60s that suggested that there was not a single qualified Latino grade school principal to be found for any of the heavily Latino grade schools in East Bakersfield. As an officer in the Association of Mexican American Educators, I lead parents and students to picket the City School Board meetings until the Board agreed to hire the first Latino principal at Mt. Vernon school. Things have never been the same as there are now numerous Latino and Latina principals in the city school district, as well as scores of teachers.

I recall, also in the late 60s, that as President of the Kern Council for Civic Unity, along with Charles Siplin, Fleming Atha, Jack Brigham and others we lead the fight in challenging the transfer of FCC license from Time/Life to McGraw-Hill broadcasting at the local NBC affiliate. We challenged license renewals at all local television and radio stations demanding that women and minorities be put in front of the camera and on the air. Louie Vega, who is now a judge in our court system, was hired as the first Latino reporter at channel 23 as a recently returned Viet Nam veteran. I recall a local station manager telling me then that women would never make it in news broadcasting because their voices were too high. The public demanded a baritone voice, according to him. But things have never been the same as we see women as co-anchors on nearly every local news program in the nation.

I recall going against the prevailing attitude that "a portly Ph.D.", liberal Latino with a mustache could never get elected to a legislative office in Kern County. With a twenty thousand dollar, grassroots campaign, and the support of teachers and students at both the colleges in the city where I had taught, the support of the UFW and other labor organizations, and even taking the unpopular position on a farm labor initiative, a death penalty initiative, a fair housing initiative, we nevertheless won election to the California State Assembly. Against the prevailing political practice, I returned checks I received after my election from corporations and lobbyists, and carried significant campaign reform legislation, which created the Fair Political Practices Commission and opened all legislative Conference Committees to the public. And against the prevailing attitudes, I voted against a death penalty bill that was blatantly unconstitutional and which in its first challenge was also declared unconstitutional by the California Supreme Court. Justice Cruz Reynoso, Chief Justice Rose Byrd of the California Supreme Court, and I, all lost our positions because of our votes on that unconstitutional law.

And in later years, as a foreign service officer stationed in Guatemala and the Caribbean, I often dissented from U.S. policy in Central America in the 80s, and on the basis of my human rights reports, Guatemala was declared the grossest violator of human rights in the Western Hemisphere in the early 80s. I went on to send numerous dissent messages to the Secretary of State and to President Reagan's National Security Council, opposing U.S. policy in Central America and the Iran/Contra scandal that I was all too familiar with.

After returning to Kern County I attempted to carry the banner for the Democratic Party in the senate race against the reactionary Don Rogers, but the gerrymandered district in which I ran, which was the size of Massachusetts, Connecticut and Rode Island combined was just too large for a grassroots campaign like mine.

After the 1990 census, as Chairman of the Kern County Latino Redistricting Committee, we attempted to design legislative and Congressional districts that would reflect the community of interest of voters rather than the protection of incumbents. With the energetic assistance of Steve and Art Arvizu, Jess Nieto, Lou Gomez, Robert Tafoya, Rosalio Bañales, Esther Torres and many others, Steve Arvizu and I successfully testified before the California Supreme Court, which accepted our recommendations, citing the reasonableness of Latino Redistricting Committee's design.

As a result, the 5th Supervisorial District, an assembly and a senate district, and a congressional district in the Southern San Joaquin Valley were drawn by the court with heavy Latino registration. Things will never be the same as Pete Parra, Nicole Parra and Dean Florez serve in these seats today.

While I have cited many instances of my dissent from the prevailing attitudes of the so-called establishment, I don't want to leave anyone with the impression that I am a totally negative character that always finds something to disagree with. I would like to think that I have devoted much of my life to challenging issues of disparate treatment of Latinos and other minorities, and all other deserving citizens seeking justice when I have felt the playing field was perpetually uneven. I would like to think, nevertheless, that like Hubert Humphrey in another age, I am a happy warrior, that I do have a positive view of life and of the world. I do see great achievements by Latinos all over this land and here in Kern County.

As we have reached critical mass with respect to our numbers here in Kern County, we have now seen a Latina president of the community college here, and a Latino as longtime president of the state university in this valley. We have come a long way from the days when I was the only Bakersfield Latino hired at either one of those colleges.

From the days in my lifetime when we had not one physician, not one lawyer, not one CEO of Latino background in the city, we now see lawyers, doctors and judges, and Latino and Latina principals, administrators and classroom teachers all over the county. Now, as Latino children make up the majority of the state's population under the age of 18, we have a responsibility to be leaders in our communities for all of our citizens, not just our own kind. Let us not forget the unfairness with which we might have been treated in the past and resolve that we will be more tolerant and more understanding of diversity than others have been towards us in another age.

I like to think that I have contributed a little to this effort. I like to think that I have tried to live by that motto of John and Robert Kennedy, "to dream of things that never were, and ask why not." I believe in the basic goodness of humankind, and the innate desire of all people to do good. And I am confident that out there among the youth of our nation there are planted the seeds of great leaders as we have known before, the John and Robert Kennedys, the Thomas Paines and Thomas Jeffersons, the Franklin Roosevelts, the Martin Luther Kings, and the César Chávezes, and the good teachers, and mothers and fathers, who have molded young minds and set them on the right course. Ultimately, I am not an angry old man. I take great joy in the promise of our youth and of our nation.

I

Politics and Social Movements

Summary of Articles

T he first section of A Lifetime of Dissent presents political writings, the first of which, "The Price of a Lawmaker's Ear" appeared in the California Journal in February of 1975. The last one, written on the occasion of Antonio Villaraigosa's mayoral victory in Los Angeles was carried by the Hispanic Link News Service in May of 2005. In between these two articles, I wrote extensively of the emerging political participation of Mexican Americans (Chicano/Latinos) in the politics of California and the Southwest. The first article presented in this section, "California's Latinos: Emerging Political Power," was written for a text on the Latino participation in the United States. In my view, it is one of the most comprehensive reviews of Latino politics in California written up to the time of its writing in September of 1997. While the evolution of Latino political participation was by no means rapid or monumental in its early stages in California, it has been solid and continuous since the day in 1973 when Richard Alatorre, Joe Montoya and I joined the only two Latino legislators, Alex Garcia and Peter Chacón, in the California Legislature. The progress of Latino and Latina politicians in California and the Southwest is now receiving national attention. Today there are 27 members in the California Senate and Assembly. The last three Speakers of the California Assembly, Bustamante, Villaraigosa, and Nuñez have been Latinos, due to the fact that Lainos/as are the single largest caucus in the Assembly Democratic wing, which as the majority, elects the Speaker. Additionally, term limits, enacted by Initiative in 1990 has had much to do with the success of women and Latinos/as winning seats in the California Legislature. Many of the other articles in this section deal with such issues as the influence of money in politics, the role of race and ethnicity in politics and other controversial issues such as term limits, redistricting, and bilingual ballots. As in most of my writing, I have often taken the less than popular view of an issue.

California Latinos:
The Emerging Political Power

Latino Politics Collection, **Sept. 1997**

In 1970 there were two Latinos among the 140 members of the California Legislature, Alex Garcia of East Los Angeles and Peter Chacon of San Diego. Today there are 18, and one of them, Cruz Bustamante, is Speaker of the 80 member Assembly, arguably the second most powerful political position in California. Also in 1970, there was only one California Latino Congressman, Ed Roybal of Los Angeles. Today there are five members of the House of Representatives from the state. What has happened to bring about this dramatic and uncharacteristic political participation of the state's burgeoning Latino population, estimated at 11 million today and expected to be 50% of the state's population by the year 2040?[1] What has occurred in the social dynamics of the state to bring this often-maligned and frequently-labeled "sleeping giant" to its feet?

One answer is simple—*anger*. Motivated by the passage of the perceived anti-immigrant Proposition 187 in 1994 and the appearance of the anti-affirmative action Proposition 209 on the 1996 general election ballot, Latinos have become citizens in record numbers, registered to vote as never before, and voted in an unprecedented turnout in the November 1996 elections. Reflecting on this Latino turn-out, Antonio Gonzales, president of the Southwest Voter Registration Education Project noted: "People are becoming citizens. They feel like they have been treated with disrespect. They want to participate."[2] Another Latino political observer in California, Harry Pachon, president of Thomas River Policy Institute agreed with Gonzales' assessment. He related that exit polls conducted by the Institute showed that the surge in the Latino vote in the election was the result of the participation of new Latino voters, most of them recent citizens eager to cast their ballot for the first time and many of them energized by opposition to Proposition 187. "I think what is catching people by surprise is that it's having such a quick impact," Pachon stated. "People didn't expect it to be translated into voting power so quickly. But if anti-immigrant bashing and rhetoric continues, you naturally are going to see the largest minority community [in the state] running out to the polls in self-defense," Pachon added.[3]

A History of Non-Participation

The 1990s will be seen as the decade of Latino political emergence in California and to some extent the nation. The role Latinos will play in the evolving politics of the 21st Century will depend on the success or failure of the new batch of elected Latino officials and community leaders who have cut their political teeth in the last decade of the 20th Century. Clearly in California the demographics would suggest that Latinos as a political force are here to stay, but changing demographics are not the whole picture. Such things as education, employment opportunities, increased spending power, and galvanizing issues such as Prpo. 187 will all tend to play a part in the development of the political sophistication of Latinos in the state. Numbers in themselves are not the only factor. The Jewish community, for example, while it constitutes less than three percent of the population in California can point to the fact that the two United States senators for the state, Fienstien and Boxer, are Jewish; and while Latinos, African Americans and Asians each significantly outnumber Jews in the state, these groups have fewer members of the state's congressional delegation respectively than does the Jewish community.

To understand the political hurdles Latinos have had to overcome, one must go back a few years to gain perspective. Just two days after the statewide gubernatorial elections in 1974 the Los Angeles Times published an article by G. Gutierrez and Cesar Sereseres, entitled "*Nada por Nada*, Nothing for Nothing, the Chicano Political Trap" which highlighted the dearth of Latino involvement in the state's political life.[4] (For purposes of this article one should assume that Chicano today has generally been replaced by the much broader term Latino which includes more than just the Mexican-American Latinos or Chicanos.) The thesis of the Gutierrez/Sereseres essay on the results of the Jerry Brown—Huston Flournoy gubernatorial contest of that year, in essence, concluded that most successful statewide candidates were under no obligation to consider the interest of Chicanos in California because Chicanos possessed "a self-defeating tradition of not voting." The authors could point to three areas of political support in which the Chicano community did not produce.

Financial support. Because the Latino community and its organizations lacked real economic power, a candidate could expect little financial support from this community. Additionally, the notion of political contributions was not something well understood or practiced in the Latino community, even for its own Latino candidates.

Endorsements. Traditionally, visible spokesmen for Latinos were minor power brokers primarily interested in landing jobs in new administrations. No Latino had ever been elected to statewide office, thus local endorsements, which were all that were available, had little impact on a statewide race. Latino political organizations in California such as MAPA (The Mexican American Political Association) tended to be viewed as ineffective, disorganized, and untalented.

Voting. Although Latinos constituted 18 to 20 percent of the state's population in 1974, they produced less than 5 percent of the vote in most general elections.[5]

Behind the Apathy

What had caused this apparent apathy that resulted in a less than five percent voter-turnout over the years? Historically, Latinos are recent arrivals to California, and although some can trace their heritage back to the area's long and rich Hispanic past, most, at the time of the 1974 election, were 20th century arrivals from Mexico. In 1909, the year before the Mexican Revolution began, there were some 4,000 Mexican immigrants that came to the United States. By 1916, in the peak years of fighting during the revolution, there were nearly 100,000 immigrants crossing the border annually from Mexico. Later, in the years of the Bracero Program begun during the Second World War, an additional 200,000 braceros a year crossed the border, with about an equal number of illegal entrants. Many of these Mexicans married and remained in the U.S. Additionally, perhaps 20 percent of California's Latino population in those years, had migrated from Texas.[6]

How did this immigration trend affect voting patterns in California? First, we must understand that there has been little democratic political tradition in Mexico. Since the Revolution of 1910 the country has been run under a one-party system (at least until the Mexican elections of 1997 when the PRI (*Partido Revolucinario Institutional*) party lost its control of the congress. The secret ballot has been viewed pretty much as a farce in Mexico during most of this century. This background has led Mexican immigrants to the U.S. to look with skepticism upon the political process in this country. Another factor has been the fact that Mexican Americans comprised the bulk of the migratory labor force in the state, making residency requirements for voting a problem. Add to this the language barriers maintained for many years in the voting process in the U.S. and there was little wonder that the Latino voter of the past appeared to be peculiarly apathetic.

Anglo politicians and the political parties took advantage of this situation and did little to bring Latino's into the political process.

In terms of supplying financial support to candidates in the past, the Latino community's inability to deliver funds was a product of both tradition and poverty. There had never been a tradition of political giving among the community, as there had been in the Jewish community, or even to a degree in the African American community. The lack of a significant professional class also guaranteed that there were few members of the Latino community economically able to contribute politically. In 1968, there were only 70 Mexican Americans enrolled among UCLA's 25,000 students, in a city of more than a million Latinos in those days.[7] As a result, it is not difficult to imagine a paucity of professionals among Latinos in urban areas, much less in rural areas like the vast San Joaquin Valley were large numbers of Latinos were found. As recently as 1970, in a community such as Bakersfield with a population of 120,000 in that year, there was not one Latino medical doctor nor lawyer and there was only one Latino among the 200 member faculty at the community college.[8] In the business community, the situation was no better. Few were the number of Latino-owned businesses with the sophistication to see political contributions as being good for business. In those days, most Latinos were found in agricultural work, railroading, and domestic or menial services—not areas likely to generate potent political contributions from the Latino community.

Finally, in the past, there had been no political "heavies" in the Latino community to whom the candidates or political parties could look to for endorsements or support. The political fratricide, suspicion and betrayal that often emerged in the Latino community did not escape the notice of Anglo politicians. At best, one hoped to avoid conflict among divergent Latino groups, but rarely was a candidate obliged to seek the support of whatever passed for Latino leadership. And at the campaign level, the training ground for future politicians, Latino political staffers were next to invisible. In 1972, with the Democrats in control of both houses of the legislature, there was not one Latino committee or political consultant among the one hundred-plus consultants that served at the pleasure of Democratic legislative leadership.[9]

The Parties' Failures

Immigration history in the country also sheds some light on the slow political evolution of Latinos over the years. Latinos arriving in California in the 20th century were not greeted in the same manner as the Irish or other European immigrants that arrived on the country's eastern shores in the last century. The Democratic party in those days had been viewed by new arrivals as a home for their political protection and aspirations. New York's Tammny Hall evolved from a mere fraternal organization that aided Irish immigrants in the 1790s to an awesome political machine in the 1800s that virtually controlled New York politics. Italians, Poles, Jews and Slovaks were added to the Democratic party machines throughout the industrial northeast as the new immigrants became the backbone of the industrial revolution and the rank and file of the emerging labor unions. By the early 1900s the Democratic party was seen as the party of the working class while the "Grand Old Party" (GOP), in characteristic immigrant-bashing rhetoric, pushed legislation to curb immigration.[10]

> Aristocratic Anglo-Saxon intellectuals in northeastern states alleged that the new immigration was bringing in inferior blood stock that would dilute and debase the racial purity of predominantly Anglo-Saxon American nation. Republican Senator Henry Cabot Lodge of Massachusetts was the leading spokesman for this point of view . . . In 1888 he began calling for the end of immigration. In the 1890s his ideas spread. The issue around which he and other nativists gathered their forces was the establishment of a literacy test for all immigrants [in English], for it would strike most severely at the new immigration.[11]

In contrast to the welcome the Democratic Party had extended to other immigrants for most of the 20th century, Latinos had not been accorded the same welcome. They were not considered a relevant part of the Democratic party machinery, much less the Republican party structure. In California, liberal Democratic party leaders made it a practice of carving-up Latino barrios to benefit white or even black politicians at the expense of the Latino community. The civil rights movement of the 50s and 60s bonded white liberals and blacks all across the nation. In California the bonding was especially effective. As a result, the West Los Angeles Jewish community was instrumental in the election of Wilson Riles, the first black statewide official in 1968 as Superintendent of Public Instruction for the state.

Riles had been a lower-level and almost invisible deputy superintendent of public instruction in Sacramento before the election. One of his opponents in the primary that year was Dr. Julian Nava, Latino president of the Los Angeles Unified School District, author and professor at Cal State Northridge. The Jewish community, led by Marian Joseph, a state school official in Sacramento, hand-picked Riles to run against the incumbent, conservative Superintendent Max Rafferty. Westside Jewish money and political expertise got behind Riles and the rest was history. Dr. Nava, who had paid his dues in California politics and was President of the board of the second largest school district in the nation, was humiliated at the polls and the bitterness among Latinos, especially those in the Los Angles community who believed Nava had earned the right to be the Democratic candidate in the non-partisan race, took many years to dissipate. (Dr. Nava later was named U.S. Ambassador to Mexico by President Jimmy Carter.)

Additionally, the local politics of Los Angeles county, home to 32% of the states population and 46% of the Latino population, has in the past pitted the interest of Latinos against the combined interest of the Jewish/Black coalition. As political writer Sherry Babitch Jaffe points out, "the black-Jewish coalition that once dominated LA politics was grounded in the civil rights movement; it had an ideological ballast." The election of LA's first black mayor in 1973 was a product of this coalition. Tom Bradley's victory required "a cross-racial, citywide coalition; and here, he was the beneficiary of support not only from blacks [who constituted 26 percent of LA's electorate though only 18 of its population] but from Jews . . . He was the beneficiary of a black-Jewish alliance that had come together for civil rights in the 10 years preceding his victory."[12]

Latinos were the political losers during these years in other ways as well. Of major significance to Latinos was the lose of potential political clout they suffered as a result of redistricting for local, legislative, and congressional districts after each 10-year census. The Westside Jewish political machine has been instrumental since the early 70s in determining political districts in the area. The results of this computerized expertise has produced Jewish legislative, congressional, and local government districts far in excess of Jewish population figures and usually at the expense of Latino neighborhoods. Blacks too, becaise pf Jewish sympathies, benefited from the talents of the Westside until the new wave of Latino and Asian immigration in the 80s has made it impossible to overlook the growing numbers.

With the increase in population figures, Latinos began to use the judicial system to rectify a historical pattern of gerrymandering of political districts at their expense. This has occurred throughout the state and most significantly in Los Angeles county, which is the most populous county in the nation, bigger than 42 states. In 1990 Latinos constituted a third of the 9 million plus inhabitants of LA county, yet they had not had a county supervisor of Latino decent since the *Californio* days of 1872.[13] But in 1990 MALDEF (The Mexican American Legal Defense and Education Fund) and other Latino organizations filed suit alleging political discrimination against Latinos in the drawing of supervisorial districts in the county. In fact, the Democratic Party establishment of the county had traditionally carved-up the barrio sections of the county to benefit white incumbent supervisors. But in a special election held in 1991 as a result of court-ordered redistricting, the only two significant candidates to run in the new district were state senator Art Torres and former assemblywoman Gloria Molina, with Molina becoming the first Latina and the first woman elected to the LA county board of supervisors.

In other parts of the state, legal action by Latino groups was also producing changes in political boundaries, which helped rectify some of the discriminatory gerrymandering usually perpetrated by white Democratic party leaders at the expense of the Latino community. It was accepted by these party leaders that the "loath-to-vote Latinos" could be overlooked when district boundaries were being drawn both at the local and statewide levels. The absence of significant numbers of Latinos in the legislature and the mediocrity and self-interest of most of those who served in the 70s and 80s resulted in little advancement of Latinos on the political scene in those days. The most significant actions did not come about because of Chicano legislators but rather as result of the activity of Latino legal groups, who were challenging boundaries and other voting rights violations on the basis of the 1965 Voting Rights Act.

Most significant in this regard were law suits won by attorney Joaquin Avila of the San Jose area who single-handedly won a number of precedent-setting cases throughout California. Avila's litigation has been significant also because it has had major impact at the local levels, in small jurisdictions like school districts, special districts and city councils which have traditionally been the training camps for higher legislative offices. While most of these cases have not had the news appeal of the LA county supervisorial board case, the impact at the grass-roots level has, nevertheless, been significant.

A Critical Mass Emerges

What is different about the political environment of California in the 1990s that did not exist in the four decades preceding this period? And further, what is it that now has political analysts and pundits making such comments as "the sleeping giant awakes . . . the Latino political slumber is over . . . time at last to slay a giant cliché . . ."? The differences are many and complex. Obviously, one of the most notable changes has been the Latino impact on the demographics of the state as a result of Latino immigration. "Since the early 1980s, California has been on the receiving end of an immigrant wave that demographers have compared with two other historic spurts of migration to the United States: the great surge of famine-induced Irish migration in the late 19th century, and the subsequent arrival of southern and eastern Europeans—a diverse population of Jews, Italians, Lithuanians and more—from the turn of the century until the 1920s."[14]

The third and present immigrant wave is coming, not from Europe but from Pacific Rim countries, the Philippines, Southeast Asia, Central and South America, and Mexico. This wave began after the 1965 immigration law removed national quota restrictions, and opened the door to millions of immigrants of color from the Third World.[15] Mexicans constituted 43 percent of the new immigrants to California with Central and South Americans becoming an ever-increasing percentage. More recently, during the 1980s, as a result of the 1986 Immigration Reform and Control Act over 8.6 million immigrants had arrived in the U.S. according to the U.S. Census Bureau. In California alone, as a result of the amnesty granted under the act, over 1.6 million illegal immigrants became eligible for legal, permanent residency.[16]

Beyond just the sheer numbers of recent Latino immigrants, the nature of these immigrants to California is a significant factor. Many of these immigrants, in large numbers, fled Central America during the 1980s, a time of great turmoil in that region. Guatemalans, Salvadorans and Nicaraguans especially, fled countries where human rights and political rights violations were the governmental policy of the day. Today, these new residents tend to have a very healthy respect for the democratic process that was denied them in their countries of origin. They are hardworking, aggressive and more politicized than the millions of farm laborers that came before them during the 50s, 60s, and 70s, especially those who came from Mexico. A large majority of these new immigrants choose to work in the service area rather than farm labor, and have joined unions such as SEIU (Service Employees International Union) and other labor groups that put a premium on political participation. With the possible exception of César Chávez' efforts with the United Farm Workers Union, most Latino immigrants of the past involved in farm labor tended to live on the margins of the political life of the country. Even the Democratic-sponsored Wagnor Act, which gave collective bargaining rights to American workers in 1935, failed to include agricultural workers, thus excluding them from the opportunity to become part of organized labor's political apparatus.[17] Today, in contrast, Latinos make up 45% of the membership of labor unions in Los Angeles county.

The close relationship between organized labor and the Democratic Party over the years has been no secret. In many instances, the marriage of the unions and the Party produced the victory of white Democratic congressmen, state legislators, and local officials in the urban areas across the country and in California. Blacks as well benefited from labor's support which often had Jewish leadership which was traditionally sympathetic to the black civil rights movement. Latinos, however, in urban areas, were expected to vote the ticket, but were seldom invited on to the ticket. Even the United Farm Workers Union which was heavily influenced by Jewish leadership such as, then general counsel, Jerry Cohen and organizer Marshal Gantz, often became more involved in the campaigns of non-Latino, liberal Democrats than in support of Latino candidates. The UFW's approach was often one of pragmatic politics, "support those who were likely to get elected and advance the farmworkers issues rather than waste time on long-shot Latino candidates." For much of the 70s and early 80s the UFW was a key component of the Democratic Party at the national level, with its leaders in conspicuous roles at party conventions. But the union was much less significant in California Democratic politics on behalf of Latino candidates.

Demographics, Registration and Rhetoric

Clearly, the sheer growth in the Latino population of California since the early 80s has been phenomenal. Today the Latino population in the state is approaching

12 million, a 48.8% increase in this last decade. In the next fifty years this same population will experience a astronomical growth rate of 125%, reaching 31.5 million. By contrast, the present majority white, non-Latino population will grow by only 19%, from 17.1 million to 20.5 million, and cease to be the majority in the state by the year 2005. Latinos will become the plurality in the state by the year 2020 and the majority by 2040.[18] But sheer numbers are not the only changes taking place. The 1996 presidential elections showed a 20% increase in the Latino vote nationwide. Of particular importance to President Clifton's re-election efforts that year and to Congressional Democrats was the fact that these Latinos voted Democratic 80% of the time.[19]

In California the results were particularly significant. From the general elections of 1994 to the general elections of 1996 the percentage of California Latino voters had increased from 9.6% to 13% of the electorate. At the end of the 80s Latinos had been less than 8% of the state's voters. The 13% Latino turn-out in the last general election indicates that the Latino vote has increased by nearly 50% in less than a decade. And new citizens now constitute 26% of the Latino vote in the state.[20] These new voters tend to be those more politicized and active voters mentioned above.

It was perhaps these new voters who were the "angriest" Latino voters that came out in 1996 as well. George Cothran, writing for the San Francisco Weekly in an article titled "La Nueva Fuerza," shortly after the 1996 election, noted:

> "The reason for the outpouring of civic participation [of Latinos] is simple. Republicans forget one prime imperative of politics—do the math. Willfully ignorant of the growing Latino population, and trends toward increased citizenship and electoral participation, the party stuck to these anti-immigrant policies, from welfare reform in Congress that ended Medicare for legal residents, to Proposition 187, the state initiative that seeks to deny services to undocumented aliens. Instead of serving the intended goal—to increase older, Anglo voters—the proposition prompted Latinos to protect, with their votes, the toehold they have on the American dream."[22]

As white voters dropped as a percentage of the total electorate in 1996, Latinos organized themselves as never before. The "mean-spirited" Republicans had added Proposition 209 to end affirmative action to the 1996 ballot, which only added fuel to the fire. Republican presidential candidate Bob Dole even boasted with pride about running on this "wedge issue."

California state senator Richard Polanco, a key figure in the ongoing statewide Latino registration drive says, "thank you Pete Wilson for the gas we need."[23] Polanco working with organizations such as SVREP (Southwest Voter Registration and Education Project), Centro del Pueblo in San Francisco, and the Legislature's

Latino Caucus won approval in the state budget for $7.2 million to fund citizenship centers at community colleges and community-based organizations. Additionally, corporate support from such organizations as PAC Bell and GTE added to the funds available for naturalization efforts, registration, voter education, and get-out-the-vote drives. In one such project at Bakersfield College in the agriculturally rich San Joaquin Valley, 3,000 new citizens were sworn-in during a single day and were promptly registered to vote.[24] While these projects are non-partisan in nature, the Republican Party's image as being "anti-immigrant," which today can translate into anti-people of color, has pushed many new-citizen voters into the hands of the Democrats. "The Republicans never knew what hit them; they didn't think people were going to respond," senator Polanco noted. "They maintained the stereotype that we were not interested in assimilating."[25]

A Sweeping Change in Vote-Rich Los Angeles

Perhaps nowhere has the increase in Latino political participation in California been more dramatic than in last April's Los Angeles city elections. Republican mayor Richard Riordan won re-election to a second term with 61% of the vote over liberal Democrat, state senator Tom Hayden's 29%. Despite his party affiliation in this non-partisan race, Riordan won 60% of the Latino vote and 62% of the Asian vote, both groups heavy with new citizen-voters. Hayden, on the other hand, seen as a 60s liberal, got 75% of the Black vote. These results signaled what Sherry Babitch Jaffe noted as a harbinger of political doom for blacks in Los Angeles.

> Demographic arithmetic is leading to the inevitable erosion of [black] political clout as growing numbers of Mexican and Latin-American immigrants become citizens and voters. Black turnout in the April election amounted to 13 percent of all voters; that is reflective of the percentage of African-Americans in the city's population. Latinos comprise nearly 40 percent of LA's residents but have historically voted in much smaller numbers—about eight to 10 percent of the voters in a typical municipal election . . . This year, however, things changed. Latinos accounted for 15 percent of the vote in the April mayoral race—an historic high. For the first time, Latino voter participation in Los Angeles elections surpassed that of blacks. The true cost of this shift for African-Americans will be felt in the next reapportionment; they risk becoming marginalized in city politics as "black" electoral districts become increasingly "brown".[26]

Indeed, two of the three current black city councilmen, all of whom supported Hayden's loosing effort, now represent districts that have become majority Latino since they last ran for office. The political rivalry between the two groups only looks to intensify over the next few years. Latinos believe they got little from Democratic black mayor Tom Bradley during his four terms in office and are already benefiting from their support of Riordan. Professor Paul Ong who heads up the UCLA Department of Urban Planning has studied the issue of the widening divide between blacks and Latinos noting, "as young blacks and recent Latino immigrants compete for work, economic and political tensions may simmer. Latinos outnumber blacks in the city by 3 to 1. But historically, blacks have been far more politically active. On Tuesday for the first time, that appeared to change, as Latinos came to the polls in greater numbers than blacks."[27] Some political analyst call this "the pivot" when political power swung from blacks to Latinos in LA politics.

In the April election in Los Angeles, Latinos also appeared to demonstrate a high sense of civic-minded self-protection. Proposition BB, a school bond measure that sought to make available 2.5 billion dollars for repairs, construction and improvements in the LA Unified School District, received its strongest support from Latinos. According to the Rivera Center exit poll, Latinos voted an amazing 91% in support of the school bond measure.[28] Officials credit the Latino vote in providing the margin for the success of the bond measure, which was required constitutionally to pass by a difficult two-thirds vote margin. Latinos, angry already about Propositions 187 and 209, appeared to be motivated by the fact that their children made up 68% of all students in LA Unified, the second largest school district in the nation. White children constituted only 11%,[29] and the white vote over the years had voted down school bonds on a regular basis. Latino leaders in the community noted after the April election, that "the strong turnout and the success in helping win passage of Proposition BB would have a dual effect, simultaneously demonstrating the growing clout of Latinos and expanding that clout as victory reinforces the idea that participation is meaningful."[30]

Beyond Los Angeles

Los Angeles is not the only area in which dramatic Latino political participation is occurring in California. The most celebrated Latino victory in 1996 was that of neophyte Loretta Sanchez over conservative incumbent Congressman Bob Dornan in Orange County. What Republicans have failed to take notice of over the years in a political sense has been the overflow of Latinos from eastern Los Angeles into Orange County and the assimilation of new immigrants in that county as well. The city of Santa Ana, for example, is made-up of a majority of citizens who are foreign born, mostly Latinos and Asians. Republican analyst Tony Quinn has asserted that, "Republicans drove away the middle-class conservative Latino voters into transitional suburbs," especially in Republican areas of Southern California, where Anglos have begun moving out and affluent Latinos and Asians have begun moving in.[31] These new citizens are, in the case of Orange County, changing the political make-up of this once conservative sanctuary in the direction of the Democratic party.

Just north of Los Angeles in conservative Kern County in the San Joaquin Valley, two Latinos sit on the five member board of supervisors, partly as a result of the efforts of the Kern County Latino Redistricting Committee which lobbied successfully for the creation of Latino dominant districts after the 1990 census. Other Latino groups throughout the state became actively involved in coordinated redistricting strategies encouraged by the success of legal efforts such as those of voting rights attorney Joaquin Avila. The results have seen a dramatic increase in Latino representation throughout the state particularly at the local levels.

The National Association of Latino Elected Officials (NALEO) points to over 800 Latino-Latina officials serving statewide today, from school board members to state senators. This is up from 460 just ten years ago, nearly a 100% increase in a decade. What has become clear as well is that many more Latinos are getting elected outside of the East Los Angeles barrio-type constituencies. For example, Debra Ortiz was elected to the State Assembly from Sacramento in 1996 with only 11% registered Latinos in the district. Assemblyman Joe Baca, who many believe will succeed Congressman George Brown in San Bernardino, only has 28% Latinos in his district. Assembly member Denise Moreno Ducheny, Chair of the powerful Budget Committee, has less than 26% in her San Diego district. In fact, only half of the 18 Latino legislators come from districts that can be characterized as Latino. Cruz Bustamante, the Speaker of the Assembly comes from a Fresno district that has fewer than 33% registered Latino voters. Bustamante is only the second Latino elected to the legislature from the San Joaquin Valley, the first, Ray Gonzales (the author of this article) was elected in 1972 in a Kern County district that had only 8% registered Latino voters.[32]

In the more rural areas of the state where agriculture dominates the economic climate and where Latino labor has for years been the backbone of the industry, Latinos have been making great strides. In years past, and to some extent, even today, local school boards, special district boards and city councils, dominated by white officials, made it a practice of stacking the deck politically. Often, incumbent board members, rather than lose a white member on a board, would appoint a new member when a vacancy occurred, instead of holding a special election. This allowed the new member, usually a crony of the other sitting members, to run as an incumbent at the next election. This guaranteed that, most rural communities would be run by white officials, though in most cases in the agricultural areas, the majority of the population was Latino. Successful legal battles challenging at-large elections in favor of by-districts elections won by voting rights attorney Joaquin Avila have also changed the political landscape in many of these rural communities, as have Latino challenges to reapportionment boundaries, and the new-found political anger resulting from the perceived "Latino bashing" of the last few years.

In the agricultural community of Lamont in Kern County, the center of the UFW grape boycotts of the 60s and 70s, where five farmers, or their wives, or their friends used to preside over a school district that was more than 85 percent Latino, two Latinos and a Latina are now a majority of the school board. In historically significant Delano, birthplace of the United Farm Workers Union, a Latino majority now sits on the high school board. There are over 400 Latino school board members serving in the state at the elementary, secondary and community college levels, from Calexico to Oroville, from Fresno to Monterey, in the San Joaquin Valley, in the Salinas Valley, in the Sacramento Valley. And they serve as well on school boards in the large urban areas of Los Angeles, San Francisco, and San Diego counties.[33]

At the mayoral and city council levels throughout the state, representation is also seeing a significant increase. Certainly Joe Serna, as mayor of Sacramento, the state's capital, represents a significant and visible move forward with respect to political respectability for Latinos. Serna earned his political spurs in support of the United Farmworkers' efforts during the 70s, and as a political science professor at Sacramento State University, he was instrumental in bringing students and Latinos into the political process in support of Democratic legislative candidates.[34] When it was time for this former Peace Corps Volunteer to run for the Sacramento City Council, and subsequently for mayor, he could call in the IOUs. His victory in 1992 was especially significant since the City of Sacramento had less than 10% registered Latino voters.

In addition to Serna, there are 36 other Latinos or Latinas serving as mayors of cities in California. From Santa Ana to Antioch, from Pamona to Pico Rivera, Latino leadership at the city level is manifesting itself as never before. Especially significant are the inroads being made in the fastest growing part of the state, the "Inland Empire". In Riverside and San Bernardino counties, for example, Latinos are mayors in the cities of Indio, Coachella, Colton and Chino. In Los Angeles county, no fewer the 13 Latinos/as serve as mayors in such cities as Montebello, South Gate, Bell Gardens, Azusa, Monterey Park, and Irwindale.[35]

Perhaps one of the most significant developments for Latinos in the rural/agricultural regions of the state, where Latinos have traditionally been far removed from the political power structure, has been the increase of their political strength in communities where they have long been the majority of the population. In the San Joaquin Valley, cities such as Orange Cove, Mendota, Lindsay, Exeter, Arvin, McFarland, San Joaquin, and Parlier are led by Latino mayors. In Orange Cove, an early manifestation of Latino political dominance in rural communities, mayor Victor Lopez presides over a city council that also includes four Latino city council members who constitute a majority of that body. In the small agricultural community of Parlier, as well, four Latino city council members form a majority with mayor Luis Patlán. These small communities are the vanguard of what is likely to come in the political future of rural California.

This new-found political strength of the Latino population in the agricultural regions is being felt not only in the San Joaquin Valley but all across the state. In Monterey and Santa Cruz counties, and in the Salinas Valley, the richest agricultural region in the nation, Latinos, many of them former farm workers, are mayors and city council members in such cities as Soledad, Gonzales, Greenfield, Watsonville, Santa Cruz, and Salinas. The high numbers of Latinos in many of these communities have always been there. Monterey County has a Latino population of 38% today, which is expected to reach 50% within twenty years. In cities such as Salinas, King City, Soledad and Gonzales, the population is already well over 50% Latino.[36] But, in the past, what was lacking was the involvement of most of these Latinos in the political process of the community.

The difference today, in addition to recognizing their own increase in numbers, has been the angry response by Latinos to the immigrant, and by extension, "Latino-bashing" that has come from some politicians in both Sacramento and Washington, D.C. Additionally, the political groundwork done by the United Farmworkers Union over the years and the increased stability of the once, very mobile, farm labor force has begun to pay-off. The growing civic-minded-ness of this very large labor force has become ever apparent. New educational opportunities for the children of these workers are also beginning to pay dividends as many college graduates return to take up professions in their communities. This dramatic surge in the political participation by Latinos in the formally conservative rural areas of the state can have an impact on future statewide elections, which have, on occasion, been determined by the rural vote whenever the Los Angeles and Bay areas have split the vote.

A Latino Political Future

Yet Latinos have not succeeded in electing one of their group to statewide office to date (1997). More militant members of the community have, in the past, attributed this to "racism." But the political success stories among other minority groups at the statewide level refute this charge. The Asian community can point to March Fong Eu who served as Secretary of State for five terms from 1974 to 1992. Her son Matt Fong, although a member of the opposite party from his Democratic mother, presently serves as State Treasurer. S.I. Hayakawa also served as U.S. Senator in the 70s. African Americans have also had Mervyn Dymally who served as Lieutenant Governor and Wilson Riles who served four terms as Superintendent of Public Instruction, and this with a Latino population in the state four times as large as that of the Black and Asian communities.[37]

Latinos, on the other hand, have had difficulty even getting past a party primary to become part of the ticket at the statewide level. Attorney and founder of MALDEF, Mario Obledo, who was appointed by Governor Jerry Brown as the first Latino cabinet member in 1975, garnered less than 5% of the vote when he ran against Tom Bradley for the Democratic nomination for governor in 1982. Herman Sillas, long-time political activist and director of the Department of Motor Vehicles under Jerry Brown, had a similar fate when he ran for nomination as controller in the 70s. The only Latino who has won the nomination of his party for statewide office has been former state senator Art Torres, who was expected to win election as State Insurance Commissioner in 1994, but was upset by Republican Charles Quackenbush. Torres, nevertheless, continues to be a leading force within the Democratic Party as he was elected chairman of the state party after his defeat. His leadership of the party, especially the role he played in delivering the Democratic votes for Clinton's huge victory in the state in 1996, has not gone unrecognized at the state and national levels. He will likely emerge as a candidate again in the future.

Other Latino office holders in the state are poised for significant roles in the not too distant future. Congressman Xavier Becerra of Los Angeles is a member of the powerful Ways and Means Committee of the House and serves as the chairman of the Hispanic Caucus of the Congress. Representative Esteban Torres, who was appointed Ambassador to UNESCO by Jimmy Carter, and is the Dean of the California Latino Congressional delegation is always to be considered for higher office. In fact, President Clinton had tagged him to be the Secretary of Labor in his new administration, only to change his mind at the last minute in favor of Doris Herman, as a result of pressure from Jesse Jackson and the Congressional Black Caucus. A move that reminded many Latino political pundits that Southern Democratic leaders think only "Black" when they think minorities.

Another on the political radar is Cruz Bustamante, previously mentioned, as Speaker of the Assembly who serves in the second most powerful political post in the state. His role is significant in identifying other Latinos as possible candidates for state assembly seats. State Senator Richard Polanco, Assemblyman Joe Baca, and Antonio Villaraigosa, who is majority leader of the Assembly, are also poised to seek higher offices. The political odds-makers are also suggesting that in the next mayoral election in Los Angeles a Latino or Latina will be the favorite, perhaps Gloria Molina, or city council member Richard Alatorre. Some even suggest that former Secretary of Housing and Urban Development, Henry Cisneros, now relocated in Los Angles as CEO of UNIVISION, might be a candidate.

Most significant, in recent years, has been the emergence of Latinas as a political force in the state. They have dramatically increased their share of mayoral and city council seats, school board post, and legislative positions. Seven of the fourteen Latino assembly members are women, with five of them serving as committee chairs. Denise Moreno Ducheny of San Diego chairs the Budget committee, the most important committee in the Assembly.[38]

Beyond the political inroads Latinos are currently making at the local and legislative levels, and conceding that the 1996 general elections will be recognized as having been a watershed year in Latino political participation in the state, the political power of Latinos has really not yet been felt. While analysts speak of the "critical mass" that emerged from the Latino community in the 1996 elections, the exploding demographics of this group in the state during the first two decades of the 21st century, which is less than three years away, will determine the roll Latinos are to play in the political life of the state. By the year 2020 minorities will be 60% of the state's population with Latinos constituting 68% of this group. And these Latinos will become the plurality in the state, at an estimated 20 million of the states projected 48 million population, by that year.[39]

Most significant, however, is the youthfulness of the state's Latino population, which is twelve years younger on average than the white, non-Latino population. The projected school enrollment figures give an idea of just how large this youthful Latino population already is. In the potentially vote-rich San Joaquin Valley, Latinos have been the majority of the 18-and-under population since 1990. While statewide, Latinos became the majority of the 18-years-and-under population this year.[40] The impact of these figures on education is tremendous. By the year 2005 Latinos will constitute 50% of all children enrolled in schools K through 12 in the state, while the white population will be only 28%.[41] High school graduation for Latinos is also expected to increase by 60% in these years. This will constitute the largest pool of potential new voters in the state.

It is in the educational future of these children where the dreams, hopes and aspirations of Latinos for a more significant role in the political and civic life of their communities rests. But one cannot assume that the Latino vote will be a monolithic vote. As a group, they have proven to be less liberal than the Black or Jewish voter, yet not as conservative as the white voter on a variety of issue. Overall, as a group, they appear to have a moderate agenda with wavering party loyalty. Assemblyman Villaraigosa suggests that, "the older Latinos will probably stay with the Democratic Party the rest of their lives, but with their children there is no guarantee. I would never argue that this Democratic vote will be for time immemorial."[42] The GOP is counting on this, as it scrambles to recoup from its recent loses by showcasing its only Latino Republican legislator Rod Pacheco from Riverside.

While the 1996 elections did reflect a historic expression of political power in the Latino community, in the future it would appear that those political parties and politicians that address the issues Latinos consider most significant in their lives will be the most successful. Today, those issues are education, job opportunities, safe streets, affordable healthcare, and a reduction of the anti-immigrant, and by extension, anti-Latino rhetoric. And quite clearly, among those politicians seeking support will be an ever-increasing number of Latino men and women who will be running for office at all levels of government. However, one thing to be remembered is that while the increased population portends a more significant role for Latinos in the political life of the state and the nation, it also carries with it an awesome responsibility for a group that is destined to become the majority of the state's population by the middle of the 21st century.

Endnotes

[1]   Dept. of Finance. Report 93E-1, May 1993.

[2]   Newton, Jim and Matea Gold. "Latino Turnout, a Breakthrough." *Los Angeles Times* 10 April. 1997.

[3]   Ibid.

[4]   Gonzales, Raymond J. "Why Chicanos Don't Vote." *California Journal* July 1975: 245+.

[5]   Ibid. 246.

[6]   Galarza, Ernesto. *Merchants of Labor*. Santa Barbara: McNally and Loftin, 1964, p.29.

[7]   Galarza, Ernesto, Herman Gallegos, and Julian Samora. *Mexican-Americans in the Southwest*. Santa Barbara: McNallly and Loftin, 1969, p. 46.

[8]   In 1969 I was a professor at Bakersfield College in Bakersfield, California. I was the only Latino faculty member at the college for the five years I taught there from 1965 to 1970.

[9]   In 1972 I was elected to the State Assembly fron the 28th Assembly district in Kern County. In 1974, as a freshman legislator, I was appointed Chairman of the Assembly Education Committee by the new Speaker of the Assembly Leo McCarthy. I personally hired Jorge Haynes as consultant to the Education Committee. He was the only Latino consultant among the staff of over 100 of the 28 Assembly standing committees and the 17 Senate standing committees.

[10] Kelly, Robert. *The Shaping of the American Past*. Englwood Cliffs: Prentice-Hall. 1990, p. 412.

[11] Ibid.

[12] Babich Jaffe, Sherry. "Tug of War: the Shifting Demographic Sand Will Profoundly Affect California Politics and Government in the 21st Century." *California Journal* July 1997: 28+.

[13] "Outlook: People." *U.S. News & World Report* 4 Mar. 1991: 20.

[14] Chavez, Ken. "Increasing Civic Awarness Takes Root in Immigrants." *The Sacramento Bee* 4 May 1997.

[15] Ibid.

[16] Ibid.

[17] McWilliams, Carey. *Factories in the Field*. Santa Barbara: Peregrine Publishers, 1971, p. 264.

[18] California. Dept. of Finance, Report 93 E-1, May 1993.

[19] Lord, Jim. "Latino Get Out the Vote Effort." *San Francisco Weekly* 1 Jan. 1997.

[20] Decker, Cathleen. "Victories in the State Senate and Assembly Underscore the Future Voting Power of Latinos." *Los Angeles Times* 4 March 1997.

[22] Cothran, George. "La Nueva Fuerza: With Attachs on Immigration and Affirmative Action, the GOP Has Fueled a New Latino Political Apparatus." *San Francisco Weekly* 1 Jan. 1997.

[23] Ibid.

[24] Chavez.

[25] Cothran.

[26] Babitch Jaffe.

[27] Rohrick, Ted. "Reorden Faces Challenge of Bringing Unity to City." *Los Angeles Times* 10 April 1997.

[28] Love, Denis and Luz Villeral. "Election Sees Rise for Labor, Latinos; Partnership's Clout Revealed in Results." *The Daily News of Los Angeles* 13 April, 1997.

[29] California Dept. of Finance. "California Public School K-12 Enrollment Projections by Ethnicity." 1996 Series.

[30] Newton and Gold.

[31] Jacobs, John. "Latino Vote Makes a Difference." *The Sacramento Bee* 23 Nov. 1996.

[33] National Association of Latino Elected Officials (NALEO). "Report on Latino Elected Officials." 1997.

[34] Gonzales, Raymond J. "The Myth of the Latino Sleeping Giant." *California Journal* Feb. 1979: 47+.

[35] NALEO.

[36] Ibid.

[37] Gonzales, Raymond J. "Missing: The Chicano Candidate." *California Journal* May 1978: 143+.

[38] California Assembly.

[39] Dept. of Finance, 93 E-1.

[40] Dept. of Finance, 1996 Series.

[41] Ibid.

[42] Cothren

Villaraigosa's Victory:
Finally, Some Respect for Latinos

Hispanic Link News Service, **May 29, 2005**

A ntonio Villaraigosa's election as mayor of Los Angeles, the nation's second largest city, was inevitable. Not so much, Villaraigosa's own election, but the election of a Latino in a city that has a higher Latino population than any city in Mexico except Mexico City itself. Some 1.7 million Latinos make up 47 percent of the total Los Angeles population.

More significantly, on Nov. 17 they comprised 25 percent of those who went to the polls, with 84 percent casting their ballots for Villaraigosa. Just 12 years ago, they made up only 10 percent of the voters in the mayoral election.

This is not to say that as a person, Villaraigosa was the inevitable winner. The difference was that as a politician, he finally brought together the qualities and strategies that an articulate and savvy Latino politico needed. Significantly, he did not run as a Latino.

Some years ago I outlined in an article for the *California Journal,* three major reasons why Latinos had until then been unsuccessful as statewide or high visibility political candidates

One: Latinos had no real economic power. Thus, a candidate could expect little financial support from the community. In contrast, Villaraigosa not only counted on wide funding support from an ever more professional and affluent group of Latinos, his experience as Assembly Speaker in the late '90s allowed him to raise more money than the incumbent mayor.

Two: In the past, Latinos had not been able to count on important endorsements. Both white and Black political leaders favored their own, and there were few Latinos in prominent political positions to offer such public backing. In 1972 there was only one Latino state assemblymen from Los Angeles and one U.S. congressman. Not a single Latino served on the Los Angeles City Council or L.A. County Board of Supervisors.

By the time Villaraigosa ran for mayor, he had locked in endorsements of Congress members Hilda Solís and Lucille Roybal-Allard of Los Angeles, County Supervisor Gloria Molina and nearly all of the Latino City Council members, who now make up nearly a third of that body. Additionally, he picked up key endorsements in the Black and Jewish communities.

Three: Voter turnout for Latinos had been abysmal in the past. While California's Latino population has been growing at astronomical rates since the 1980s, political participation had not kept pace. In most statewide elections, Latinos could be counted on producing only 5 percent of the vote. Political parties, especially the Democrats, were loath to spend heavily on politicizing Latinos at election time because of the poor turnout in the past.

Things began to change in the '90s. Latinos became motivated by the passage of the perceived anti-immigrant Proposition 187, supported by Republican Gov. Pete Wilson in 1994. Antonio Gonzáles, president of the William C. Velasquez Institute, noted at the time, "People are becoming citizens. They feel they have been treated with disrespect. They want to participate." And they did.

Villaraigosa has been the beneficiary of this anger and newfound pride. Since the '90s, Latinos have been making significant political gains that have led to this sense of inclusion in the state's political process. Nineteen Latinos, males and females, serve in the State Assembly. They are the largest caucus in that chamber and generally have the votes to elect the Assembly Speaker. Three of the five speakers since 1998, Cruz Bustamante, Villaraigosa and the present Speaker Fabián Núñez, have come out of the Latino caucus. *Los Angelinos* can also look to the positive political image of Gloria Molina on the County Board of Supervisors as well as four Latino/a congressional members from the area.

These gains have not come easily. Despite their phenomenal growth in the last decade of the 20th century, nothing has been given to Latinos in the political arena. At redistricting time, California's Democratic Party leaders made a practice of carving up Latino *barrios* to benefit white or Black politicians. Lawsuits by the Mexican American Legal Defense and Educational Fund in 1988 and 1990 changed council boundaries in the city and redrew county districts to create winnable offices for Latinos.

Villaraigosa's 18-point victory this month came at a time when immigrant-bashing was again taking center stage. Yet he won in every income group, among nearly all religious groups (44 percent among non-Catholic Christians), among whites, Latinos and Jews (Blacks 48% Asians 44%), and among all age groups except seniors over 65. He won because of his experience, his political connections, and his ability to fashion a coalition,

While having a compelling life story of being raised by a single mother, dropping out of high school and eventually gaining a law degree, he was the right person at the right time for Los Angeles, for California, and perhaps for the nation.

Villaraigosa's election as the first Latino mayor in the City of Angels since 1872 was both historical and prophetic. Its historical significance is obvious. But prophetic—how can we gage that?

Hopefully, as mayor of the nation's second largest city and in a state with the world's fifth largest economy, he can command a little respect. And Latinos, lacking political recognition and respect for so long, can shed the Rodney Dangerfield reputation that has dogged them politically for most of the last century.

The New Democrats

Latino Political Wires, Feb. 1, 2004

E ditor, Bob Price's, recent piece in the *Bakersfield Californian* on the emergence of State Senator Dean Florez as a Democratic Party power broker in Kern County, much like the roll played for the past 20 years by Congressman Bill Thomas (Chairman of Ways and Means of the U.S. Congress), is right on point. Price was referring to Florez' role in gaining the endorsement from the Democratic Central Committee for his former aid Mike Rubio for 5th District Supervisor over the incumbent, Pete Parra,.

Price noted that, "in fact, he (Florez) probably has a firmer grasp on power among local Democrats than Thomas has on local Republicans." Price also noted that this victory by the Florez forces in gaining an endorsement by the Democratic County Committee in a primary race for his guy, was unusual, but justified because Florez had paid attention to local Democratic politics by attending Central Committee meetings or sending staff, and packing the committee with staff and supporters. Parra, on the other hand, hardly ever attended meetings and was criticized for failing, over the years, to take positions on issues supported by the local Democrats.

Unfortunately, this long simmering dispute between the Parra and the Florez forces recalls an article I wrote for the *California Journal* (Why Chicanos Don't Vote: CJ 7/75) some years ago in which I recounted an often told story that circulated in the Latino community:

> A tourist walking down a seaside street one day happened upon a man selling live crabs from a tub on the sidewalk. As the two men conversed about sight-seeing attractions and anything else a crab vendor and

tourist might wish to discuss, the tourist noticed that the crabs were all moving slowly toward the side of the tub and forming a pyramid by stacking themselves one upon the other. The vendor, who had been paying no attention to the activity of the crabs, dismissed the tourist's expression of concern that the crabs might escape. As the crabs' pyramid reached closer and closer to the top of the tub, the tourist became increasingly amazed at the vendor's nonchalance. Finally, unable to restrain himself any longer, the tourist blurted out, "Those crabs are going to get out in a minute!"

"Oh don't worry," the vendor replied, carelessly. "Those are Chicano crabs. When one finally gets ready to make it over the top, the others will pull out from under it."

The dispute between Parra, the senior Democrat in the County, and Florez, the highest ranking state Democratic office holder in the region, is lamentable. That these two are Latinos adds another wrinkle to the political equation. As I pointed out in the *Journal* article, there is little likelihood that the Latino community will ever be unanimous in its political behavior. I noted that it didn't happen among the Democratic and Republican parties nor among the black, nor Jewish communities. I hoped in those years of the 1970s when I wrote the article, that Latinos would reach a level of political sophistication that would be needed to ensure adequate representation for its millions of people in California

To his credit, Florez did the right thing by paying attention to local Democratic issues by working with the Democratic Central Committee. Parra discovered this too late. As political leaders they had this obligation. In 1990, when I was a member of the Kern County Central Committee, and as Chair of the successful Latino Redistricting Coalition that essentially created the assembly, senate and congressional districts adopted in the court mandated redistricting plan, I tried to convince my colleagues on the Central Committee that they should expand their numbers to included more Latinos and blacks. I felt that the complexion of the Democratic Party in Kern County was changing, as the old-time Dixicrats in the party had been fleeing to the Republican party in the county over the years. I was rebuffed in my efforts by a committee that was dominated by trade unions and women's groups that naturally were seeking to retain their own political power. They were not at all disposed at the time to make room in the party leadership for minorities, especially Latinos.

They were shortsighted. I was not after control of the party, but coalition, a coalition that would be more reflective of where the party was heading as we headed into the 21st century.

In another article written for the *Californian,* shortly after the defeat of Democratic Assemblyman Jim Costa by Phil Wyman in a special state senate election in 1993, I noted with concern that: "the defeat of Jim Costa in the April

17 election does not bode well for the future of the Democratic Party in Kern County nor is it surprising. Local Democratic leaders and State Party leaders have not changed their failed attitude that none but conservative, good ol' boy Democrats can win in Kern County. The fact is that they have not won."

At the time, not even I could anticipate such a dramatic growth in the Latino community in the San Joaquin Valley that has now impacted the political scene. But Latinos are here and they are becoming middle class, active and political. My hope is that they will seek to participate politically by practicing the principles of inclusion, coalition, and respect for others within their party. Hopefully, Latino Democrats will have learned from the past political history in Kern County, that they should only win when they demand political courage, sensitivity and inclusion and that their candidates seek to serve all of the people of their political districts.

Big Win for Latinos: Democrats and Latinos Dominate State Election Results

The Bakersfield Californian, Dec. 7, 2002

L atinos were winners in this November's elections, nationally, statewide, and in Kern County, too.

The final count in favor of Nicole Parra, ostensibly giving her the victory in the 30th Assembly District, added to Dean Florez's election as state senator, signal the growing strength of Latinos on the political map in the Southern San Joaquin Valley. If there are any skeptics, just focus on the fact that another Sanchez will join sister Loretta as congresswoman in Orange County, previously recognized as the most conservative county in the State.

Not too long ago, Kern County and Orange County were the two counties in California that served as the mother lode for the Republican Party. When I won an Assembly seat in Kern County in 1972 it was seen as an aberration, which it proved to be, as I was promptly defeated in the next election. It took 20 years for another Latino to win an Assembly seat in the San Joaquin Valley; Cruz Bustamante of Fresno was elected in 1992.

The results of this year's elections are also being hailed as a great victory for the Democratic Party in California, bucking the trend nationally in favor of the Republicans. In California, Democrats picked up every statewide office from governor down, despite the abysmal weakness of Governor Gray Davis at the head of the ticket for the Democrats. This is the first time in 120 years that Democrats have held all statewide offices. They also hold 33 of 53 congressional seats and both U.S. Senate seats. And as gravy, Rep. Nancy Pelosi of San Francisco was elected Minority Leader of the House of Representatives by her Democratic caucus.

With respect to Latinos, this political growth has been anticipated for a number of reasons. Certainly their population growth through birthrate and immigration is nothing short of phenomenal, projected to be 40 percent of the state's population by 2010, and already the largest minority group in the U.S. But in California it hasn't only been population growth; many credit former Republican Governor Pete Wilson for the accelerated political activism of Latinos in the state.

"In 1994 his media-focused support of Proposition 187, which sought to deny public services to illegal immigrants adults and children alike shocked the Latino community, which in turn prompted a massive effort to register Latinos," according to the *Los Angeles Times*.

More specifically, with respect to Latino candidates like Parra and Florez in Kern County, other elements are involved. Some years ago, in an article I wrote for the *California Journal,* I noted the some of the reasons the Democratic Party and the Republicans Party for that matter did not take Latinos seriously as political players were:

* **Lack of financial support: Because the Latino community and its organizations lacked real economic power, they could be counted on for little financial support.**
* **Endorsements: Traditionally visible spokesmen and groups in the Latino community were only considered minor players, political lightweights.**
* **Voting: Although the Latino community constituted 18 to 20 percent of he population (at that time), only 5 percent, at best, could be counted on to vote.**

Now, 20 years later, all of this has changed. The Latino community is able to generate significant political funding from its own community, and more importantly, from significant political groupings, such as the unions they are members of. A significant entrepreneurial class has emerged, and an increasing number of professionals have graduated from colleges. Endorsements of Latino groups, such as League of United Latin American Citizens, the G.I. Forum, the United Farm Workers Union and others are actively sought by candidates Democrats and Republicans alike. With respect to voter turnout, in 2000 Latinos significantly surpassed the black turnout in California, reaching nearly 13 percent, and this year, the potential for a turnout of 17 percent was there, but not realized because of the poor showing of both gubernatorial candidates.

More specifically, the reason Latinos are having so much success in getting elected to the California Legislature (23 seats out of eighty in the Assembly) or the Congress is that they now have become players, using the same methods of gaining support as many other candidates have in the past.

By this I should explain the Ray Gonzales maxim. Candidates for the Legislature or Congress generally evolve from three sources: They have experience as elected officials in local government. (A Roy Ashburn or Kevin McCarthy for example in Kern County.) They have worked as staff for other office holders. (Congressman Cal Dooley worked as staff for the late Sen. Rose Ann Vuich of Dinuba.) Or they have deep pockets, using their own money to buy a seat. (Former Congressman Michael Huffington in Santa Barbara is an example.)

Florez and Parra are classic examples of the second category, which is perhaps the most effective way of getting elected in these days of excessive political spending. Dean Florez served as staffer for influential state Sen. Art Torres, who today is head of the Democratic Party in California. And Parra, of course, spent a number of years working for Cal Dooley. Having her father serving as a Kern County supervisor was an additional plus.

What these former staffers attempt to do is scare out most competition in primary elections because of the influential political connections they bring to the race. This, in turn, allows them to raise astronomical sums of money because the same groups that support their mentors will generally financially support the staffer-candidates. It is not likely that Nicole Parra would have been able to raise nearly $2 million for an Assembly race had she not been able to count on the same unions, lawyer groups and other political PACs that she was already familiar with, having worked as a staffer for a successful congressmen in the area.

As I think of the $20,000 that I raised locally with barbecues and enchilada feeds to win an Assembly seat in a much larger district than Parra's, I am staggered by what is being spent on legislative elections these days. My only hope is that these new Latinos winning elections all over the state with massive sums of money can withstand the temptation of saying thank you to the many groups that contributed to their elections without selling out.

I recall sadly the two Latinos who were elected with me out of Los Angeles in 1972, from very safe districts. They were not able to resist the temptation of the "mother's milk of politics." One ended up at Boron Federal Prison for extortion and bribery and the other was convicted of federal campaign offenses. Both are ex-felons today who let down their constituencies, as well as their families and friends, not to mention the Latino community.

If we are moving into a new era in California politics, let us hope that it will be a political era where ethical campaigns will be waged, using local money and treating one another with civility. Anything less will surely be a step backwards.

Of Mustaches and Accents

Latino Vote, Oct. 15, 2003

The "Supper Bowel of Debates" as one candidate called it, proved to be very entertaining, if perhaps not too informative, as the five leading candidates in California's gubernatorial recall election squared off for a nationally televised debate this week. While most voters who plan to vote in this first recall election in the state's history may have already decided on whether to vote yes or no on the recall question, there may still be significant indecision on the choice for a replacement for Democratic Governor Gray Davis, if the yes vote results in a recall. The debate probably did little to catapult any of the five candidates into a significant lead. At last count, Cruz Bustamante was only a few percentage point ahead of Arnold Schwarzenegger in opinion polls, followed by Senator Tom McClintock, Peter Camejo of the Green Party, and Arianna Huffington an Independent, in that order.

What is significant about the debate was not the entertaining exchanges between the candidates, but the profiles of the five candidate. Their very presence on the stage at Sacramento State University was as graphic an illustration of the demographics of the State of California as one could find. There were four obvious immigrants or ethnic representatives and one, what we might call, traditional "white" male in the group. Senator Tom McClintock represented that less than 50% of the traditional white population that remains in the state. Both Schwarzenegger and Huffington, as indicated by their obvious accents, are foreign born, Huffington having immigrated from Greece and Schwarzenegger from Austria. Bustamante and Camejo are Latinos. This is the remarkable fact of this gubernatorial recall race. Four of the five top candidates are clearly representatives of the ethnic population of the state who are vying to replace a typically white male in Governor Davis.

At another stage of the campaign, Bustamante's mustache was raised as an issue as it seemed to reflect a stereotype of the Latino, with references to the Frito Bandito of another period. Schwarzenegger's accent was also made an issue with Davis commenting that no one should be governor who could not pronounce the name of the state, CALIFORNIA, properly. Huffington's accent was not made an issue directly, but does not go unnoticed. Camejo's Latino accent is barely traceable, but his willingness to defend the plight of immigrants as well as his Spanish surname have clearly identified him as an ethnic.

Significantly, the only "traditional" white candidate, McClintock, seems to be the furthest to the right, and out of step with the other four candidates. His desperate clinging to the far-right positions on immigration and his reflection of the rest of the conservative agenda even makes the Terminator look like the poster boy for moderation. McClintock unabashedly opposes abortion rights, equal rights for gays, and is in lockstep with other traditional conservative positions.

Bustamante, Schwarzenegger, Huffington, and Camejo have all made positive statements about immigrants and the contributions they have made to American and California life. Schwarzenegger credits his personal success to the opportunities he had in California in realizing the American Dream after arriving penniless from his native land. Huffington has expressed sympathy for the many immigrants that have had to pay for services at a disproportionate rate while the very wealthy use tax loopholes to avoid paying taxes. Camejo supports the granting of licenses to undocumented immigrants since the economy depends on the labor of these immigrants to perform the tasks that Americans will no longer do. Bustamante recalls his early years working in the fields of the San Joaquin Valley along side of the Mexican *braceros* who were legally imported as labor to support the agricultural industry of the country.

McClintock stands out as the only candidate that has nothing kind to say about immigrants or ethnics for that matter. His campaign, with the support of national conservative mouth pieces like Bill O'Rilley and Joe Scarborough, attacks Bustamante for having been a member of a college, Latino student group and assails Schwarzenegger for supporting a woman's right to choose or support of gay unions if not marriages.

When the tumultuous recall season comes to an end, if the polls are correct, there will be a new governor. And symbolically, since this state no longer has a single majority group, the next candidate will either be wearing a mustache and have a Spanish surname, or be foreign born with a very detectable accent. Either way, the state will again have chosen moderation as a direction and have come of age with respect to recognizing the diversity of the most populated state in the nation.

Latinos the Losers in the Recall Election

Latino Political Wires, **Nov. 6, 2003**

L atinos were the big losers in California's historic recall election. They were the losers because, despite all of the pre-election talk about the potential role of the Latino vote, it proved fairly irrelevant and certainly of little import to Latino candidate Lt. Governor Cruz Bustamante. While he garnered 52% of the Latino vote, Schwarzenegger, McClintock and Camejo together got 44% of the Latino vote. Bustamante's 52% translated into a small percentage of the total vote, perhaps 11%. Ironically, blacks were more supportive of Bustamante at 65% than were Latinos at 52%.

Twenty-five percent of all Democrats voted yes on the recall question, while a remarkable 46% of Latinos voted for the recall. Some of these votes by Latinos may have been to support Bustamante's effort, but since only 52% of Latinos voted for him, it is not very likely that many were a yes on the recall and a yes for Bustamante. Why did Bustamante make such a poor showing, even among Latinos? One answer certainly was the "perfect storm" created by Governor Davis' historically high negatives and the Terminator's arrival on the scene.

Arnold Schwarzenegger was bigger than life, both physically and symbolically, relegating Bustamante to the role of bit player. Bustamante also ran a disastrous campaign on his own. While he was the front-runner in the early stages, he began to slide after his very poor showing in the one and only debate that Schwarzenegger participated in. Bustamante came across as timid, almost even frightened in exchanges with Schwarzenegger. All of the other candidates on the dais did better than Bustamante. Schwarzenegger demonstrated that he could handle himself and Camejo and McClintock appeared much more knowledgeable than Bustamante. Arianna Huffington served as the perfect foil for Schwarzenegger, while Bustamante came across as the least inspiring, showing few signs of any leadership qualities. For Latinos, overall, the debate was a very bad showing, except for the other Latino, Green Party candidate Camejo's articulate, though, sometimes extreme, positions for the California electorate. Bustamante began to self-destruct soon after the debate.

He also disappointed by falling into the political greed trap. He was willing to accept several million dollars from the Indian gaming lobby, just at the time that Californians were warming to the charge against Gray Davis' of "extortion," as some called it, of his fundraising tactics of the past among the gaming lobby. Schwarzenegger succeeded in painting Bustamante with the same brush strokes he was using on Davis. And embarrassingly, Bustamante was even ordered to return the Indian money by the Court in the final days of the campaign.

Davis' transparent efforts to court, event pander to various constituencies to save himself was also hurtful to the Latinos of the state. While his appointment of Dolores Huerta, co-founder of the United Farmworkers Union with César Chávez, to the Board of Regents of the University of California, was a late but welcomed honor, some of his other actions did more harm than good. After having vetoed the bill to grant drivers' licenses and identification cards to illegal immigrants twice before, Davis' sudden changes of heart in the midst of the recall election only guaranteed that the new statute would become a wedge campaign issues where Latinos, in general, would come out the losers.

California Latinos were losers at a national level as well. While there was continuous talk by pundits and the various cable news channels of the importance of the Latino vote, it would appear that there were no Latinos to be found in the state who could be called upon to discuss the impact of the recall election on the Latinos of California. CNN, Fox, the NBC cable channels paraded their line of experts to comment on the California recall election, inviting such regular pundits as Peggy Noonan, Howard Fienman, even Ben Stine to pontificate on the impact of the recall vote on Californians and on Latinos. On one occasion, Chris Mathews of MSNBC's Hardball invited two unknown reporters from Telemundo to serve on a roundtable. Other than this slight gesture and an occasional comment from New Mexico governor Bill Richardson, the Latinos, as commentators were virtually invisible, as they usually are on these news programs. The only bright spot was Art Torres, who as Chairman of the California Democratic Party was forceful and articulate in presenting the Democratic Party view on numerous television interviews, though he was not actually speaking on behalf of the Latino perspective.

And finally, the images of the victorious Schwarzenegger camp, on election night, was the symbolic final blow to the Latinos of the state. At other times in the Latino struggle for justice and equality in the state, one could remember images of Bobby Kennedy taking holy communion with a fasting César Chávez in Delano back in the Sixties, or Senator Kennedy chairing a Senate hearing on farm labor

abuses in Kern County where he gave the local sheriff lessons on upholding the
U.S. Constitution. One also had memories of Ethel Kennedy, Bobby's widow
and some of her children, marching in Delano in 1993 in the funeral procession
for César Chávez.

Now, instead, we were greeted with front page pictures and television images
of Maria's mother, Eunice Kennedy Shriver (JFK's sister), her children, and
husband Sargant Shriver, the first Director of President Kennedy's Peace Corps
and the 1972 Democratic vice-presidential running mate for George McGovern,
all standing arm in arm with, Schwarzenegger, the new Republican Governor
of California. Just as Cruz Bustamante was supported by the Indian gaming
tribes, Schwarzenegger received millions from the agricultural interest of the
state, suggesting that the almost spiritual Kennedy connection with the Latino
community now belongs to another age and another generation.

Bustamante Owes Assembly Speakership to Term Limits' Long-term Cleansing Effect

Hispanic Link News Service, Dec. 1996

Cruz Bustamente, a moderate Latino Democrat from Fresno, has been elected speaker of the California Assembly, arguably the second-most important political position in California. Speakers are generally selected by the members of the majority party caucus of the Assembly. But with all due respect to his political skills and the support of the 14-member Latino caucus, it seems clear that Bustamante owes his success to term limits as much as anything else.

With only three years in the Assembly, it is not likely that he would have emerged as speaker at this point had not such veterans as Phil Isenberg, John Vasconellos or Tom Bates been forced to move on by term limits.

Despite how much others might criticize term limits, I continue to believe that it is one of the most wholesome changes to our political system in this century. As far back as 1973, while serving briefly in the California Assembly, I introduced a term limits bill of my own. Having seen the influence of lobby money and the shady methods many legislators used to raise campaign funds, and recognizing the fact that incumbents won re-election 95 percent of the time in general elections, I believed, and still do, that only term limits could bring about political reform.

I think, moreover, that the Founding Fathers clearly intended that our elected officials should be "citizen servants" and not career politicians. But my colleagues in the Assembly did not agree with me. In my first effort to get a term limits bill out of the Rules Committee, then chaired by career politician John Burton, I couldn't muster a single vote.

Bustamante's selection as speaker is a direct result of the term limits initiative the voters eventually adopted, over the objection of the politicians. Even though tenure in office is not as important in the California Legislature as it is in Congress for gaining positions of power, it still made a difference in the past. It took time for a would-be speaker to get his ducks in a row. It took Willie Brown two tires and seven terms before he could put it together. And it also took millions of dollars of special-interest money raised by Brown and other speakers to help them win seats for their political supporters. Hopefully, Bustamante will not be encumbered with as many special interest monkeys on his back, and that is as it should be.

At the national level, Congress should take note and move toward term limits as well. The courts, which have already done much to retard political reform, should not tamper with California's term-limits initiative. The present system has opened up a greater number of opportunities for women and minorities, as well as for many other worthy candidates who want to do the people's work and shouldn't have to wait until someone dies in office.

Term limits at the national level could have sent into retirement this November such decaying institutions as Strom Thurmond, Jesse Helms and Robert Byrd. Just count the millions of dollars of special interest money they were able to raise because of their incumbency over the years. Who can tell how many of the scandals that beset the Legislature in recent years could have been avoided if term limits had been adopted here much earlier? There are currently members of the U.S. Congress from California who spent years in the state legislature and now as many as two decades in the Congress. These individuals, in most instances, have hardly ever had real jobs. They are the epitome of career politicians, and come from both Parties.

Term limits makes it possible for the politician to prove his/her stuff in a short period of time, and if, a big if, he/she is recognized as having done a good job by the electorate, the individual can seek higher office. Bustamante will have only a few years to prove if he has the right stuff and then he might chose to move on to a position of more responsibility. This is as it should be. I do not believe that it was ever intended that our elected officials should become career residents of elected office.

The Price of a Lawmaker's Ear

The California Journal, Feb. 1975

S ince I carried the original lobby-control legislation, AB768, which was prepared with the assistance of governor Brown's staff when he served as Secretary of State, and since this bill eventually became Chapter Six of Proposition 9, (The Political Reform Act of 1975), I feel compelled to respond to Congressman Tom Rees' remarks in the November issue of California Journal [see "The ten-dollar trick" p. 395].

The thesis of Rees' commentary was that the noon luncheon tradition of Sacramento (Derby Club, Clam and Choral, Moose Milk, etc.) and other forms of wining and dining guaranteed that there would be communication between legislator and special interest lobbyist. He insisted that "for laws to be written there has to be communication among all parties—lawmaker, constituents, colleagues and people or interests affected by a change in law."

I certainly have no quarrel with this statement. In fact, during my two short years in Sacramento, I attempted to promote this type of communication by insisting on a strict open-door policy. Neither constituent nor lobbyist was required to make an appointment to see me in my office. On the other hand, if Congressman Rees believes the Derby Club to be the best place for the free exchange of ideas between lawmakers and lobbyists, one might ask why membership to the Derby Club is by invitation only. I was not invited to join. Nor were other legislators who were publicly critical of the wining-and-dining circuit. Indeed, female legislators are still not invited to join. Neither are Blacks. Some Chicano members were just recently declared acceptable. If the Congressman truly feels that such an institution as Derby Club results in better legislation, then we should insist that it be open to all members.

Congressman Rees declared in his article that, "at times I got more bills through at Derby Club than in a dozen committee rooms." If this indeed was the case with legislators, perhaps the business of state could more effectively be conducted at Posey's, Ellis', the Firehouse, Frank Fat's or any of the other fine Sacramento restaurants. And if the lobbyist picked up all the tabs, we could lock up the committee rooms, fire consultants, secretaries and sergeants, and conduct all legislative business in public pubs and dinning rooms. This surely would be a tremendous tax savings for the State of California.

It may be true that much legislative business is conducted at lunch or dinner in Sacramento and at other more glamorous settings, such as Lake Tahoe or Mazatlán, Mexico. But if one is to believe the promoters of the lunches and the trips, the purpose of these affairs is not to discuss legislation, but rather to get to know the legislators. In fact, I was told repeatedly by third-house members, that they simply wanted to get acquainted. This is all well and good, but what in fact happens is that the intimacy that develops between the third house and the Legislature becomes the subject of intense public scrutiny. It leads to exaggeration by the press, suspicion by the general public and ultimately, to a sense of persecution on the part of lobbyist and legislator. In reality, what we are discussing here is not a situation that results in outright violations of the law or of political propriety. What we are discussing is, in essence, a question of degree, the degree to which an elected or appointed official will go into a relationship with the special-interest lobby groups and the effects of this relationship on a suspicious public.

The public is concerned today about the relationship that exists between special interests and government officials. And since the general public and the more poorly funded grassroots consumer groups do not have the means to carry on an extensive wining-and-dining operation of their own, they seem to be at a disadvantage when competing for the legislator's ear.

Perhaps, the biggest shortcoming of the California lobby law prior to Proposition 9 was that it was both ambiguous and devoid of clears guidelines. There was, for example, no prohibition on a lobbyist's giving gifts of any value to a legislator. The entire membership of the California Legislature last year received a pound of butter from a local dairy. This, of course, was certainly not enough to win favors nor was it intended to do so, but what can be said of an all-expenses-paid trip to Acapulco? Or a weekend at Lake Tahoe?

Congressman Rees should recognize that the true virtue of Proposition 9 is that it ends all the ambiguity in the law. Chapter six makes it quite clear that "it is unlawful for a lobbyist to make a contribution or to act as and agent or intermediary in the making of any contribution. It is unlawful for lobbyist to make gifts to one person aggregating more than $10 in a calendar month. It is unlawful for any person knowingly to receive any contribution or a gift which is made unlawful under this article." There appears to be little ambiguity in this language.

In essence, what the new law does is to insure that all citizens can compete on more equal terms for the public official's time and consideration. If Congressman Rees truly feels that "the important thing will be to keep the legislative branch in Sacramento from becoming isolated from itself and from the world," he should recognize that this is most likely to happen if the archaic and somewhat exclusive traditions such as Derby Club and Moose Milk go the way of other questionable political traditions. Then, perhaps, we can truly begin to open up the political process to the less financially potent segments of society.

California Lobbyists Once Again Have Free Rein

The Sacramento Bee, **Feb. 17, 1980**

The 1970s have been characterized in various end-of-the-decade articles as the years of the "me first" generation, or the years in which Americans came face to face with "the limits of growth." But perhaps a more profound commentary on the '70s is to repeat the term that W.H. Auden used to describe the 1930s: "a low, dishonest decade."

It was, in fact, the decade that gave us Richard Nixon and Watergate, Spiro Agnew, Koreagate, Wayne Hayes' secretarial services, Wilbur Mills' dive in the reflection pool, the Talmadge closet caper . . . The cynicism and disgust prevalent among Americans as a result of these and other political scandals was perhaps the most dominant tone of the decade.

It is no doubt true that these scandals were partly responsible for the backlash passage of California's Proposition 13 (tax reform), and Proposition 9 (The Political Reform Act of 1974), and will likely result in the passage of Jarvis II in June of this year. Indeed, politicians now rank 20th, at the bottom, of a list of professions parents would choose for their children.

All of this brings me to a moment of serious reflection on an issue that has long been a private crusade of mine—the manner of controlling the extraordinary power and influence of special interest groups and their lobbyists in our political system. As a result of a California Supreme Court decision in the last half of 1979, and despite the public outrage at influence peddling in politics, there appears to be a regressive movement afoot that may very well end the efforts for political reform that sprang out of Watergate and other political scandals.

The California Supreme Court ruled in 1979 that part of The Political Reform Act of 1974 was unconstitutional. A group of lobbyists (The Institute of Governmental Advocates) had pooled their money to challenge the law. Specifically, the court held that "Government Code 86200, which prohibits lobbyists contributions, is invalid in that it is a substantial limitation on associational freedoms guaranteed by the U.S. Constitution's First Amendment."

The court was by no means unanimous in its decision. Chief Justice Elizabeth Bird in her dissent invoked the immortal words of former speaker of the Assembly Jess Unruh when she wrote, "Today's decision moves California farther from, not closer to, a First Amendment society where individuals are able to speak meaningfully with their representatives and be heard. Once again, 'money will be the mother's milk of politics,' with the Third House lobbyists owning the dairy."

Following on the heels of the California Supreme Court decision, the U.S. Supreme Court began the new year with its own action in respect to California's Political Reform Act. In a 7-2 decision, the court let stand the California Supreme Court ruling, which had been appealed by the Fair Political Practices Commission.

I feel a personal sense of frustration by the current situation brought about by the court ruling, since a large portion of the Political Reform Act of 1974 was originally my legislation, introduced in March of 1973 when I served in the California Legislature. At that time, before Watergate had really exploded, the *California Journal* referred to my proposals as "tilting at windmills."

I had been thoroughly amazed at having been sent gifts and money from lobbyists shortly after my surprise victory in the 1972 elections. As a result of several news stories about my returning the gifts and money, Jerry Brown, then Secretary of State, but already running for governor, had offered two of his very dedicated aides, Dan Lowenstein and Robert Stern, to help me draft a lobby control bill. While Brown obviously had political motives in mind, Lowenstein and Stern truly were reform minded, as I felt I was. Thus, when the bill finally was drafted, *The Journal* concluded that, "the Brown-Gonzales measure, AB 786, is the most extensive lobby-control measure put before the California Legislature since the substance of the present law was enacted in 1950."

Not surprisingly, I was unable to get even a single co-author for my bill, and it suffered an ignominious death in the first committee hearing. Not long after the bill was killed, the lid blew off the Watergate scandal in Washington, and Jerry Brown, Lowenstein, and Stern succeeded in incorporating my defunct bill in what became known as Proposition 9, the Political Reform Act of 1974. By the time the June primary rolled around, legislators were tripping over themselves to support the initiative because they could read the polls on the issue. The proposition was subsequently passed, overwhelmingly by the voters.

Ironically, I lost my bid for re-election, but the legislators who survived, henceforth were supposed to be limited to the proverbial "hamburger and coke" at the lobbyists' tables. Before the passage of Proposition 9, it was not uncommon for the major restaurants in the downtown area of Sacramento to host sumptuous luncheons every day of the week for legislators—lunches that were paid for by the major lobby groups. I am even told that dinners and lunches at such places as Lake Tahoe, Mazatlán, Acapulco—with a week thrown in to aid digestion—were not uncommon.

I personally received few invitations, since I had not endeared myself to the Third House, a result of having introduced my bill. There were some lobbyists, however, who privately communicated to me their support for my efforts. One even went so far as to say that, "the way some legislators squeeze money out of me for their fundraising dinners is nothing short of extortion."

It now appears that as a result of the Supreme Court rulings, the milk shortage that was supposed to have lasted from 1974 to 1979 has come to an end. Indeed, it may never have occurred. While the law was supposed to have limited lobbyists to $10 a month to spend for each legislator and public official, the reality was that the lobbyists' employers, usually large corporate interests that hire them, were actually able to buy the fundraising dinner tickets and pay for the vacations, making sure to send the lobbyists along to guarantee a close relationship with the public official.

Thus, it would seem that even before the court repealed the lobby control portions of Proposition 9, the industrious Third House found other means of exerting its influence. Spending by lobbyists actually climbed to $40 million in 1975-76 and to $50 million in the 1977-78 legislative sessions.

Obviously, the courts' decisions and the realization that the lobby controls envisioned by the Political Reform Act were never truly accomplished, have shattered a small dream that I had about equal access in government. I, like many other citizens, had become increasingly disheartened by what was perceived to be the "dirty game of politics." Unfortunately, while much of the criticism of elected officials and lobbyists may be unfounded, the bottom line seems to be that as long as money continues to play such an important part in our electoral process, the cow will continue to be sacred and politicians will continue to be attached to their udders.

Now, as Chief Justice Bird predicted, lobbyists for the many special interests can continue to exert their disproportionate influence with full abandon. The two most prestigious courts in the land have given them *carte blanche* as it were. In the first few weeks of this legislative session, lobbyists for the beer and soft drink industries have opened up their checkbooks and successfully killed legislation aimed at eliminating non-returnable bottles and cans; medical industry lobbyists led the attack to defeat a medical cost-containment bill; and by the end of the legislative session millions will be spent by the lobbyists to either kill or get passed some special interest legislation.

It would seem that the time has come for Americans, both at the local and national levels, to bring and end to the exaggerated length of political campaigns, the excessive dependence on private funding, and the abuses of the wealthy and powerful special interests. Unless some sort of public financing of campaigns is instituted with limited terms in office for politicians, and equal access to lawmakers by the public is assured, the political abuses of the '70s will pale in comparison to what we will likely see in the future, now that the courts have taken a major step backward.

Jerry Brown Tilts Towards Latinos

Nuestro, December 1978

Governor Jerry Brown of California is in trouble. At least that is what most political experts and a cadre of pollsters are saying on the eve of the statewide general election in California. Brown fell from a record high popularity rating of 85% shortly after his 1974 election to a near-record low for an incumbent governor of 25% after the June primary election. By last month as the campaign headed into the home stretch, one poll said that only five percentage points separated him from Attorney General Evelle Younger, his Republican rival in the November election. But perhaps the group Brown is counting on most heavily is California's Latinos. The governor's expectation is understandable.

Thus far, the group that has remained the most loyal to Jerry Brown during his first term and into the campaign has been the Chicano community. When he hit that 25% dip in his "good job" rating, 42% of Chicanos were still admirers. This has been no accident. Brown has worked hard to maintain Chicano support. Indeed it would be fair to say that Brown is probably the best-known national politician to have recognized the enormous potential of the Latino vote. In his recent book, *Jerry Brown: The Man on the White Horse,* former Brown aide Jim Lorenz reports that shortly after his election, the new governor began developing a Chicano strategy. "In December of 1974, Jerry told me he was going 'to tilt towards Mexican Americans' which meant tilting away from the Blacks," says Lorenz. Brown also told Lorenz, "Blacks are the wrong symbols in the 1970's." Says Lorenz, "I gathered he felt easier, more relaxed, with Mexican Americans, as well as regarding them as virgin territory."

Virgin territory it may have been. But four years have passed now. And if Brown is looking to Chicanos for support, Chicanos have also been looking at the governor's record. And the assessment of that record as it relates to the Chicano community not surprisingly is mixed. Does that mean, on balance, that Brown's tilt has held his Chicano support steady, or will that support topple? The polls say 67% of Chicano voters will back the governor, compared to 87% that voted for him in 1974. but the real answer will not be in until the first Tuesday of November. Meanwhile, judge the record for yourself.

There is agreement that in the number and scope of his appointments at the highest levels he cannot be faulted. Soon after his inauguration, he appointed Mario Obledo as the first Chicano cabinet secretary in the history of the state. Although he has been the agency secretary most often criticized by Brown detractors, he has tenaciously hung on to his post as Secretary of the huge Health and Welfare Agency (NUESTRO, June, 1978). In fact, he is the only Secretary left of the original Brown cabinet.

There have been many other appointments, too. Brown has named more Chicano judges than any other California governor, 30 at this writing. Adding those judges and Obledo to various department directors, plus members of public boards and commissions, Brown can claim nearly 200 high level Latino appointees—more than any governor since the US took over California.

The total has impressed a leading Chicano legislator who was an early critic of Brown. Assemblyman Art Torres now believes that "Brown's efforts have been exemplary. He has been the only Governor in the history of California to have appointed so many Chicanos to so many diversified positions within government and the judiciary." Dr. Arnold Munoz, appointed by Brown as deputy director of the Department of Social Services, also contends that, "Brown has done an incredible job. If you look in the area of Chicano judges, they will be there forever, or at least until they die. Then there's Irene Tovar, appointed to the State Personnel Board for 12 years, Vilma Marinez to the Board of Regents of the University of California, also for 12 years. They'll have influence over the entire system for a long time after the governor has gone."

Not all Brown's critics are completely satisfied with his appointment record, however. One noticeable absence, for example, is the lack of any Chicano in the governor's immediate staff. Though Rudy Ahumada serves as the Director of Administration, there is no serious dispute about the fact that Brown's inner circle is made up of a select group of "gunslingers" who initially at least tended to be upper middle class poverty lawyers whose only connection with minorities was somewhat paternalistic. Today, the inner group has shifted and broadened somewhat, but there is still no Chicano.

The same was true at first of Brown's campaign staff, and many Chicano leaders had to exert pressure to have the first Chicano, Leo Gallegos, put on the staff in a midlevel position. More recently because the Chicano vote has come to be viewed more importantly in the November election, George Pla, the Chicano former deputy director of the Department of Economic and Business Development, was added as one of the campaign deputies in charge of the

Southern California effort where most Chicanos are located. Pla, who built a reputation as a top economic analyst while with the East Lost Angeles Community Union (TELACU), is viewed as a key selection by most Chicanos, who feel the campaign has finally seen the light. And there are other signs that Pla's addition to the campaign staff marked a change in outlook. An estimated half-million dollars have been earmarked for voter registration, mostly among Chicanos on the assumption that those newly registered voters could make a difference for Brown in November. Additionally, the Chicano community is being counted on to raise more than a half-million dollars by the end of the campaign—which is different but no less welcome way of taking Chicanos seriously.

Still even those who think Brown's heart is in the right place are often unsure of where his head is. They remember unhappily Brown's past penchant for surrounding himself with exotic types; French expatriates with shaved heads, astronauts on leave from NASA, storefront lawyers, and the like left little room for real minorities. A common feeling among critics is that he has dealt more in symbols than in realities. "He's on his own trip," declares one critic.

That trip—and the often unclear nature of his motives—can lead to criticisms even of his achievements. Early in 1975, for example, César Chávez had a farmworker bill introduced to the Legislature by Assemblyman Richard Alatorre. Assemblyman Torres, Secretary Obledo and others tried to get Brown to support the Chávez bill which was virtually identical to Brown's own bill; it was to no avail. Instead of a natural alliance, Brown chose to have an unnaturally bitter fight. "I'll use Obledo against Chávez," Brown was reported to have said. "I'll out-fast Chávez."

Jim Lorenz suggested in his book that the issue all boiled down to a primal struggle between Brown and Chávez. "Jerry had to subdue César in order to be the man on the white horse. César was the last charismatic man in California. If Jerry was to gain charisma too, he couldn't tag along on César's bill . . . The father figure had to submit to the new sun of the firmament." Brown won the battle by passing the first farm labor bill in the country, and that helped him emerge as a national charismatic leader. Chávez, on the other hand, declined somewhat on the charismatic scale. The following year, for example, Chávez suffered a staggering defeat at the polls, almost 2 to 1, on a proposed farm labor ballot initiative.

Brown's reported desire to cut down Chávez even as he fought for the farmworkers cause is just the sort of compromised commitment that critics say is typical of the governor. One top Chicano legislative aide, who is among those critics, observes: "Sure, he's made some significant appointments, but then he lets those Chicanos hang out to dry." He continues with an example. "Look at Obledo. That poor guy got stuck with the Health and Welfare Agency, then Brown proceeds to do a Reagan number on him. He wouldn't give him a dime to do anything. All show and no go."

Again the Lorenz book fills in an unflattering picture that, if accurate, demonstrates why many Chicanos felt that Obledo made a mistake in accepting a "no win" job as Secretary of the enormous Health and Welfare Agency. "Once it was so bad," Lorenz writes, "that Mario sat mute, almost comatose, for two days while Jerry blue-penciled the Welfare Department's budget." The acting director of welfare reportedly said, "I couldn't believe it. Here was a noted Mexican-American public interest lawyer letting the welfare recipients take it in the ear, while I, a former member of the Reagan administration, was arguing on their behalf."

Obledo disputes the charge that Brown put him in the saddle but gave him no horse. Obledo points out that Brown has substantially increased the medical programs and welfare for children and has supported Assemblyman Peter Chacon's innovative bilingual school legislation. However, the belief continues among many Chicano activists that, Obledo has been used by Brown as the flak-catcher for what was supposed to be a liberal administration.

So the true picture is hard to be sure of—like one of those novelty postcards that changes depending on the angle of your viewpoint. Is Jerry Brown the liberal governor genuinely anxious to improve the situation of Chicanos, or is he the ambitious politician whose appointments reflect only the skin-deep concerns of an opportunist? Latino voters also will get a chance to assess Brown in the final campaign weeks on how much he continues to support affirmative action programs in civil service, bilingual education and the positive aspects of the controversial Bakke decision on affirmative action in light of the conservative tilt of the electorate, as indicated by the passage of Proposition 13. Programs and jobs most affecting minorities will receive closer scrutiny and under the guise of cost efficiency may well be cut first. The Chicano legislative caucus must insure that his sincere commitment to Latino people is not compromised by political considerations.

Most California political observers believe that Brown, who opposed Proposition 13, is now making a public appeal to the 65% who voted for Prop. 13 by promising frugality and lowered expectations. Assemblyman Joe Montoya is among those who believe that the governor is facing as tough as race as he is because he already has gone too far in that direction. "He may not have the same loyalty in 1978 as he had in 1974. Many Blacks, Chicano labor leaders, and barrio Raza are disappointed in his handling of Proposition 13. In 1978, there won't be the same type of illusion that existed in 1974."

But whatever may be true of his post-13 turnings, there is no indication that Brown has forgotten the importance of the Latino vote. Quietly, the campaign continues to work toward bringing in a record number of loyal Chicanos on election day. He knows that those voters are important not only in his re-election, but for his presidential ambitions as well. During his brief run at the 1976 Democratic presidential nomination, Brown drew much organizational support from the national network of those active in the cause of farmworkers. Brown is aware that such support is not likely to be there again if he has lost the backing of California's Latinos. But right now, no one knows whether he has lost that backing or not. That is what the state's Chicano population and the nation will find out in November when Jerry Brown's Chicano strategy is put to the test.

Of Hacienda Mexicans and
Aging Liberals
(Party Abandons Liberal Tradition)

A shorter version appeared in The Bakersfield Californian, **Aug. 8, 1993**

S tate Assemblyman Jim Costa lost the 16th District Senate seat in last month's special election because he didn't run as a Democrat against his Republican opponent, Phil Wyman. Costa, like so many other Valley Democrats before him, tried to position himself to the right of his conservative opponent. Comments like, "I'm more conservative than Mr. Wyman on many issues," are hardly the type of phrases that will get moderate-to-liberal-voters to come out in huge numbers to offset the loyal Republican vote. And against Wyman, whose dubious claim to fame among Latinos was calling them "wetbacks," Costa was a fool to think that a "more conservative than thou" position was going to warm the political hearts of Latino voters.

Costa's political error was the same one made by Kern County Democrats since the 1950's, which is, subscribing to the notion that only a "good ol' boy" Democrat could win an election against a Republican in Kern County. Over the years, Sacramento's Democratic leadership has bought into this theory as well. In 1986, Dave Roberti, the Democratic State Senate leader, thought he had come up with a winner to replace retiring Democratic Senator Walter Stern by hand picking Kern Community College Chancellor Jim Young as the party nominee. The politically untested Young certainly had what appeared to be ideal credentials for Roberti and Kern County's conservative Democratic clique. He was an Oklahoma boy, locally educated and a friend of the farmers. Even with a million and a half dollars (a Kern County Record) that Roberti put into the race, Young came up short. And again, a conservative Democrat lost to the conservative Republican, Assemblyman Don Rogers.

Money has seldom been the issue, for in the case of Young vs. Rogers, the Democrat outspent the Republican by nearly two-to-one. In the case of Costa vs. Wyman, the Democrat outspent the Republican by more than two-and-a-half-to-one. So what's the problem? Why has it been impossible for Democratic challengers to beat Republicans for state legislative seats in Kern County since the 1950s, when all the legislative seats were held by Democrats. The only exception to this was the 1972 victory of Ray Gonzales (the author) who ran as an under-funded liberal against three term Republican incumbent Kent Stacy. This was certainly an anomaly.

What has occurred in Kern County since the 1950s is exactly what has happened to the Democratic Party in the Deep South. In years past, the South was commonly referred to as the "Solid South" because of its loyalty to the Democratic Party since the Civil War. In the 1950s and 60s the Southern Democratic party was irreparably split by the Civil Rights movement that swept across the nation. The efforts to gain civil rights, including voting rights for the Negroes throughout the South, effectively destroyed the Democratic Party unity of that region. We must remember that it was Democratic Governors such as George Wallace and Orval Faubus who stood in schoolroom doors with ax handles to keep black students out. In those days before Civil Rights, virtually all Southern Governors, Senators and House Members were Democrats. A common refrain was that a Republican politician in the South was as rare as a nudist at a Baptist convention.

The Civil Rights movement, along with the perceived unpatriotic anti-Vietnam War protests, and changing lifestyles combined to make conservatives even more conservative. In the South, this meant causing Democrats to turn Republican. A significant numbers of white Southern politicians, as well, changed their party colors. Some very visible figures such as Mississippi's Senator Strom Thurmond changed from being Dixiecrat Democrats to being unflinching conservative Republicans. The exodus from the Democratic Party in the South continued throughout most of the 60s and 70s when such Conservatives as John Connolly and Phil Gramm of Texas became Republicans for ideological reasons as well as the practical reason of wanting to be on Ronald Reagan's winning team. It was, in fact, a Democratic President from Texas, Lyndon Johnson, who predicted the eventual defection when he signed the 1965 Civil Rights Act. "We will see the end of the Democratic Party in the South as we have known it," he commented.

But the South was not the only place where Civil Rights caused Conservative Democrats to show their true colors. In Kern County, where the Dixiecrats from Oklahoma, Arkansas and East Texas had been transplanted during the Dust Bowl days of the Depression, the reaction to Civil Rights was the same. Conservative Democrats could not accept the efforts of "uppity Negroes" and long-haired radicals who were upsetting the tradition of the country. The same reaction to the Civil Rights movement by such Democrats as George Wallace in the South occurred here in Kern County. When Wallace bolted the party and ran as an American Independent, he garnered more votes in Kern County than any place outside of the Deep South, 28 percent.

Additionally, in Kern County, another civil rights movement that was born locally and gained national attention added to the split among local Democrats. The emergence of César Chávez' Farm Worker Union in the Sixties which was clearly identified with the Democratic party, put the finishing touches on Democratic party unity in the county. It pitted liberal Democrats and Chicano activist Democrats against the grower interests identified in the image of the transplanted Dixiecrats. Many of these growers had been Democrats when they had arrived in their impoverished conditions during the Thirties.

The story of the Democratic Party in the South and in places like Kern County and Orange County where Dixiecrats also eventually settled, is the story of the emergence of a new class. Southern novelists William Faulkner in his books writes about a Post-bellum South where the lower class, uneducated, white Southerners take over control of the region from the plantation aristocracy. In his trilogy SNOPES, "Faulkner creates the archetype Flem Snopes, who in his sheer negativism and lack of humanity is one of the most terrifying characters in fiction." But sadly, the Snopeses were not just fiction. They represented the class of anti-intellectual, bigoted tinkers and peddlers who emerged as the dominant force for much of the South up to the Civil Rights movement. They were the backbone of the Klan and the bigots that denied a chair in the lunchroom or classroom to any Negro in the region. But then the social revolution of the 60s set the South on its ear and did the same in those regions of the country where this new breed had taken over. In Kern County, it has been in the triumvirate of agriculture, oil and land development interests where the Snopeses have dominated since WWII. This group too, like their Southern counterparts bolted the Democratic Party, primarily though not exclusively, because of the Civil Rights movement. Economic factors were also often at play.

In the 60s, César Chávez' farmworker movement threatened to alter the economic balance that heavily favored growers at the expense of underpaid and poorly protected agricultural workers. Chávez began to organize the previously voiceless "Hacienda Mexicans" who began to get their faces out of the mud and look to the horizon. This is what revolutions are made of according to the accepted theory. A man does not revolt when his face is in the mud, but rather when he raises his head and begins to see the horizon and the world that is around him. This is why Chávez became the most hated man in the county, at least by the growers and the petty politicians who were supported by them. Locally, Democrats began to bolt the party in record numbers and any Democrats holding office began to feel that the only way to stay in office was to be more conservative than Republican opponents.

The result of this most recent election and the spinelessness of Democratic office holders, and the preference of party leaders in Sacramento for conservative

Democrats over moderate or liberal Democrats resulted in the disillusionment among the remaining liberal-to-moderate Democrats. While they did not all defect and join the Republican ranks, many of them merely dropped out. The aging liberals in Kern County can now be seen packing their cars for the coast on weekends or skiing the slopes at Mammoth in the winter months. And no one can blame them. Local Democrats have nothing but conservative candidates to offer them and State Party leadership in Sacramento has long since washed its hand of Kern County politics.

Thus, the defeat of Jim Costa in the April 17 special election does not bode well for the future of the Democratic Party in Kern County nor is it surprising. Local Democratic leaders and State Party leaders have not changed their failed attitude that none but conservative, good ol' boy Democrats can win in Kern County. The fact is that they have not won. In spite of million dollar campaigns, they have not won. What is apparent is that the growing number of Latino residents in Kern County, 160,000, and the already Democratic Afro-Americans find little to vote for among the local Democrats that have been put forth in the past. And when candidates from these minority groups decide to run, they get little to no support from Party leaders. It is no wonder that voter turn-out and loyalty is low in the county. Why should any self-respecting Democrat go to the polls to vote for a candidate who tries to align him/herself to the right of the opponent and goes after the same grower/oil/developer money that lines the pockets of Republican politicians.

Like the Negroes described in Faulkner's *Sound and the Fury*, and the Latinos described in Rudolfo Gonzales' epic poem, "I am Joaquin," those once Hacienda Mexicans of Kern County "will endure." Just as those black politicians who have emerged as the hope of the Democratic Party in the New South have been winning mayorships in cities like Atlanta and Congressional seats throughout the old Confederacy, Latinos throughout the San Joaquin Valley will endure.

Those Hacienda Mexicans are fast disappearing, being replaced by Chávez inspired activists and other middle class Latinos who have already seen the horizon. Together, with the black party loyalists and the children of the aging liberals of the 60's, they may retake the heart of the Democratic Party, or at least demand that no Kern County Democratic Party will sell out the humanitarian principles on which the Party was based. Otherwise, there really is no reason for Latinos, blacks or liberals to vote for the Democratic candidates the party has been giving them over the last two decades in Kern County.

No Democratic candidate or office holder should ever be allowed to carry the party label while at he same time being afraid to stand for those principles that make one a Democrat. Latinos, Afro-Americans and true Democrats in Kern County should demand that their Party nominees be made of sterner stuff. They should demand that political courage, sensitivity and inclusion be the hallmarks of the Party and the candidate, for as Tom Paine, an early political motivator in American politics, once said, "these are the times that try men's souls . . ."

Nasty Racial Politics

Somos Magazine, **February 1979**

I n a recent article I argued that perhaps 1978 was not the best year for
a Chicano to be seeking statewide office since "several socio-political
factors (had) developed which would virtually guarantee that in 1978 any
Chicano candidate for major office would have to run a defensive campaign."
My reasoning was that attacks on Health and Welfare Agency Secretary Mario
Obledo, DMV Director Herman Sillas, and the problem of Mexican migration
north were scapegoats for the conservative elements of the state.

As it turned out, even though no Chicano candidate was on the ticket of
either major party, the Chicano community figured prominently in this year's
statewide elections. It soon became evident that the Republican candidate for
governor, Evelle Younger, appeared to make the Chicano community the target
of his campaign rhetoric. It is hard to assess just what effect this tactic had on the
ultimate vote, but it presented an interesting phenomenon. Chicanos were taken
seriously in a statewide election, even if in a negative way.

Younger's Attacks

Lt. Governor Mervyn Dymally perhaps best characterized the tone of the Younger
campaign in a speech delivered to 500 delegates at the annual convention of the
Association of Mexican American Educators held in San Francisco on October 28th,
a little more than a week before he was defeated at the polls. "It is very interesting to
note that the Attorney General of California (Younger), in the course of the campaign,
has selected three people for attack: Two Chicanos and one black; Mario Obledo,
Herman Sillas and Merv Dymally . . . I believe the entire state of California ought

to be offended regardless of ones party affiliation at the irresponsible statements the Attorney General has been making about Mario Obledo.

Indeed, the attacks by Younger, who gave the appearance of running more against Jerry Brown appointees than against Brown himself, were so irresponsible that even President Lopez Portillo of Mexico, in an immediate response to the comments about Obledo, issued from Peking, China, where he was on a presidential visit, a strong denunciation of the racist policies toward the Hispanic people in the United States.

In an effort to discredit Brown appointees, Younger had singled out Obledo and declared that, "I would prefer a smart crook rather than an incompetent administrator as head of the Health and Welfare Agency." Younger argued that a smart crook would only rob the state of several million dollars, implying that Obledo would cost the state much more.

Herman Sillas, the U.S. Attorney in Sacramento, and former Brown appointee as the Director of the Department of Motor Vehicles, was also singled out by Younger. He accused Sillas of purposely delaying indictments by a federal grand jury that Younger felt would embarrass the Democratic Party.

Dymally was one of the Democrats whom Younger accused Sillas of trying to protect. Interestingly enough, Younger as Attorney General had conducted an investigation of Dymally less than a year before the election and had concluded that there was no evidence of criminal wrongdoing.

In what some have described as a desperate effort to salvage his faltering campaign, Younger engaged in an exchange of public letters with U.S. Attorney General, Griffin Bell, attempting to discredit Sillas by both attacking him personally and professionally. One thing is certain, by making his letters public, Younger was obviously functioning in the role of gubernatorial candidate rather than as California's Attorney General.

After failing to gain any public opinion points in the polls by his attacks on individual Chicano leaders, Younger seemed to shift his attack towards the entire Latino community by developing a "them and us" argument. In a November 4 press conference in Los Angeles, Younger, while declaring he had to go after uncommitted Democratic and Republican voters, stated that "I think we ought to be honest about it and say there's a certain kind of service that can best be performed by people from Mexico willing to perform it and, for one reason or another, OUR OWN people aren't." (Emphasis added.)

Chicanos all over the state were enraged by the comment, feeling that Younger obviously didn't include them as part of "our own people." One Chicano politician responding to Younger's suggestions of issuing "fool-proof" identification cards to Mexicans remarked, "Yeah, maybe we should all have a Star of David tattooed on your foreheads."

While Younger concentrated his attacks on Chicanos, Mike Curb, the eventual Republican victor in the Lieutenant Governor's race, took over the attacks on

Dymally by flatly stating that "he was guilty of felony crimes." And almost in the same breath, in an attempt to separate himself from Younger, Curb declared that he, was a Chicano because one of his relatives had been one. Both the Younger and Curb campaigns seemed to demonstrate an almost paranoid mixture of politics and prejudice with the question of race ever present in the background.

Chicanos at all levels should be aware that the current attention being paid to the Latino community by the press in articles such as the series in *the Washington Post, Time, and New West,* while appearing to be favorable comments about the awakening of the so-called "sleeping giant," carry with them an element of fear for the present majority community.

Chicanos should avoid any temptation of falling into the trap of being as racially biased as those who have traditionally been in power. Recent reports from Sacramento explain how a takeover by Chicanos of certain state offices can be avoided if we make sure to put a little salt and pepper into our salsa. (Meaning white and black employees.) If such high ranking individuals as an Attorney General and a new Lieutenant Governor do not hesitate to raise the racial specter, we must assume that the average citizens of the state will be quick to criticize what they perceive to be excessive Chicano gains.

The truth of the matter is that the facts are on the side of the Latinos. While all other groups have reached parity with the labor force in state service, the Spanish surnamed population is barely at 7 percent while it constitutes 16 percent of the labor force in the state. These things take time, but *mañana* seems a bit too far away.

Wilson's Attack on Affirmative Action Continues

Hispanic Link News Service, **March 1996**

There is no limit to how far Governor Pete Wilson of California will go in his quest for the Republican nomination for president in 1996. Having already championed the immigrant bashing Proposition 187 on last year's California ballot, he most recently led the trustees of the University of California system to vote to end affirmative action programs at the nine campuses of that institution. Now his most recent insidious action is to sue his own state "to rid it of minority and gender preferences in state-sponsored construction contracts." Also included in the suit filed in the state appellate court in Sacramento was the proposed repeal of two state laws that require state agencies and community colleges to meet affirmative action hiring goals.

The proof of Wilson's less than subtle attempt to gain points on the polling charts in anticipation of the election is that he is taking this action on the advice of political consultants who believe he must push the "hot buttons" in order to move out of the pack of the those Republicans presently trailing Robert Dole for the presidential nomination. The fact of the matter is that no group is asking Wilson to take this action. There is no organized group pushing for an end to affirmative action or race and gender preferences in the state. No one is asking him to lead the charge. Certainly, there is sentiment in favor of an end to affirmative action among right-wing groups, but it is the politicians like Wilson who seek to become leaders through demagoguery and malevolent opportunism rather than by more noble example. So much for profiles in courage.

Wilson's attack on community college hiring is especially insensitive, since community colleges in California have long been the best hope of students of color for beginning a college career. These institutions' revolving door policy has made it possible for millions of minority students to go on to greater heights in academia. I began my own journey towards a Ph.D. at a community college. Today, across this country, community colleges enroll over 52% of all minority students entering higher education. Many community colleges, which are located in the inner cities of California, are predominately minority because they are, in fact, truly community colleges. Tribal Colleges on many U.S. Indian reservations also provide community college opportunities to Native Americans who have long been passed over by higher education in this country.

For Wilson to say that these institutions should not be sensitive to race and gender in hiring is to take a giant step backwards in civil rights history. In my own academic career, I began teaching in the mid-1960s at the same community college I had attended in California. For the five years I was there as faculty, before moving on to a state university, I was the only Latino faculty member of 200 instructors employed by the institution. Not coincidentally, there was also only one African American and one Asian on the faculty.

The year I left, 1968, was perhaps one of the most turbulent years on college campuses throughout the United State. At my own campus, located in the Central Valley of California, the stirrings of civil rights and equal justice were no less evident. Because the Latino MECHA students, the Black Student Union and sympathetic faculty were supportive, I succeeded in getting the academic senate to pass a resolution demanding that the school administration hire ten minority faculty for the coming year, barely five percent, but certainly more than the three tokens I and my two minority colleagues represented. The administration accepted the resolution, not because of our reasonable arguments, but because students were sitting-in on college campuses throughout the country.

For Wilson to suggest that the good ol' boy network, that has dominated state agencies and academic institution for all of our history will do the right thing, is to expect us to believe in the tooth fairy. Left to their own devices, institutional bureaucracies will perpetuate themselves. The English colonialists would not have left India except for Ghandi and the movement he inspired. The Deep South would not have been desegregated except for Martin Luther King and a host of other civil rights workers and the movement they engendered. Our own American Revolution would not have occurred except for the farmers and shopkeepers who took up their muskets and began a revolution that put an end to monarchy in our own country. Wilson and his kind should read a little of Thomas Paine and Thomas Jefferson if they wish to become leaders. Those who would lead should be inspired by great and noble thoughts on how to bring a people together, not on how to divide and fragment them so as to eke out an election victory with the support of a small plurality of the most narrow minded and angriest voters among us.

Wilson, despite his mild-mannered demeanor, has during his political life, made it a practice to seek to divide the electorate on emotional issues that often spawn hatred and bigotry. His appeal to the lowest aspects of American character make him unfit for any higher public office.

A Living Wage? Shame, Shame

Hispanic Link News Service, **March 1995**

There should be no debate over the minimum wage issue, especially in this town, Washington, D.C. This is a town where Congress and federal employees earn their money and spend it lavishly. To argue over the paltry forty-five cent raise proposed for the first year to raise the minimum wage from $4.25 an hour to $4.70 an hour and to $5.15 in the second year exposes our crassness to the world. Others have calculated that the $4.25 an hour equals $170 a week and $8,840 a year. If we deduct a modest 10% social security and state and federal taxes, we are talking about $7,956 as an annual net income. Nobody, but nobody, really believes a single person, no less a family can live on $7,956 a year—maybe in a third world country.

But this is not really the issue. What we fail to point out when talking about the absurdity of the business sector's response that they will have to layoff workers, is the fact that those who hire workers at the minimum wage are already getting away with murder. Not only do they pay a less-than-living-wage, in most cases they do not provide even partial health insurance for their workers; they routinely stagger hours of employees, making them less than full-time so that the employer won't have to pay for certain benefits required by law for full-timers, or give sick leave or vacation time.

And who are these minimum wage employees? In almost every news account seen on T.V. recently discussing the issue, the busboys, dishwashers, maids, janitors and farm workers shown in the background were people of color. Certainly, there are thousands of whites working at minimum wage, but statistics demonstrate that roughly seventy-five percent of those entering the service labor force are minorities and women. One need only walk into a McDonalds, Burger King or Taco Bell to see who is passing out the food. Even in suburbia, local, middle-class kids shy away from these jobs, resulting in residents of the inner cities commuting to the suburbs for these minimum wage jobs. And the response from some of these fast-food super powers that they will have to lay off workers is a bit hollow when the fact is that a new fast-food franchise opens every thirty minutes in this country.

To allow corporate America, which ultimately sets the agenda for wage disputes in the workplace, to claim that a higher minimum wage will cause them to layoff workers, is to fall for more than another Colonel's Chicken Little story. Do we really believe that the McDonalds Corporation or PepsiCo, which owns Taco Bell, Pizza Hut and Kentucky Fried Chicken are really going to be hurt by an increase of 90 cents an hour over two years. We all know we will all just be required to pay more for our hamburgers and fries. And certainly we can afford it. Estimates are that the price of a burger would not have to be raised by 2 cents in order to cover the increase in the minimum wage that is being proposed.

As federal employees, last year we got a 2.5% COLA (Coast of Living Adjustment) increase passed by the Congress for the District of Columbia. This amounted to $1,289 increase a year for a federal employee earning $50,582. Add to this the automatic step increase that every federal employee gets every year and that $50,582 federal employee gained $2,771 automatically last year because the Congress took care of him/her. Just this total, automatic raise given to the federal employee in this region last year amounted to 35% of the total annual take home pay of the minimum wage earner.

But federal employees are not overpaid nor treated well beyond reason. The fact is that their coast of living and step increases are based on averages compiled by the Bureau of Labor Statistics of wages paid around the country in the private sector. What makes this debate on the minimum wage almost immoral is the fact that this group of minimum wage workers are already the most ill-treated workers in the American labor force. Nearly all of the millions of minimum wage employees in this country also work without healthcare benefits being provided for them by the large corporate employers who employ the bulk of these workers.

Additionally, federal law has never included farmworkers under the labor protection of the National Labor Relations Act. Farm workers have no right to bargain collectively in this country. Minimum wage workers, because they are subjected to part-time status in many instances and work in small groups, have never been able to organize into unions for their own protection. And because so many of these minimum wage workers are recent immigrants (mostly legal), they find it very hard to fight for their rights.

So it should be the Congress, speaking on behalf of those among us who have the least, and work the hardest that should end this shameful debate and vote to increase the minimum wage without delay. It is hypocritical to argue "work instead of welfare" and then expect someone to support themselves and perhaps a family on $8,840 a year.

Why Chicanos Don't Vote

The California Journal, July 1975

The Crab Vendor

A *tourist walking down a seaside street one day happened upon a man selling live crabs from a tub on the sidewalk. As the two men conversed about the weather, sight-seeing attractions and anything else a crab vendor and tourist might wish to discuss, the tourist noticed that the crabs were all moving slowly toward the side of the tub and forming a pyramid by stacking themselves one upon the other.*

The vendor, who had been paying no attention to the activity of the crabs, dismissed the tourist's expression of concern that the crabs might escape. As the crabs' pyramid reached closer and closer to the top of the tub, the tourist became increasingly amazed at the vendor's nonchalance. Finally, unable to restrain himself any longer, the tourist blurted out, "Those crabs are going to get out in a minute!"

"Oh don't worry," the vendor replied, carelessly. "Those are Chicano crabs. When one finally gets ready to make it over the top, the others will pull out from under it."

The story of the crab vendor is one that Chicanos tell on themselves and, in spite of its humor, it is also taken by Chicano activists as an all-to-accurate description of their own political behavior. A recent example occurred when two Chicano legislators criticized Governor Edmund G. Brown Jr. for his appointment of Mario Obledo as secretary of the Health and Welfare Agency. Their action drew a cry of dismay from the Chicano community. And the story of the crab vendor once again made its rounds.

Enough has been said and written about the occasional fratricide that occurs and may continue to occur among minority communities. And there may never be an end to the internal struggles that erupt within minority communities. Assemblyman Richard Alatorre was denied success in 1970 in his first political effort by the presence in the race of a Raza Unida candidate that denied victory to a Democrat and gave success to an Anglo Republican in an otherwise Democratic district. Last November, when I was up for reelection as an assemblyman, Raza Unida accused me of being unsympathetic to Chicano causes while the Anglo press in the district attacked me for being "part and parcel of the political coalition of venal White politicians, power-hungry White labor leaders, education professionals, Negroes, self-styled Chicanos, welfare-rights professionals and other minorities whose ideology is out of step with the White majority."

There is little likelihood that the Chicano community will ever be unanimous in its political behavior. It does not occur within the Democratic or Republican parties in the Black community, in the Jewish community nor even in the John Birch Society. But perhaps the Chicano community will begin to develop the political sophistication that it will need to ensure adequate representation for its four million people in California.

Chicano Trap

Just two days after last November's election, the Los Angelas *Times* published an article by G. Guitierrez and Cesar Sereseres, entitled, "Nada por Nada, Nothing for Nothing, the Chicano Political Trap." The thesis of their essay was that most successful statewide candidates are under no real obligation to make any concessions to Chicanos in California because Chicanos possess "a self-defeating tradition of not voting." Neither Brown nor his Republican opponent, Houston Flournoy, was under any obligation to court the favor of Chicanos during the last gubernatorial campaign, Gutierrez and Sereseres wrote. They could point to three areas of political support in which the Chicano community did not produce:

> ***Financial support.*** Because the Chicano community and its organizations lack real economic power, a candidate can expect little financial support.

> ***Endorsements.*** Traditionally visible spokesmen for Mexican-Americans have been minor power-brokers primarily interested in landing a job in the administration.

Voting. Although Chicanos constitute 18 to 20 percent of California's population, in most general elections they can be expected to produce only about five percent of the vote.

"California candidates have been fully aware that Chicanos over the years have been incapable—or unwilling—to employ their vote with the same degree of sophistication as, say, Blacks," Gutierrez and Sereseres concluded. The writers expressed openly what many political observers have known for some time: Chicano spokesmen tend to place all of the blame for electoral failure on the White establishment. Though it is true that reapportionment plans over the years have avoided developing Chicano legislative districts by splitting up *barrios* such as in East Los Angeles, it is also true that Chicano voter apathy has resulted in the election of non-Chicano legislators and local officials in areas with significant Chicano registration.

Behind the apathy

What causes the apparent apathy that results in a five percent voter turnout? Historically, Chicanos are recent arrivals to California, though a few of them trace their heritage back to the area's long and rich Hispanic heritage; most are 20th-Century arrivals from Mexico. In 1909, the year before the Mexican revolution, there were some 4,000 Mexican immigrants in the United States. By 1916, in the peak years of fighting during the revolution, there were as many as 90,000 legal immigrants crossing the border form Mexico. During the years of the *bracero,* when field labor was short in the United States, as many as 200,000 *braceros* a year crossed the border, plus about an equal number of undocumented entrants. Many of these Mexicans married and remained in the U.S. Additionally, a good percentage—perhaps 20 percent of California's Chicano population—has migrated from Texas during the last few decades.

How does this affect voting patterns? First, there is little true political tradition in Mexico. The country is run under a one-party system. Moreover, the secret ballot there is a farce and has been for most of this century. This background has led Mexican immigrants both to maintain close relationships with relatives in Mexico and to look with skepticism upon the political process in this country. Add to this the language barrier maintained for many years in the voting process and the fact that Chicanos have compromised the largest migratory labor force in the state, and it is little wonder that the Chicano voter appears to be peculiarly apathetic.

In terms of supplying financial support to candidates, the Chicano community's inability to deliver funds is a product of both tradition and poverty. In 1968, there were fewer than a hundred Chicano students among UCLA's 25,000 students, in a city of more than a million Chicanos; it is not difficult to imagine a paucity of professionals among Chicanos. In the business community, the situation has been no better, though there is a beginning. For many years Chicanos were found in agricultural work, railroading and domestic services—not areas likely to generate potent political contributions for the Chicano community.

Finally, there have been no political "heavies" in Chicano communities to whom the candidates could look for endorsements. The fratricide, suspicion and betrayal that produced the crab-vendor story have not escaped the attention of Chicano and Anglo politicians, not to mention party leaders. At best, one hoped to avoid conflict among divergent Chicano groups, but rarely did a candidate seek the support of whatever passed for Chicano leadership.

There are stirrings, however. In 1970, there was one Chicano legislator in California. Now, there are two senators and four assemblymen. And there is a growing number of local Chicano elected officials.

Perhaps the most dramatic change for Chicanos occurred with the inauguration of Governor Jerry Brown. In the past, there was never any real doubt that qualified Chicanos were available to serve in government; there was, however, also great difficulty in winning for them the support of the major political parties. Now, however, the new Governor has made appointments to state government that can be expected to have a lasting effect on the State of California. Health and Welfare Secretary Obledo heads the largest state agency in the nation. Herman Sillas is director of the Department of Motor Vehicles. Julian Camacho has been named deputy director of the Department of General Services.

And Brown is not alone: Lieutenant Governor Mervyn Dymally named Joe Serna as chief education advisor, and Assembly Speaker Leo McCarthy selected Ralph Ochoa to head his Los Angeles office.

Yet, despite this increase in elected and appointed officials, a feeling of frustration and skepticism persists among Chicanos. For one thing, no Chicano has ever held a state-wide office. To do so, however, will require wide support outside the Chicano community. The successful candidate will make it on his or her own merits, not on the basis (or in spite of) a surname or skin color or Chicano affiliations. California voters have already demonstrated the fact that they will accept minority leadership in the persons of Dymally and Superintendent of Public Instruction Wilson Riles and Secretary of State March Fong Eu. It may be that Blacks have had it easier because of guilt complex prevalent among many White liberals, but that advantage was seized because of the political sophistication that exists in the Black community. Fong was elected on the basis of her popular appeal, not her ethnic background.

Everyone's Problems

The failure of a Chicano to have fared as well lies also in the fact that the dominant culture has never really fully understood the Latin culture, and that

Latins have never really grasped how the political process works in California. A Chicano candidate *can* succeed, but the successful state-wide politician's commitment must be made to human beings, not to Chicanos, Democrats, Republicans, or minorities generally. The issues are *people* issues, the problems everyone's. At the same time, while no Chicano candidate will be successful state-wide by relating only to Chicanos, he or she must nonetheless be an inspiration to Chicanos. Since five percent of the vote offers a small operating base—even if it is secured—the successful candidate must also inspire the Chicano community to raise that percentage.

Chicanos appear to be ready for such a candidate. California is ready for full Chicano representation. And potential candidates probably abound. But before one reaches the top of the pyramid, or tub as it were, one must succeed in each step and not fear the legacy of the vendor's "Chicano crabs".

Missing: The Chicano Candidate

The California Journal, **May 1978**

With the June primary election only a month away, the political stage is crowded with a cast of hundreds. But conspicuously absent from that cast is any Chicano candidate of stature seeking statewide office. Some militant Chicanos claim this is because the California electorate is "racist," but the political success stories among other minorities refute that charge.

The Asian community can point to March Fong Eu, virtually unchallenged for her second term as secretary of state, and to U.S. Senator S.I. Hayakawa. Blacks have two incumbent state office-holders seeking reelection: Lieutenant Governor Mervyn Dymally and Superintendent of Public Instruction Wilson Riles. In addition, a popular Black congresswoman, Yvonne Brathwaite Burke, is running for attorney general.

In terms of numbers alone, the Chicano population should be on the political rise. The *Los Angeles Times* recently reported that 28.8 percent of Los Angeles County is currently Chicano, and the percentage is increasing yearly. Other studies indicate that Spanish-surnamed people will be the dominant population in California by 1990—by which time minorities will outnumber whites in California, and Chicanos will outnumber any other minority.

Yet there are a variety of political realities that do support the theory that the California electorate is not ready for a Chicano candidate. Or, perhaps more accurately, a Chicano candidate is not ready for the California electorate. Several socio-political factors have developed which would virtually guarantee that in 1978 any Chicano candidate for major office would have to run a defensive campaign. These factors, producing an image problem for the entire Chicano community, include the following:

- *Gangs and gangland*—Chicano prison gangs, La Familia (a rural-oriented group) and the Mexican Mafia (urban-oriented), represent a new movement of a nonpolitical nature among the criminal element in the Chicano community. The wide media attention these groups receive distorts the reality of their small numbers. The state Justice Department estimates that there are only "between 150 and 200 hard-core members of the Mexican Mafia." Yet, even with these small numbers, there is no dispute that they are involving themselves to a considerable degree in criminal activity in California. The department indicates that the Mexican Mafia is involved in "drug dealing, protection rackets and assaults in prisons. On the street, the Mexican Mafia is active in narcotics, robbery, extortion and homicide."

The recent emergence of the Chicano gangs as "high rollers" in the underworld is a rather strange sociological phenomenon. It results from a series of events for which the Chicano community is certainly not responsible but for which it is suffering. It was the end of the Vietnam War the catapulted the petty Chicano gangsters into the higher levels of crime. With most of Southeast Asia falling under Communist control, the lucrative drug traffic shifted from that part of the world to Mexico and South America. Suddenly the Chicano gangs emerged as high-level drug dealers rather than "the street-corner hustlers" they once were. Suddenly the language of the drug deal became Spanish and the entry-point was the Mexican border.

A recent Associated Press story reporting on the subject indicated that U.S. drug officers have discovered that "narcotics traffickers search out peasants in isolated areas (of Mexico) offering them money, goods and sometimes guns to plant, cultivate and harvest opium poppies and marijuana." But Mexico is hardly the only source for the drugs coming into the United States. Justice Department officials now calculate that Columbia currently receives as much money from illicit drug production as from the production of coffee.

The role of the Chicano gangster in the drug traffic has obviously become indispensable in the business. The gangland killings, the prison assaults, the protection racket and related crimes such as extortion are not dissimilar to the style and techniques employed by the original Mafia.

- *The immigrant problem*—Related somewhat to the drug traffic is the ever-increasing entry of Mexican immigrant into the United States. Certainly most immigrants—estimated at between 8 to 12 million now—are in no way involved in bringing drugs into the country. Sometimes, though, the price an undocumented Mexican pays for getting across the border is serving as a carrier of heroin or other drugs.

Most illegal immigrants from Mexico, however, come to the States for purely economic reasons. The *Wall Street Journal* reports that "the disparity between economic conditions and opportunities in Mexico and the U.S. is too great . . . So long as the Mexican birthrate yields a sky-high 3.5 percent annual population growth, far outstripping the nation's capacity to create jobs, and so long as employers in the U.S. yearn for cheap labor that will work hard and work scared for wages that would be princely in Mexico, and army of the jobless will continue to plod north."

They are plodding north at an accelerated rate. U.S. Border Patrol officials indicate, that "the 1,017,000 captured in the year that ended September 30 made the highest total since 1954, when 1,092,000 were caught." And they estimate that for every one they catch, two escape This staggering increase in illegal border crossings and the resultant media attention had divided the American citizenry and once again fanned the flames of bigotry, just as it did during the arrival, legal or illegal, of the Italians, the Irish and the Eastern Europeans during the early 1900s.

In fact, the issue has become so emotional that the Klu Klux Klan this year initiated its own "border patrol," attempting to keep out "the unwanted foreigners who take jobs from Americans." Even though statistics indicate that Mexican illegals generally take only the jobs that American citizens don't want, the impact of their presence sends shudders through those who are always made uncomfortable by the mere presence of "foreigners" with darker skins and a different language.

- *The Mondanaro affair*—Partly because of their increasing numbers, Chicanos are now waging a new concerted effort to find jobs in all sectors, including public service. César Chávez's courageous efforts on behalf of farmworkers have been overshadowed in the past few years of Health and Welfare Secretary Mario Obledo and others to find meaningful positions for Chicanos in civil service.

Though Obledo and his former assistant, Xavier Mena, have been criticized severely by the media for their roles in Governor Brown's firing of Dr. Josette Mondanaro, they emerged as heroes in the Chicano community. Obledo made no bones about his efforts on behalf of the Spanish-speaking. Testifying in the Mondanaro hearing, he said, "I'm going to do all within my power to make certain the Spanish-speaking people are brought into state government." But he added, "I'm friendly with all kinds of people. That's why I'm in trouble now—because the office of the Secretary has been open to people who had never been able to see an Agency Secretary."

Ironically, the gay community feels it won a victory in the Mondanaro affair, while Chicanos suffered a setback. Even ex-Police Chief Ed Davis of

Los Angeles supported Mondanaro, but Chicano affirmative-action efforts were generally denounced.

As a result, there is a growing frustration among Chicano state employees and Chicano leaders, who are aware of the backlash among white co-workers and the general public but helpless to counteract it. It appears, too, that overly aggressive affirmative-action officers in some state departments have played into the hands of their critics. Appellate Court Judge Cruz Reynoso has suggested that Obledo and other state Chicano leaders "may be victims of over-zealous staff members" who have implemented affirmative-action programs with somewhat "heavy-handed tactics." Whatever the tactics, two things are certain: Chicanos have gained less than 2 percent in state employment since the beginning of the Brown Administration—and their gains are far less significant than their critics believe.

Obledo, fact and fiction

The central figure in the controversy over affirmative action in state government is obviously Obledo. As the highest Chicano appointee in California, Obledo would be the logical choice for statewide candidacy if it were not for the current climate and the fact that he has always said, "I'm not a politician."

Governor Brown, in a recent statement to the *Los Angeles Times* in defense of his beleaguered agency secretary, echoed the same sentiment: "Mario is not a politician. He does not play the political game . . . He is a highly moral, highly religious person who tries to do his job in a very straightforward way . . . He's not hanging around bars in Sacramento talking to legislators or bureaucrats. He goes home to his family, and now he is paying a certain price for that . . ."

It was Obledo who, in the early days of the Brown Administration, urged the Governor to end the evening cabinet meetings and shift to a day schedule so that cabinet members could spend a little more time with their families.

The truth is that Obledo inherited an agency that had nearly as many problems as it did employees. With such departments as Corrections, Youth Authority, Health, Narcotics and Drug Abuse, to name a few, he took on a "no-win" job. The Health and Welfare Agency deals with people problems, and there appears to be no end to people problems. Obledo took the job against the advice of many Chicanos, who said, "You will be crucified in that job." The more politically sophisticated Chicanos felt that a minority person in that position would be a sitting duck for the conservative elements of the state, as well as a scapegoat for a liberal administration.

Steve Barber, a former deputy director in the now-defunct Office of Educational Liaison in the Health and Welfare Agency, says, "Mario inherited a real mess left for him by Earl Brian and company. While he (Brian) used the agency as a thinly disguised campaign organization for his U.S. Senate aspirations, the mental hospitals were . . . neglected, social services to Californians were broken up and submerged to be replaced by a highly visible and politically marketable, public-dole system called the Department of Benefit Payments. What really bothers me now is that no one recalls that under Brian there wasn't a single woman or minority on the agency's professional staff."

Barber writes off Obledo's troubles to election-year politics: "One thing the Governor and Mario refused to do when they took over the kitchen was to clean out the middle-management pantry of all the Reagan leftovers who had run for cover at the first hint Flournoy couldn't beat Brown. Now these leftovers have started to spoil."

Nevertheless, Obledo left his teaching job at Harvard Law School to return to California to, in his words, "take on the only job I would have accepted in the administration, a job where I could do something for people." Unfortunately for Obledo, his tenure as Secretary has caused him and the entire Chicano community a great deal of anguish. The press has been less than sympathetic. Accusations of cronyism in the employment, underworld ties and other charges against Obledo have depressed him and angered many Chicano community leaders who want him to "come out fighting."

Because of Obledo's style and his adamant disinterest in political office, it is unlikely that he will ever seek elected office in California. But he has become perhaps the most popular Chicano in the Spanish-speaking community. The strong support for him was demonstrated by a gathering in Sacramento of nearly 2,000 persons last December, and more recently in Los Angeles where 5,800 gathered to show Chicano solidarity. Obledo is able to attract this support precisely because he is not a politician and does not constitute a threat to any of the elected Chicano legislators. Also, unlike most politicians, he has not been afraid to speak out on controversial Chicano issues.

His recent dispute with the Youth Authority Director Pearl West is a case in point. Obledo was adamant in pointing out that in the 30-year history of the CYA, there had never been a Chicano deputy director. He rejected the idea that there were no "qualified" Chicanos among the 4,000 employees of the department. This concern of Obledo's has endeared him to the Chicano community, but at the same time has not made him a favorite among many state employees. Yet, despite his efforts over the last three years, the employment rate of Chicanos in the Health and Welfare Agency is still only 8.6 percent compared to the 6.8 percent they constituted when Obledo arrived. (Chicanos constitute 13.7 percent of the labor force in the state.)

Another of the visible Chicano leaders, who was twice a candidate for statewide office, has opted to follow a path other than the political trail. Herman Sillas, former director of the Department of Motor Vehicles appointed by Governor Brown in 1975, was recently selected by President Carter to serve as U.S. Attorney for the eastern district of California. Sillas will, no doubt, tackle his new post with same vigor he displayed at DMV; but, for the political present he has removed himself from California politics.

If not Sillas or Obledo, who will be the first electable Chicano candidate for statewide office? Many Sacramento observers see Assemblyman Art Torres of Los Angeles as the brightest star among the Chicano legislators. But for a Chicano legislator to succeed, he would have to have a much broader base than East Los Angeles. One Chicano political figure who holds no elected office, but who has very strong ties in the Democratic party throughout the state, is Ralph Ochoa, chief of staff to Assembly Speaker Leo McCarthy. Ochoa, however, is considering pursuing his legal career rather than continuing in politics at the present time.

The loyal constituents

Although there will not be any efforts in 1978 on behalf of a major Chicano candidate, the role of Chicanos may take on new significance. The fact that Jerry Brown appeared at both Obledo functions, proclaimed that "I am only as strong as you are," and indicated that Obledo was "his proudest appointment," obviously indicates that Brown—a master at pulse-taking—realized even before the latest California Poll that his most loyal constituency was the Chicano community. While his popularity as a "good" governor had fallen from 53 percent in March 1976 to 29 percent in February 1978, his "good" rating remained highest among Chicanos at 42 percent. Another survey among Chicano leaders throughout the country indicates that Brown received a "good" to "outstanding" rating from 83 percent of those Chicanos surveyed, while President Carter received only a 20 percent rating.

So—even though this will not be its year—the Chicano community may be a political force to reckon with in the future. It has three big assets: increasing vote-power; a growing middle-class that is more politically sophisticated; and a loyalist's tie to an ambitious governor. Now the Chicanos must find the leaders to translate these assets into statewide electability.

The Bilingual Ballot:
Plus or Minus for Chicanos?

Somos Magazine, Sept. 1978

B efore the 1964 Civil Rights Act, there were fewer than one hundred Black elected officials in the Deep South. Now there are nearly two thousand. As a result of marches, the militancy, and the voter registration efforts facilitated by federal legislation, Black citizens in the South, always a sizable population, finally began to exercise their franchise in the 1960s. Gone were the poll taxes and the bias local laws and elected officials that discouraged Black citizens from voting for over one hundred years.

In 1976, the U.S. Congress was required to extend the Voting Rights Act of 1964, and as a result of the emerging Chicano and Asian militancy and such court decisions as *Lau* vs. *Nicoles*, the Congress added a new dimension to the voting rights legislation—bilingual voting materials.

While the results of the initial Voting Rights Act among the Black community in the South is quite demonstrable, its bilingual component in the Southwest has, up to this point, had little tangible impact. In fact, the backlash among the Anglo community is so severe that the program appears to be in jeopardy. At a time when the fiscal conservatism embodied in California's Proposition 13 is enjoying such success, the costliness of the bilingual ballots seems to outweigh any positive aspects that might be embodied in the legislation. While one opponent exclaims. "If they want to be citizens, let them learn English," another retorts, "There is nothing in the Constitution that says English is the national language."

The emotion and rhetoric surrounding the issue is heightened in the weeks preceding an election and the backlash begins to surface in the "Letters to the

Editor" section of most newspapers as the bilingual material begins to arrive in the households of California and throughout the Southwest. Even supportive Latinos are somewhat embarrassed by the cost factors that are attached to this new voting requirement and find it difficult to defend the concept.

"Sure, there is a real need for bilingual ballot programs so that certain voters can vote effectively and intelligently," declares Ray Ortiz, a top election official in the Secretary of State's office in California, "but all the time and effort and expense is not necessary." Ortiz believes that the counties are now in position to target the bilingual voter. "At the time of registration, the voter can specify if he/she wants the ballot sent to him/her in another language," declares Ortiz. He feels that there are many counties in California that shouldn't be covered by the federal law or the state law. Ortiz concludes, however, that "there is no much we can do about it."

Basically, what the Federal Voting Rights Act states is that if a minimum of five percent of the citizens of voting age in any single language minority group live in a county, the voter pamphlet, sample ballot and the ballot must be printed in both languages. In California, the state legislature has even gone one step further. By statute, the Legislature has reduced the five percent figure to three percent. This has resulted in an extreme application of what is basically a sound principle of guaranteeing the right to vote.

What has caused the negative reaction and the numerous expressions of the *vox populi* attacking the bilingual ballot are the dismal figures that underline the impracticality of the method in which the law has been applied. For example, in Contra Costa County, where figures are readily obtainable for the June, 1978 primary, the results were that 265 bilingual ballots were requested of the county clerk, but only seven voters of the 31,000 in the county cast a bilingual ballot. In Sonoma County, which also falls within the three percent minimum, 52,000 bilingual pamphlets were printed and only twelve bilingual ballots were requested.

In Sacramento County, where all of the nearly 250,000 ballots were printed bilingually, only 583 bilingual ballot pamphlets were requested prior to the election. There is no way of calculating how many voters read and used the bilingual portion of the ballot as all voters punch the same holes on the ballot depending on their choice of candidates or issues. In other northern California counties covered by statute, the results were as bleak. In Mendocino, there were five requests for bilingual pamphlets and ballots; in Colusa, eight; in Stanisluas, 150; and in Sutter County, a request for 16.

By far the greatest demand for bilingual material comes from Los Angeles County where over a million and a half Chicanos live, but even there the request was not that significant. Margaret Miller, the election count supervisor in LA County indicated that 59,000 bilingual ballots were requested prior to the election. Much of this material is used by foreign language teachers for classroom use and "just people who are curious," Ms. Miller declares. In Los Angeles County, like Sacramento County, all of the ballots are printed bilingually so there is no practical way of knowing who voted using the Spanish version of the ballot.

Statewide, in the June primary, the Secretary of State's office found that there were 192,000 requests for bilingual material among the nine million or so registered voters. Of this figure, 12,500 requests were for Chinese voting materials and the remainder of 180,000 were for Spanish language material.

The small percentage, 2.1 %, in the eyes of many, hardly warrants the expenditure. This year the Secretary of State's office has shifted the fiscal burden to the counties, a burden that is considerable. The Secretary of State's office spends only $54,090 on the translation, printing, and proofreading of the bilingual materials for the state ballot. Sonoma County, alone, for example, spends $52,000 for all of its voting material and in Sonoma County this material produced only 12 Spanish language voters. This results in nearly $4,000 per voter spent on bilingual materials, the critics contend. In 1976, Los Angeles County spent $854,000 for bilingual materials for the June primary. For the 1978 general election, Dean Smith, the head of the LA County Budget and Fiscal Services, indicates that the cost will be between $400-$450,000 for bilingual materials. He indicates that the County has succeeded in reducing the cost factor by half in comparison to the 1976 totals.

Most election officials, like Ortiz from the Secretary of State's office and Frank Taggart, Chief of the Election and Registration unit for Sacramento County, are sympathetic to the concept of bilingual voting materials. Taggart states that, "if it helps people who vote, I am all for it, but we are caught in the middle. The Grand Jury says we are spending too much money while the US Attorney for the Sacramento region, Herman Sillas, sends us a letter saying he is going to keep his eye on us because we are not doing enough."

Ortiz believes that the solution is in getting the people who want bilingual materials on computer tapes and then sending only that group the material requested. Many Latinos agree with Ortiz. The cost, both monetarily and in public relations, is too high to pay. If every time an Anglo voter receives bilingual material in the mail he is going to have a negative reaction, the price may indeed be disastrous.

Militant Chicano activists see no room for compromise, however. "Voting is a constitutional right," they declare. "We have the Congress and the courts on our side." Yet on the other side are the 65 percent of California voters who supported Proposition 13 and its attack on wasteful government spending, and interestingly enough, a majority of Latinos in California were among those who voted for Proposition 13.

Perhaps the most positive thing that can be done at this time is to follow the advice of Ray Ortiz of the Secretary of State's office and develop a method whereby those who need the service are guaranteed of receiving it. Otherwise, those voters who continue to receive bilingual materials, which they consider to be basically unwanted junk mail that they have to pay for, may eventually put pressure on those very legislative bodies that perhaps went too far in implementing a good thing.

Latinos as Political Day Laborers

Latino Political Wires, March 1, 2004

O ver the last several weeks the citizens of the United States have been incessantly exposed to the discussions and activities surrounding the Iowa and New Hampshire Democratic presidential primaries. Hours upon hours of coverage were devoted to the two political events. The nation was treated repeatedly to the now famous Dean scream and Al Sharpton one-liners. We saw the candidates in living rooms, VFW halls, restaurants and pubs, shaking hands, kissing babies and doing effectively all the things that candidates do. There was, however, also a very serious discussion of the issues facing the citizens of the country as we head into the last 10 months of this presidential year. Individual candidate positions were staked out on the Iraq War, the Bush tax cuts, terrorism and homeland security, and indictments of the Bush administration were plentiful.

While these primary contest took place in states with minimal minority populations, the events taking place, specifically the votes there and the impact of these votes on the national political scene are, nevertheless, of some import to the minority populations within the Democratic party. But what the coverage of the two primaries demonstrated was that at the national political level, Latino Democrats remain invisible on the national scene. And on this occasion, they have been placed there both by their own party and the national media.

As far as the discussion of American politics goes, Latinos are unfortunately not involved in the national dialogue. They number zero among anchors or lead reporters on any of the four major networks, and zero as anchors or panelists for any of the variety of news and current affairs programs on the cable systems. And in this instance, there was also a total absence of any Latino commentators or pundits on the primary process in Iowa and New Hampshire. Also, among the twenty high level staffers for the seven Democratic primary candidates that have been repeatedly interviewed by networks and cable systems, only one Latino/a staffer, Maria Echeveste of the Dean campaign, was interviewed on any of the news and commentary programs. Among the tens of "experts" invited to comment on the elections as they played out over the last two weeks, not one Latino was observed commenting on the build up to, or the results of the elections. Not one Latino Congressman, governor, nor academic was presented as an expert to discuss the nuances, the impact, or the meaning of the election results. What does this say about the role of Latinos in the American political process? What does it say about an obvious bias, or at least neglect by the national electronic media? And finally, is it important that Latino media professionals and political pundits and experts be involved in the American political dialogue at all?

In this election season, over one hundred anchors, reporters, pundits, campaign staffers, election experts appeared on the electronic media repeatedly to discuss the very exciting elections in Iowa and New Hampshire. All of the T. V. regulars appeared repeatedly, Chris Mathews, Pat Buchanan, Cambell Brown, Robert Novack, Paula Sahn, Judy Woodruff, and on and on. Political pundits, Dee Dee Myers, Susan Estrich, James Carville, David Gergen . . . African American news reporters and political experts were also well represented: Donna Brazil, Juan Williams, Carlos Watson, among others. Even elected or former elected officials were called upon either to handicap the races or comment on the impact of the results, Robert Dole, Ted Kennnedy, and a parade of senators and congressmen. But glaringly significant was the fact that not one Latino Congressman, political expert, or media personality appeared on national television during the two weeks of this exciting and meaningful primary election period.

As a group on the national political scene, except for the expectation that they will vote as a block for the party nominee, Latinos seem to be considered either intellectually incapable or uninterested in participating in the national political discussion. The media and the political parties seem to believe no Latinos can be found to contribute intellectually, or even emotionally to the national political debate. While it is true that there were few Latino voters in Iowa and New Hampshire, there were few black voters as well. Latinos, like blacks, do have an opinion on politics and other national issues, but it would seem that the national media continues to keep Latinos beneath the "Tortilla Ceiling." And the Democratic Party, too, should look within itself to see if it, in fact, is also guilty of looking upon Latinos as little more than political day laborers.

McGovernizing Howard Dean

LatinoPolitical Wires, **Aug. 12, 2003**

A ny discussion of former Vermont governor Howard Dean's surge in the scramble for the Democratic nomination for next year's presidential election usually concludes with the comment that he may be too liberal for his party. The press and right of center political pundits, as well as some Democratic leaders, inevitably throw in the comment that a Dean nomination may be a McGovern experience all over again for the Democratic Party. George McGovern, of course, lost the 1972 presidential race to Richard Nixon, winning only the State of Massachusetts and the District of Columbia.

None of the pundits bother to discuss the 1972 presidential race, preferring instead to pontificate on their analysis of Dean's chances. Let us recall here for the millions of voters who were perhaps only infants in 1972, or may not have even been born yet, that George McGovern lost the election that year to Richard Millhouse Nixon, the most disgraced president in the history of the nation. How soon we have forgotten as a nation, what a mockery of democracy was the 1972 presidential election, thanks to the winner of that election. Most voters under the age of forty remember Watergate only as an abstract as they may recall World War Two or the Depression. They did not live the Watergate scandal as a daily T.V. soap opera, or see it daily in the pages of the Washington Post or other newspapers.

Only months after he was sworn in for a second term, Nixon's White House began to crumble around him as the scandal of Watergate consumed him and most of his administration. Even before the election, we know now that Nixon had unleashed his minions in a series of "dirty tricks" to disrupt the Democratic nomination process. The break-in of the Watergate offices of the National Democratic Party was only the tip of the iceberg which Nixon's press secretary Ron Ziegler had called "a third-rate burglary" at the time.

Before it was all over White house staffer James McCord had revealed to the court that the break-in had involved other Nixon operatives and that perjury had been committed at the trial of the Watergate burglars. Senator Ervin's Select Committee heard testimony from a parade of Nixon White House staff and administration officials such as Attorney General John Mitchell, presidential counsel John Dean, and aid Alexander Butterfield, among others. It was Butterfield who almost accidentally revealed the existence of tape recordings of Nixon's entire West Wing exchanges with staff and visitors alike. As the Watergate scandal unraveled, the Nation saw an administration that had illegally used the Committee to Reelect the President (CREEP) "to crush its political opponents and illegally hide its acts." The list of felonious activity was a long one and included:

- Administration operatives breaking into the office of Dr. Daniel Ellesberg to look for evidence to use against him at his trial for leaking the classified "Pentagon Papers" revealing unfavorable positions on the Viet Nam war;
- Under pressure from the White House Acting Director of the F.B.I. L. Patrick Gray had destroyed evidence in the Watergate case;
- Don Sigretti had headed up the CREEP (Committee to Re-elect the President) "dirty tricks" team to disrupt the Democratic primary;
- CREEP had collected large sums of money from corporations promising favors or threats of retaliation, then tried to conceal this activity;
- The White House had drawn up an "enemies list" which included members of the media, university personnel, members of the entertainment community, all of whom were to be harassed by Internal Revenue Service audits;
- The Administration had used illegal wiretaps to spy on its enemies and members of its own staff to gather dirt and plug leaks;
- And a spokes person for many of the Administration's policies, Vice President Spiro Agnew, had to resign in disgrace to avoid prosecution for extortion and tax evasion while serving as governor of Maryland. (from Erwin Unger's, *United States: The Quest for Our Past*)

Perhaps the most damaging blow to Nixon came as a result of his effort to preserve the hundreds of hours of tape recordings by claiming "executive privilege." After the Ervin Committee's Senate hearings ended it was up to special prosecutor Archibald Cox to subpoena the tapes and ultimately for Judge John Serica to require Nixon to hand them over. The "Saturday Night Massacre" then followed when Attorney General Elliot Richardson refused to fire Cox as Nixon had ordered and was himself fired along with his deputy. Solicitor General Robert Bork ultimately fired Cox who was replaced by Leon Jaworski who proved no more supportive of Nixon's claims of "executive privilege" than Cox had been.

What the tapes ultimately revealed was a man driven to stay in power at any cost. Historian Irwin Unger noted that "the transcripts revealed Nixon as a profane, confused, and peevish man, willing to use any tact against his enemies and prone to mean-spirited and bigoted remarks."

Within two years of defeating George McGovern, Nixon resigned from office after it became apparent that he had attempted to stop an F.B.I. investigation of the burglary and had conspired to obstruct justice only weeks after the burglary had occurred and before the presidential election had taken place. Most of the president's men, Dean, Haldeman, Ehrlicman, Mitchell, Colson, and other operatives Jeb Stuart Magruder, Howard Hunt, J. Gordon Liddy, Don Sigretti . . . ended up serving time in federal prison or coping pleas.

Thus, Nixon was the man that a decent South Dakota U.S. senator lost to in the election of 1972. For his part, McGovern had opposed an unpopular war in Viet Nam that the country has since concluded was one of our nation's greatest tragedies and biggest mistakes. McGovern had also attempted to raise concerns about the Watergate affair during the campaign but was drowned out by the Nixon juggernaut. Ironically, Nixon's place in history will be remembered, not so much for defeating McGovern in a landslide, but for being the only U.S. president who to date has had to resign the office in disgrace. (He was pardon by President Gerald Ford and thus avoided criminal prosecution.) McGovern is remembered as the Democratic candidate who lost a very one-sided election to Richard Nixon in 1972.

Pundits who are suggesting today that presidential candidate Howard Dean may be an albatross around the Democratic Party's neck, should recall the facts about the 1972 election and keep an eye open to the real facts emerging around the 2004 election. Facts such as the role of Howard Dean as Governor of Vermont where he reformed the state's welfare system, slashed state spending and cut businesses taxes, as well as the fact that he balanced the state's budget, supported the death penalty, and supported gun control as a state's right to determine.

Many in the media are attempting to McGovernize Governor Dean. We should not be totally put off by this notion if we remember that George McGovern was a decent and honorable Democratic Party standard barer who lost an election to a most disreputable opponent who had broken the law and was surrounded by party operatives who joined him in the violation of both the law and the trust of the American people. Howard Dean, on the other hand, appears to embody that same basic decency that McGovern possessed and this decency has resulted in the fact that the citizens of Vermont have elected Dean state legislator, Lt. Governor and Governor for a total of twenty years.

Incumbency not Race O.K. as a Community of Interest?

Hispanic Link News Service, **June 2001**

That the Supreme Court should reverse itself on post-census redistricting and the merit of the 1965 Voting Rights Act should be no surprise, given the success of Reagan and Bush in stacking the Court with "an aggressive conservative majority." The ultimate irony is perhaps the vote of Justice Clarence Thomas who would never have been appointed to the Court had he not been a black man, selected to replace the retiring black Jurist Thurgood Marshall. Marshall, of course, was the champion of fairness and equal protection, having won the Brown vs. the Board of Education decision, which ended school desegregation, as lead counsel for the NAACP,.

Perhaps the most hypocritical aspect of the High Court's ruling was the notion that somehow "race" was different than other standards of "community of interest," which the Court in previous decisions, used as guidelines in determining the constitutionality of redistricting plans. Justice Kennedy writing for the majority stated, "When the state assigns voters on the basis of race, it engages in the offensive and demeaning assumption that voters of a particular race, because of their race, think alike, share the same political interests, and will prefer the same candidates at the polls."

In the past, the Court allowed for the creation of extremely gerrymandered districts that defied logic on the assumption that the community of interest of poor people, or rich people, or Democratic people or Republican people, or city people or rural people, or blue collar people should be put into a single district, based on what they had in common.

In the State of California, which I am most familiar with, having served in its legislature and having chaired a Hispanic Redistricting committee, I can tell you that, in the past, the only real community of interest in redistricting or reapportionment was the protection of incumbents. The entire redistricting process, which comes about after the census at the end of each decade, has always been solely a political process. The leadership of both political parties go into the redistricting process with one guiding principal, every incumbent of each party shall be protected. If there are districts with no incumbents going into the next election because of retirements or individuals seeking other offices, the majority party will usually get the party registration advantage in these new districts. This is a political deal generally agreed to by both parties in most state legislatures, which ultimately draw the new congressional and legislative boundaries.

In the 70s in California, the Democratically controlled legislature, with Republican concurrence, drew an Assembly District in conservative, Republican Orange County for the Democratic aide for strongman Speaker Jesse Unruh. The District boundaries meandered through Orange County, picking up nearly every Democratic and minority household in a dozen cities. The district was jokingly called the "Corridor" after its new Assemblyman, Ken Cory. It resembles the Georgia congressional district, which was the subject of the present Supreme Court decision.

In my own case after, then, Governor Reagan had vetoed the 1971 redistricting plan worked out by the Democratic and Republican leadership of the California legislature, and it should be pointed out, vetoed over the objection of the Republicans in the legislature, the Court allowed the 1972 elections to be held using the pre-1970 boundaries. Thus, when I entered the legislature in 1973, we were again faced with attempting to pass a redistricting plan.

In perhaps one of the most bizarre plans ever concocted by a legislature, the Democratic and Republican leadership of the Legislature drafted a plan that had my proposed district cross the Kern County line west into coastal Santa Barbara County in a twelve foot path to the beach. The proposed District was designed to protect the Republican incumbent in Santa Barbara County who did not want the coastal campus of the University of Santa Barbara or the radical (then) anti-Vietnam War, college community of Isla Vista in his district. The problem was that he needed the Republican-strong portion of Santa Barbara County to the north of the campus. In order to reach this population, the western boundary of the district was to be the high tide line for the Democrat and the low water line for the incumbent Republican so that he could swing around and reach the population to the north in order to maintain contiguity. As I was the closest Democrat to the campus, across a mountain range and in another county, it was agreed by the leadership of both parties and over my objections because of the absurdity of the design, that I should represent the campus and Isla Vista. Governor Reagan vetoed the plan, not because of the many gerrymandered legislative and Congressional district in the plan, but because he felt that not enough congressional and legislative districts had been given to the Republicans.

That the Supreme Court should now suddenly proclaim that it cannot accept "traditional race-neutral districting principles," is a mockery of justice. Where was the Court when basically all white male legislatures designed districts for decades that protected incumbent white males regardless of party? Where was the Court when five white males repeatedly carved up the minority populations of Los Angeles County to benefit the five white male Supervisors of both Parties. In the past, when the Supreme Court upheld the 1965 Voting Rights Act, it did so to hopefully end forever the drawing of districts, which purposely minimized the voting power of minority groups. To say that there is no community of interest among minorities, to say that those who support racially based districts engage in "offensive and demeaning assumptions," is to deny the fact that virtually all minority congressmen and state legislators come from predominantly minority districts and that it is virtually impossible for a minority to get elected in a majority white district. In the Court's view, there seems to be no community of interest in being represented by someone who is like you with respect to race while there is a community of interest if someone is like you with respect to income level, occupation, choice of dwelling place, party affiliation and the like. Quite obviously the Supreme Court, like the Conservative Controlled Congress is taking us back in history to a time when the "White man's burden" was to lead and control the unfortunate darker peoples of the world, because certainly, they cannot be led by one of their own.

The Global Village Is Here

Hispanic Link News Service, September 1995

P residential politics is a curious circus. Instead of producing at least one "man for all seasons," it creates men without reason.

Most recently, we saw GOP presidential candidates scurrying to Washington, DC, to address 4,000 core members of the Christian Coalition at its annual convention.

The candidates produced, out of one side of their mouths, a pledge to get government off our backs; from the other side came pledges to have government determine a woman's right to give birth, require prayer in schools, and have government censor books, television, and movies.

Just before that gathering, presidential candidate Robert Dole, pandering to the American Legion, pledged to lead a fight to make English the official national language. He joined the likes of Phil Gramm, Pete Wilson, and Pat Buchanan in pushing the hot buttons of electoral politics to gain in the polls.

California's Gov. Pete Wilson is the most notorious practitioner of pollster politics. Guided by public mood swings, he has reversed his "bedrock convictions" on such issues as affirmative action, immigration and taxing policy in recent times.

The 30 second TV spot heralding Wilson's official entry into the '96 presidential contest in August proclaimed: "The first leader in America to have the courage to stand up against illegal immigration . . . The first to outlaw affirmative action quotas in state hiring and end preferences for college admission . . ."

The voice-over accompanied pictures of Mexicans dashing across the Tijuana-San Ysidro border into California.

Christian coalition Executive Director Ralph Reed led this month's attack on amoral liberals, portraying his own followers as saviors of the American family. His words served as the bible for most of the invited GOP candidates at the convention.

The speakers chorused that their audience was, in fact, the heart of America, the collective true guardian of family values. Clearly, however, the group was a homogenous gathering of white Americans who represent neither the diversity of color nor of ideas.

Just as advocates of linguistic and cultural chauvinism are gaining strength in their backward move toward isolationism internationally, intolerance domestically, and fundamentalism intellectually, there is a dearth of leadership speaking out on behalf of the other side of these issues.

Instead, those who would be king, like Senator Dole, pander to far-right constituents. He is joined by the likes of USA Today columnist Linda Chavez, who accuses bilingual education proponents of having "a far-reaching political agenda" that keeps children in the program longer than necessary.

Sally Weymouth, another columnist writing in the Washington Post, goes even further. She proclaims that, "bilingualism, in its current mode, leads to multiculturalism. And multiculturalism is a pathway to separatism."

A reader may easily conclude that bilingual education is a subversive activity that will soon lead to guerrilla warfare. In case you haven't noticed, it is the far-right, mono-lingual militia groups who are taking up arms against the government.

Attacks on bilingual education, affirmative action, and immigrants should be responded to by our moderate and liberal leaders, if there are any left not too frightened to pull their heads out of the sand.

The Kennedys, the Feinsteins, the Boxers, Dellumses, Dodds, and Daschles should not expect President Clinton to respond alone to these mindless, mean spirited attacks.

After all, the Doles, Wilsons, Gramms, and Buchanans get plenty of help from their friends as they seek to pave their path to the presidency with the corpses of some of the reasonable and humane laws of the past.

Far-right groups plan to co-opt the stage during the presidential election season and force candidates to champion English only, immigrant bashing, affirmative action retreat, and a host of other narrow-minded, simplistic policies.

This group's answer to the crime problem is to build more prisons, not more schools. Their answer to health-care reform is to deny medical attention to illegal immigrants and end school lunches, and immunizations.

Their response to the emergence of the global village is ethnocentrism and withdrawal from the United Nations.

If there were ever a time when profiles in courage were needed, it is now. The elections of 1996 will lead us into the 21st century.

What a sorry state of affairs it will be if we are led into the new millennium, not by men or women of vision, but by those who promote division.

A recent survey of the nation's employers published by Michigan State University noted, "Many employers are looking for new job entrants who possess, among other things, international experience and hopefully another language."

The mono-lingualism and isolationism advocated by Dole and others is in conflict with what the U.S. business sector and futuristic thinkers are telling us.

The global village is here, and many languages are spoken in that village.

Equality in a Diverse Society

Hispanic Link News Service, **September 1996**

While I have lived in Washington, D.C. for the last couple of years, I have a home in California and am registered to vote there. I recently received my absentee ballot and voting materials, including the pros and cons of the ballot items for the November 5th election.

As is fairly well known around the country, California is initiative crazy. Over the years the state has given us Prop. 13, the so-called tax reform initiative, and Prop 187, the anti-immigration measure, among others. This year, it is Prop. 209, the anti-affirmative action initiative which is drawing attention in other states. The reason for its notoriety is that many political pundits and politicians nationwide subscribe to the notion that "as California goes, so goes the nation." This was the case with Prop. 13, Prop.187, and many other California ballot items over the years.

But let us look at the underlying reasons for the initiative craze in the Golden State, which has been an ongoing phenomenon for more than three decades. Plane and simple, the reason so many initiatives are qualified for the ballot in California is that it has long been a Republican Party strategy in the state to level the political playing field with Democrats at election time by the use if initiatives.

As recently as the 1960s, Democrats outnumbered Republicans in the state by two to one. The Republican Party strategy has been to qualify a number of wedge issues, hot-button items for the ballot at each election—anti-gay, English only, death penalty, bilingual education, and so on. The purpose for this is that these hot-button, wedge issues often lead to the defeat of moderate Democratic legislative and congressional candidates, and occasionally, statewide office candidates. It has been concluded by political experts that former State Senator Art Torres' loss, as Insurance Commissioner in the 1994 elections, was a direct result of Prop. 187, the anti-immigrant initiative being on the ballot. In legislative contests, the Republican Party has always believed that any district with less than 60% Democratic registration was winnable by a Republican, by forcing moderate candidates in marginal districts to take the less popular position on wedge issues.

This strategy has worked as the Republican Party has steadily cut Democratic registration and most recently picked up the Speakership in the state assembly by winning a majority of the seats. Republican gubernatorial candidates like Pete Wilson have also reaped political advantage by pinning their campaigns on the hot-button issues. He overcame a 22% deficit in the polls, defeating Democrat Kathleen Brown by and equal margin, nearly a 44% move, on the strength of anti-immigrant Prop. 187 in 1992. Wilson's predecessor, George Dukemegian, rode the Death Penalty initiative to the Attorney General's office and subsequently to the governorship, no matter that both the initiatives were subsequently declared unconstitutional.

The crafty use of the initiative process that "hangs moderates out to dry" is no more evident than in this year's Prop 209. Cynically and deceptively, it is called the California Civil Rights Initiative (CCRI) and would no doubt cause deceased civil rights activists of the Sixties to turn over in their graves as it has little to do with civil rights. Any linguist or English professor, reading the Arguments in Favor of Prop. 209 in the sample ballot, signed by Governor Wilson and Republican Attorney General Dan Lungren, would have little difficulty discovering the cleaver, but not too subtle use of the English language to make a clear distinction between the "white" authors of the proposition and the "minority" targets of the measure.

The first paragraph reads, "We (read white Congress) passed civil rights laws to prohibit discrimination. But special interests (read minority groups) highjacked the civil rights movement." Farther on it states, "Students (read white students) are being rejected from public institutions because of their RACE (emphasis Wilson's). And again, "Contracts are awarded to higher bidders because they are of the preferred RACE (read minorities, emphasis Wilson's).

Probably the most obvious appeal to race, (the white race, majority voters in the state,) is the line that reads, "We are individuals! Not every white person is advantaged." (For whom are the authors of the arguments writing?) And the Attorney General in his rebuttal to the Against Argument writes, "Under the existing racial preference system, a wealthy doctor's son may receive a preference for college admission over a dishwasher's daughter simply because he's from an 'underrepresented' race. THAT'S UNJUST" (emphasis Lungren's). We are supposed to believe that the doctor's son is a minority and the dishwasher's daughter is white. YEA SURE! (emphasis mine).

The Governor's and the Attorney General's arguments would almost be funny if the issue were not so serious, for it not only will affect minorities and women in California, but potentially the entire country. We could even buy the lame arguments presented by the far-right if statistics indicated we already had a truly level playing field in the state of California and the nation. But the facts are these, even after 40 years since the Civil Rights Acts were passed, white males, who constitute only 33% of the entire population, dominate employment statistics:

> White males are:
> 85% of tenured Professors
> 85% of Partners in Major law firms
> 80% of Members of the House of Representatives
> 90% of Members of the U.S. Senate, and
> 97% of School Superintendents.

In California, Latinos and African Americans make up 33% of the population as do white males, yet, white males are 58% of the police force and 74% of firefighters. And interestingly, while women are 71% of the teaching force, white males are 97% of all school superintendents. Clearly, women must loose their competence as they try to ascend the education ladder.

This election of 1996 is very important to the country as it will lead us into the 21st Century. The race-bating, homophobia, xenophobia and chauvinism of some politicians and right-wing religious groups recalls the elections of one hundred years ago when the nation was being stirred-up to hate the arriving immigrants and continue the Jim Crow laws of the South, and the denial of the vote to women. In referring to the Democrats and their immigrant friends at the end of the last century, the supporters of Republican Senator Henry Cabot Lodge, standard barer for the extremists, said, "They (immigrants) are a danger that threatens the destruction of our national edifice by the erosion of our moral foundation."

Instead, as voters go to the polls in California, we should all hope they heed the words of a true American, U.S. Supreme Court Justice John Paul Stevens, "Individual discrimination is an engine of oppression, subjecting a disfavored group to enhance or maintain the power of the majority. Remedial race-based preferences reflect the opposite impulse: a desire to foster equality in society . . ."

Ray Gonzales campaigning for Assembly in 1974

Ray Gonzales as diplomat in Brussels 1989

Ray relaxing with children in Guatemala 1981

Latino Caucus California Legislature 1973. L t.R Richard Alatorre, Joe Montoya, Ray Gonzales, Alex Garcia, Peter Chacon

II

Latino Movement

Summary of Articles

T his section presents articles that covered a variety of issues dealing with the Latino social and cultural movement that began in the 1960s and accelerated in the 1970s and 80s. The first piece is the Keynote Address I gave at the Heritage of America awards presentation in 2005 and deals with my own evolution as a Latino activist from my days as a community college instructor to my role as a U.S. State Department diplomat and university professor. I am especially proud of the three articles, "Some Came to Praise César . . . , and the Strawberry Pickers Shall Lead them . . . , and the California Farm workers," which deal with the plight of California farm laborers and César Chávez' leadership role. Chávez and Dolores Huerta, Co-founder of the UFW were constituents of mine when I served in the California Legislature and I saw the development of their movement first hand while they emerged as national civil rights leaders. Some of the pieces in this section like "the Chicano Movement of the 70s, Hispanic Heritage Month, and Rodeos," appeared in the *Latino Encyclopedia* and the *70s Almanac*. The Hispanic Link News Service, founded by my good friend Charlie Erickson, also carried many of my articles in this section like "Vasconcelo's Cosmic Race" and "The Other Migrant Workers." I call the readers' attention to the article, "Pachuco Character's Search for Identity and Recognition" which ran in the McClatchy Bee newspapers in February of 1979. It is an article, which has some relevance to the gang phenomenon now affecting many cities in the Southwest. "The Rodney Dangerfield Syndrome" is also a telling piece on how the Latino community has still not gained the respect of the media, despite the community's significant percentage as the nation's largest ethnic group.

Keynote Address, Heritage of America Awards Banquet

Latino Political Wires, **November 18, 2004**

I would like to thank Dr. Jess Nieto and his wife Peggy, both of whom were students of mine longer ago than I care to remember, but I thank them now for their long friendship and for the efforts they have continued to make to provide a healthier and a more caring community in which they live. And I would like to thank the Heritage of America and its members for bestowing on me the honor of addressing you all tonight. I and my family were honored by you at your most successful event last year when I was inducted to the Heritage of America Hall of Fame with César Chávez and Dolores Huerta, and it is indeed an honor for me to be able to contribute in some small way to the event this evening.

My friends, we have just come through a very stressful, and at times, less than uplifting political season. Talk of red states and blue states, negative ads and counter ads, hurtful pundits and in general, a less than glowing reflection of our political process. I, by no means, want to continue the negativity. Instead, I hope that when I am through with my comments, you might agree that I have sounded a positive note, and hopefully, taken the high road.

I do believe that as a nation, despite the many things that seem to separate us, we are, in fact, coming closer together. Certainly at times it may not seem that way. But please bare with me as I comment, to the chagrin of my children, who often lament, "don't ask dad a question. He'll go on forever." But as a historian, let me take you back a bit into our American past, so that we can indeed conclude that we have come a long way in making ours a better nation. Of course we have not always been perfect, and in fact, we have more than once failed to admit our mistakes or failed to challenged the faulty assumptions or even the faulty actions of our leaders.

While we have called ourselves a nation of immigrants and while our own governor, born in Austria, ran in a special election in California not long ago that also included a candidate born in Greece, and two that had Spanish surnames, we have not always been so accepting of racial or ethnic differences among us. In some respects, that recent recall election was a beautiful thing if you consider the background of all the candidates, Swartzenegger, Camejo, Bustamante, McClintock and Areana Huffington. But there has always been a strain of xenophobia beneath the surface of our national character. We can recall the words of others in the past, who were not so accepting of differences that immigrants brought to our shores.

> "They are an invasion of venomous reptiles . . . long-haired, wild-eyed, bad-smelling, atheistic, reckless foreign wretches . . . . crush such snakes before they have time to bite. They are a danger that threatens the destruction of our national edifice by erosion of its moral foundations."

These words were, in fact, spoken by a preacher of Christian doctrine, the Reverend Josiah Strong from his pulpit and in his book (*Our Country*) in 1885. The attack then was not against Latinos, Southeast Asians, Arabs or Haitians. Rather it was against Italians, Irish, Jews, Poles . . . Europeans, who were streaming into the United States to ultimately become the backbone of the American Industrial Revolution. These immigrants were attacked in those times because of their Jewish or Catholic faiths, their foreign languages, their impoverished condition, and their willingness to do the jobs that more established Americans were not willing to do.

We have always been confused and tortured by our own national paranoia as it relates to those different than ourselves, against those who have arrived after us. Recall the words of Emma Lazarus, herself the daughter of Jewish immigrants, that so nobly grace the base of our Statue of Lady Liberty who opens her arms to the world: "Give me your tired, your poor, your huddled masses, yearning to breathe free." The words stand in deep contrast to the Reverend Strong's comments, and together, these two statements reflect the struggle we have had as a nation over the years to reconcile the two attitudes. We have had our own Proposition 187 in California, and Arizona has just passed its own version this month. The courts will again, no doubt, have to test these new laws to decide what kind of treatment of immigrants, even undocumented ones, will fall within our national Constitution. But regardless of the outcome, we continue to struggle with our view of the very notion of immigration in general, legal or illegal, then and now.

There were politicians then as now who ran on people's fears, exploiting the basest levels of our humanity. In the 19th Century there was already an "anti-immigrant" party. Nativists, such as Senator Henry Cabot Lodge, epitomized the animus towards the "mass of the unwashed" as they were called, by passing the Immigrant Literacy Bill aimed at stopping the influx of those "twisted, unassimilable, filthy, un-American immigrants." Buoyed by election victories of 1894, the nativists continued their immigrant bashing which culminated in Cabot Lodges' legislation that was fortunately vetoed by President Grover Cleveland.

Now, as we reach the midway point in the first decade of the 21st Century, there are still those among us who would try to divide us along racial and ethnic lines. But no amount of politics, rhetoric, nor doomsdayism has been able to stem the influence of immigration, nor maintain what the early nativists called the "racial purity of the predominantly Anglo-Saxon American nation." In the past, this "American Nation" had accepted such philosophical, political policies as "Manifest Destiny, Social Darwinism" and "the White Man's Burden" which nearly resulted in the extermination of the Native American population and in the illegal deportation of millions of legal residents and citizens among the Chinese, Filipinos, Italians and Mexicans from this country.

Let us consider another way of looking at immigration, by looking, in a rational and tempered way, at the movement of peoples around this planet we call Earth. In 1925, the Mexican philosopher and educator Jose Vasconcelos published his essay on futuristic demographics called *La Raza Cosmica* (The Cosmic Race). Vasconcelos' work was controversial from the start, because it challenged the European Social Darwinism that had motivated Mexican intellectuals to reject the very Indian portions of their own heritage. Radically, Vasconcelos postulated in his essay that a new race would be born in the Americas, a race that would combine all of the best qualities of the black, white, red and yellow races. Vasconcelos concluded that this fifth race would emerge in the Amazon Valley of South America where African blacks, Amazon Indians and white Spaniards, French, British and Portuguese were already mixing their racial lines. He said: "We will reach in America, before any other part of the globe, the creation of a race created with the treasures of all the previous races, the final, universal race, the cosmic race." This was certainly the opposite view of the super European race envisioned in Nietzshez's work.

But Vasconcelos' conclusions were based as much on philosophical wishful thinking as they were on sound anthropological facts, one of which was that the mixture of bloods and cultures in the Americas was far surpassing anything the European continent had ever experienced in such a short period of time, except, perhaps for the melding of Arab, Visigoth, Iberian, Jewish and Roman bloods that occurred in Medieval Spain.

What Vasconcelos anticipated, the emergence of a new race, a cosmic race, while not evolving as rapidly as he had postulated in the Amazon Valley is, in fact, occurring in another place, it is occurring in the United States today. This is perhaps what frightens the neo-nativists, descendants of the 19th Century nativists who believed in maintaining the purity of "the single Anglo-Saxon stock." Robert Kelly in his book, *The Shaping of the American Past,* noted that "aristocratic Anglo-Saxon intellectuals in the northeastern states alleged that the new immigration in those days was bringing in inferior blood stocks that would dilute and debase the racial purity of the predominantly Anglo-Saxon American nation." This fear culminated in the 1920's when President Calvin Coolidge signed the National Origins Act, declaring that, "America must be kept for Americans." This legislation ushered in a period of unlawful abuses perpetrated against many American citizens who were not native born.

Vasconcelos' theme was revisited in a 1993 special edition of *Time m*agazine, devoted entirely to the "browning of America" or "The New Face of America: How Immigrants Are Shaping the World's First Multi-Cultural Society." In this issue *Time* presents significant evolving demographic facts affecting the population of the United States. As an example of the "changing face of America" *Time* cites the notion that "intermarriage is as old as the Bible. But during the past two decades, America has produced the greatest variety of hybrid households in the history of the world."

The incidence of births to mixed race couples has increased 26 times as fast as that of any other group, according to *Time*. Japanese Americans, for example, marry non-Japanese 65% of the time. Among Native Americans the figure is 70%. Jews marry outside of their faith, or cultural group, 52% of the time. Of individuals contacted in a national poll by *Time*, 72% indicated they were aquatinted with interracial couples.

Other indicators also note the impact of recent immigration on the changing face of the country. In New York, Los Angeles, Chicago, and Fairfax County, Virginia over 100 languages are spoken in the public schools of each of these cities. By the year 2040 California which is presently 48% white will only be 32% white, and even less white, if one factors in the incidents of inter-racial marriages, and how we will count the children of these mixed marriages. In cities as distinct and as geographically separated as Miami Florida, Union City New Jersey, and Santa Ana California, more than half of the population is foreign born.

Time cited the case of twenty-nine year old Cindy Mills, the daughter of black and Native American parents, married to a white European immigrant, who believes that "her two Native American, black-white-Hungarian-French-Catholic-Jewish-American children may lead the way to an unhyphenated, whole American society."

This new American "whole" is what José Vasconcelos was envisioning in his essay on the Cosmic Race. He, of course, uses America to speak of the Western Hemisphere, while we, erroneously, refer only to the United State. Nevertheless, as hard as legislators may try, as high as emotions may run, and as unlikely as it may seem in Davenport, Iowa or Little Rock, Arkansas, the Cosmic Race is being born in the United States. The Jewish delicatessen in Brooklyn has become an Arab Sub-shop, and the Portuguese crab stand on Fisherman's Wharf has become a Vietnamese establishment, and all across the land, the migrant stream has dropped off Gonzaleses, Martinezes and Garcias in Chicago, Portland, Saginaw and St Paul. And for more than four hundred years, from the days of slavery, the black and white races have been mixing in this country. Today 88% of all the school children in Los Angeles, the second largest school district in the country, are minorities. In the largest, New York City, 89% are minorities, or more correctly, now the large majorities in both instances.

The xenophobia and isolationism that caused some of our countrymen to fear immigration in the past, has in more recent years led to another fear, the fear of affirmative action and all that it implies. We have to recognize that as Americans, we have always favored immigration when there was work to be done that we did not want to do ourselves, but opposed it when there were not enough jobs to go around. Thus when The Hudson Institute's 1993 study, *Workforce 2000,* pointed out that by the year 2000 in our country, 85% of the new job entrants into the workforce would be women, minorities and immigrants, there was the typical historic reaction, one of fear and foreboding.

What the Hudson Institute Study and many other reports of the time suggested, was that these changes in employment figures were reflecting the change that was occurring in our American population, what the Time Magazine article reflected and what was really occurring in our country. Today, the new buzz word is DIVERSITY. In the U.S. we have had two versions of diversity. In the past our DIVERSITY was called ASSIMILATION.

The ethnic groups of the past were expected to become part of that melting pot theory. Less than a stew, they were supposed to become a puree. Thus: "those long-haired, wild-eyed, bad-smelling . . . reckless foreign wretches" . . . were expected to blend in as Americans. And they did.

In many instances, names like Stein became Stone, Papandracopulis became Papan, Brileski was changed to Brill, Banducchi becomes Bandy, Albert Swartz becomes the actor Tony Curtis, and Victoria Caranza becomes the singer Vickie Carr, Antonio Oaxaca becomes Academy award winner Anthony Quinn, Ricardo Valenzuela becomes Richie Vallens, of La Bamba fame.

Certainly this did not happen in many cases, perhaps not in most cases, but there certainly was pressure for it to happen. It was important in employment, in higher education, in social status. I once challenged a radio stations here in town because they did not have any Hispanic announcers or disk jockeys on the air. One station manager responded, "certainly we do, we have Bobby Benton. It's a better radio name than Pedro Lozano."

Having mentioned already the use of stage names, those real American Sounding names like Vicki Carr or Tony Curtis, let me point out that today

DIVERSITY does not mean ASSIMILATION as it did in the past when Native American children were taken from their parents and sent to Indian Schools, their hair cut, their traditional clothing burned and their native languages prohibited. This was a national policy in the late 1800s headed up by the Director of the Bureau of Indian Affairs who proudly displayed a sign over the entrance to his office in Washington, D.C. that read: KILL THE INDIAN AND SAVE THE MAN. They almost succeeded.

Today we have Arnold Swartzenegger, Carlos Santana, Connie Chung, Sanjay Gupta, Cruz Bustamante, Wilma Mankiller. No need now to Americanize these Americans.

As Roosevelt Thomas points out in his article, "From Affirmative Action to Affirming Diversity" published in the Harvard Business Review: "Today the melting pot is the wrong metaphor even in business, for several good reasons: If it ever was possible to melt down Scotsmen and Dutchmen and Italians into an indistinguishable broth, you can't do the same with Blacks, Asians, (Latinos) and women. Most people are no longer willing to be melted down, not even for eight hours a day."

Today women, minorities, immigrants refuse to be treated like second-class citizens. Indeed, the melting pot is a metaphor that no longer applies. Women will no longer be content with only being secretaries and serving coffee to the men in the office. Lani Guinier, an unsuccessful Clinton nominee as Attorney General writes about her experience at Yale when she attended law school in the Seventies. She recalls the first day in class as she, a black woman, joined by a single white female student sat in the class full of male law students, as the professor walked into the classroom. The gruff old professor, she recalls, greeted the class, "Good Morning gentlemen," he intoned. As he noticed the only two female students seated in the class, with consternation he added, "I've been saying good morning gentlemen for twenty-five years. I'm not going to change now." An he didn't, Ms. Guinier recalls, but things have changed at Yale law school and law schools throughout out the country where women are now surpassing men in enrollment, as they are in universities in general across the land.

And in other influential areas like the media, things have changed considerably. I recall, as President of the Kern County Council for Civic Unity, leading an effort here in Kern County back in the late Sixties to have women and minorities included in broadcast news in local channels and radio stations. I recall a good friend, Ken Crows, then general manager of Channel 23, looking me in the eye and saying, "Ray, women will never make it in broadcasting. The public won't accept it. They want deep baritone voices. Women's voices are too high." Well I wish Ken were alive today to see that no self-respecting local T.V. news program goes on the air without a female co-anchor. And nationally, Judy Woodruff, Gwen Ifel, Connie Chung, Dianne Sawyer, Elizabeth Vargas have certainly changed the public's minds about who they will accept on televison screens delivering the news. Locally, we made a little history back in 1969 when we challenged the transfer of license from Time-Life to McGraw-Hill ownership here at Channel 23. We were able to improve broadcasting, eventually at a national level by breaking down barriers for women and minorities. Our own Judge Louie Vega, fresh from the Viet Nam war, became the first Latino T.V. reporter at Channel 23. The rest is history.

In many areas of the social fabric of our country we have had to challenge prevailing assumptions. I recall being the only Latino faculty member on the faculty of Bakersfield College, along with only one black and one Asian, when I taught there in the Sixties and how we had to fight to change things. And as I mentioned earlier, how we had to struggle to get the first Latino principal hired in the Bakersfield City Schools. Well now, we have had a Latino Presidents of Bakersfield Community College and at Cal State University and numerous black and Latino/a principles in city and county schools.

But changes here locally and changes at the national level in the social fabric of our country have not always come easily. Sometimes the public has to be brought to the change kicking and screaming because, as human beings, we are naturally resistant to change. I tell you my friends, prophets in their own lands quite often are not honored, as the Good Book tells us. Often it is those in the vanguard of change that sacrifice their own lives in the struggle for human dignity. Martin Luther King was slain at a young age as he struggled to end discrimination in our land. César Chávez was often scorned and criticized as he led the struggle to gain some dignity for those in our midst who toil at the lowest rung of the employment and economic ladder. Now, in our own time we finally honor both of them. Streets and bridges, schools and libraries carry their names. The State of California dedicates a day in César Chávez' honor and the nation now recognizes Dr. King for his leadership. But we must not wait until it is too late. Dolores Huerta, who herself was criticized and ridiculed along with Chávez as she served as Vice President of the Union, is still among us. Finally, she is receiving the honor she deserves as one of the most courageous and dynamic women and Latinas of our age

Because of the efforts of so many courageous leaders in our land, over the years, we now live in a better age, in a more hopeful period of our history. I began by talking about the theory of the Cosmic Race. Let me conclude by sharing with you the hope and promise of another Kern County boy, our own Gerry Haslam, an Oildale Oakie that I went to school with at Garces, who has become, along with William Saroyan and Joan Didion, one of the foremost writers that the San Joaquin Valley has produced. In his collection of personal essays entitled *Growing Up in California,* Gerry writes, "I was born in El Valle de los Tulares, now called the San Joaquin Valley, of California, and my life has taken ethnic mixtures a step further because I married a woman whose father is métis, a French and Cree combination originally from Canada, and whose mother is Polish and German.

Our five children—all *gueros*—illustrate a variation of what Jose Vasconcelos called "la raza cósmica." We are southwesterners—El Paso and Paso Robles; we are Californians dwelling en *la frontera*, on a cusp of culture and races and perspectives." Gerry, beautifully describing his own coming of age in California goes on: "I early on came to believe with James Baldwin that, 'All men are brothers. That's the bottom line. If you can't take it from there, you can't take it at all.' I chose to take it." Gerry says. He goes on, "A number of my closest white friends only tolerated my attitude and I only tolerated theirs. It was certainly easier for me to ignore at least some racial stereotypes because by then I thought of myself as either an Okie or a Hispanic, I wasn't certain which."

Like Gerry, in those early years coming from Bakersfield, I was confused by the world around me too. I recall traveling alone by train at the age of fourteen to attend a seminary in Ann Arbor, Michigan. I remember getting off the train in El Paso Texas during a two hour layover and going into the train station looking for a restroom. And there they were, two of them, one with a sign over it that read WHITES ONLY and another which red, COLORDES. I stood there, at the age of 14 in the 1950s America and didn't know which restroom I should enter. I was too young and too afraid to venture into either one. I did not know what I was. I waited to get back on the train. I had never had to ask myself what I was before. It was a new world I would be facing.

It has taken me a lifetime to answer that question. Like Gerry, my family is Californian. My children's mother is Scott and French. My grandchildren are Mexican, English, French and Indian. I have nieces and nephews that are Mexican and Irish, Mexican and Black. My cousins are products of the United Nations. We are the Cosmic Race here in California. Gerry Haslem has perhaps put it best in one of his essays which he calls *A Braided California*. He recalls a colleague of his at Sonoma State questioning him about his origins. "Just what are you anyway?" "He had seen a story of mine," Gerry writes, "in a collection of Chicano writing, another in a collection of Native American tales, and yet another presented as an Okie story in a national collection. I replied, 'what makes you think I can't be all three of those things, and more too. You ought to see my kids; they're like the *reatas* (lariats) my *bisabuelo* (great grandfather) used to braid—this and that mingled and pulled tight into a single strand. Hey this is California! This is America!"

Thankfully, Gerry's children, mine, and your children are growing up in a more racially tolerant, less legalistically xenophobic society than their parents or grand parents did, despite the politicians, and the fearful nativists, and the occasional efforts to self-segregate. The challenge will be to maintain those "beautiful treasures" of each race that Vasconcelos wrote about, thus maintaining diversity, while living harmoniously together.

My friends, Gerry Haslam is right. This is California. This is America and we are now living in a wonderful age. While there may still be vestiges of racism in some corners, bigotry should never again raise its ugly head among us. We have come from the *Grapes of Wrath* in our own county to the land of the Cosmic Race. We are a beautiful people, bringing together the wonders and glories of all of our races. Lets us all look forward to tomorrow which, my friends, will be greater than yesterday and more glorious than today. We live in a wonderful land, which has been the beacon of liberty for so many. Let us leave this hall tonight, determined to see the good in our neighbors and the wonder in our children, for we have chosen the path we now travel; we are on our way to making our land and our society even grater than our founding fathers had envisioned. It is no wonder that peoples of the world still want to land on our shores. We are truly the land of the free and the home of those brave Americans who will seek to do good and respect one another as brothers and sisters of our Cosmic Race. I thank you for this honor to share my thoughts with you tonight.

The Chicano Movement in the 1970's.

1970s Almanac, **Salem Press, June 2005**

During the 1970s Chicanos in the United State expand their efforts to consolidate the civil and political rights they began to gain in the 1960s to become full participants in the social, cultural and political life of the country. The 1960s had certainly been a decade of major changes in American society. The struggle of the Black community for economic and civil rights was aided by the many members of white society that had also come to grips with the injustices that had been perpetrated against communities of color over the years. The Civil Rights Act and the Voting Rights Act of mid decade did much to encourage minority groups to actively pursue expanded rights. The Chicano community of the Southwest, Mexican Americans who had decided to challenge the system, were battling discrimination and seeking their civil rights in a more pluralistic society.

As the 1970s began, students and teachers at five East Los Angeles High Schools had led walkouts, demanding the hiring of Chicano teachers and counselors, and expanded curricula that would reflect Chicano culture and history. At the college level, students from throughout the Southwest had gathered at the University of California at Santa Barbara and organized themselves into a single student organization, *Movimiento Estudiantil Chicanos de Aztlán* (MEChA) and drafted the *Plan de Santa Barbara* which called for the development of college programs that would create Chicano Studies courses and even departments of Chicano Studies. The Mexican American Legal Defense and Education Fund had been established in San Antonio and Los Angeles; the Southwest Council of La Raza had moved its headquarters from Phoenix, Arizona to Washington, D. C. becoming the National Council of La Raza; and César Chávez' United Farm

Workers Union was in the midst of a major labor struggle with the powerful grape growers of California.

Major Gains in the Decade

These were the events and movements that ushered in the 1970s. What was to follow was a decade that would see an expansion of the Chicano's role in American society. A focus of the Chicano movement took place on college campuses with more that 50 institutions, not all of them in the Southwest beginning Chicano/Mexican American studies departments and initiating the celebration of *Cinco de Mayo* as a national cultural event. High schools and grade schools too were beginning to reflect more realistic curricula. Educational institutions were prodded into action by the U.S. Supreme Court's 1974 ruling in the Lau v. Nichols case that mandated the establishment of bilingual education in the land. Both the introduction of Chicano studies and bilingual education resulted in a doubling of college attendance by Chicanos.

Political Action

Likewise the 1970s saw a 200 percent increase in Chicano elected officials. Chicanos also used the courts to increase their political opportunities. Using the language of the 1965 Voting Rights Act, they challenged at-large elections in many of the cities and school districts of the Southwest. In San Antonio, Texas, the first term City Councilmember Henry Cisneros won the battle to have the single member district system established as the law. This success by the young, articulate Chicano politician had much to do with his eventual election as the city's mayor, thrusting him onto the national political scene. In California, the legal challenge of the at-large elections also resulted in the dramatic increase of Chicano local elected official. Both California and Texas were becoming more important to the two national political parties because of the growth of the Latino population. Texas passed Pennsylvania to become the third largest electoral vote state to join California and New York. Adding to increased political clout, two moderate Mexican American governors won election in 1974, Raul Castro in Arizona and Jerry Apodaca in New Mexico. In California, the state with the largest Chicano population, the Chicano voting age population increased by 117 percent during the decade. For much of the 1970's the United Farm Workers' Union played a key role in the Democratic Party efforts in the Southwest, providing campaign workers and using union officials César Chávez and Dolores Huerta as motivators.

Another important political advancements of Chicanos during the decade was the appointment of Chicanos to significant positions in government. President Carter appointed Esteban Torres and Mari-Luci Jarramillo as United States ambassadors, among his other Chicano appointments. Governor Jerry Brown of California perhaps did the most to advance the role of Chicanos as appointed officials. After his election in 1974, Brown had told one of his top aids that he was "going to tilt toward the Mexican-American." True to his word, Brown appointed record numbers of Chicanos to office. He appointed dozens of Chicanos to the court, with Cruz Reynoso being the first Chicano appointed to the California Supreme Court. He also appointed Mario Obledo as the first Agency Secretary to the Health and Welfare Agency, the largest unit of state government. Brown was the first national political figure to recognize the growing economic and political power of the Latino community.

Business and the Arts

In addition to political gains, Chicanos began to emerge in the business sector, with Chicano businesses growing by 200 percent during the decade. In many cities of the Southwest, branches of the Mexican American Chamber of Commerce were established. Also, by mid-decade, half a dozen national Chicana organizations would be formed to advance women's issues in business, education and the arts.

A cultural and artistic renaissance was also the product of the activities on the college campuses and in the political and business arenas. National magazines like *Nuestro, Hispanic, Caminos* and *Quinto Sol* Publications brought news and art to the Chicano community. In 1970, novelist Tomás Rivera came out with . . . *y no se lo tragó la tierra* and Rudolfo Anaya published *Bless Me Ultima*, two of the most influential novels yet written by Chicano authors. There were many other writers and poets produced by the Chicano movement during the decade. Chicano and Chicana artists were also establishing themselves as contemporary muralist, sculptors and painters. Luis Valdez' Teatro Campesino produced the successful stage play *Zoot Suit*. As the decade ended, Chicanos were on the threshold of what was to be called the "decade of the Hispanic," the 1980s.

Impact

In the 1970s Chicanos significantly increase their participation in American life in the areas of politics, education, business and culture, emerging as the minority group in the United States with the most dramatic ascendancy. Significant Chicano leaders become national figures as representatives of their community.

Further Reading

De la Isla, José, *The Rise of Hispanic Political Power.* Los Angeles, Archer Books, 2003.

Meier, Matt S. and Ribera, Feliciano. *Mexican Americans/American Mexicans.* New York, Hill and Wang, 1993.

Montejano, David, ed. *Chicano Politics and Society.* Austin, University of Texas Press, 1999.

Gonzales, Raymond, J. "Missing: The Chicano Candidate." *California Journal.* May, 1978.

Gonzales, Raymond, J. "Chicano: California's Virgin Territory." *Nuestro*, 1979.

Latinos and the Rodney Dangerfield Syndrome

Latino Journal, October 1996

R odney Dangerfield, as we know, is the bumbling Hollywood "character" who claims he gets no respect. Whether this is true or not shouldn't really matter much to him as his shtick gains him some respect at the bank where he cashes in on his acting credits.

Latinos, as a group in this country, like the Daingerfield character, seem to suffer from perpetual disrespect. Presidential candidate Pat Buchanan vented his disrespect on the national news referring to "Jose" whenever he made disparaging remarks about immigrants from the south coming into the U.S. And in a grotesque manner, Sheriffs deputies in Riverside County, California showed little respect when brutally apprehending a group of suspected illegal immigrants not too long ago which was captured on video.

When I think of the image Latinos have in this country among some people, I am concerned that to the many like Buchanan, all Latinos are lumped into a "Jose" category which seems to refer to dark skinned, undereducated, and unskilled Latinos who have crossed our southern border looking more for a handout than for work. As wrong as this generalization may be, one thing is certain, Latinos coming into this country, legal or illegal, get no respect, despite all the data that exists which indicates that they contribute more to the country in taxes, consumer purchases, critical workforce, than they take out.

But of interest to me here is the fact that even the highest intellectual level and economically viable members of the Latino community get little respect as well. They seem to be invisible when it comes to expressing views and opinions on the issues of the day. We are talking about Latino university professors, entrepreneurs, political figures, internationalists and the like. Whenever a Latino issue does make it into national news, such as the Riverside beating incident, network news, wire services, and print median may ask Raul Izaguirre of the National Council of La Raza or other isolated Latino community leaders for comments on the event, but on issues of national importance without a Latino content, Latino leaders and experts are seldom asked to comment.

It would seem that we, as Latinos, either do not care or are ill-prepared to comment on the situation in Bosnia, the condition of the economy, the race for the presidency . . . We are considered experts only on one thing—the Latino thing. One need only peruse the Sunday morning news-talk programs, NBC's Meet *the Press,* CBS's *Face the Nation,* ABC's *This Week, The McLaughlin Group, The Capital Gang,* and a myriad of other national news commentary programs or talk shows to see that there are no Latino regulars on any of these programs.

There always seem to be a least a token Black and a handful of women on these programs, but Latinos-*nada.* Occasionally, as a guest, you might see conservative columnist Linda Chavez or an ethnically confused Richard Rodriguez on the air. But here too, they are generally only invited to give the Latino conservative view on "English Only" or other such divisive topics. They are seldom ever invited to comment on broader national or world issues.

As a group, Latinos seem to be considered either intellectually shallow or possessed only of Latinomindedness, as if we had no knowledge nor interest in other topics of concern to America. It is as if there are no Latinos to be found in this country who can make relevant comments on the issues of the day. None can be found to comment on Dole's quest for the presidency in '96 or the impact of increasing the minimum wage. Surely, a "Jose" can be found somewhere in these United States with greater knowledge and more honor and civility than a Pat Buchanan, or convicted felons Ollie North or J. Gordon Liddy who make millions spouting their venom over the airwaves.

It is time for Latinos to demand a little respect, which is not likely to be given naturally. One approach might be to contact the sponsors of these news commentary programs on the air today. While they are seriously going after the Latino consumers' dollars, they should be pressed to act more fairly on who gets to speak to the issues on the nation's airwaves. Perhaps then we might see an end to the "Tortilla Ceiling" hampering Latinos in broadcast commentary. It would also be wise for Latinos themselves to comment more frequently on non-Latino issues of importance to the country.

The Rebirth of Cultural Pride:
Cinco de Mayo

Cal State University Monterey Bay, May 5, 1997

C inco de Mayo (the 5th of May) has relevance to the Mexican People and to Americans of Mexican decent in the U.S., but the festivities with which it is greeted every year in this country is both a curious and extraordinary phenomenon. Historically, the date is considered almost as a second day of independence in Mexico. The date commemorates a military victory in 1862 by a rag-tag Mexican army made up of peasants and a limited number of troops of the Mexican army that remained loyal to the Zapotec Indian president Benito Juarez. Mexican conservatives opposed to Juarez' efforts of land reform, including the expropriation of millions of acres of land controlled by the Church, foreigners, and a small number of Mexico's elite families, had gone to Europe seeking the support of Napoleon III in identifying a European member of a royal family who would return the monarchy to Mexico. Napoleon III, himself just a commoner who like his famous relative Napoleon Bonaparte, had lived out Thomas Paine's axiom in *Common Sense,* of a group of *banddite* assuming power and naming themselves kings by wielding bigger clubs against their foes, sent an army to invade Mexico and place the young Archduke of Austria Maximilian on a new thrown of Mexico.

The invading French army, taking the same route into Mexico City as had Cortez three hundred years earlier, were greeted outside the city of Puebla by the Mexican General Francisco Zaragoza and his impromptu army. Surprisingly, they defeated the French troops, then recognized as the best soldiers in Europe, in a ferocious battle. The victory was short-lived, however, as Napoleon III sent reinforcements and soon controlled the country and established the innocent Maximillian on the thrown. Juarez, in the meantime, lived as a presidential exile in his own land, being hidden in Indian villages and remote regions of the country. The French had succeed with their invasion despite the Monroe Doctrine, which had decreed that the U.S. would not tolerate the intervention of European powers in American (North and South) affairs. The French had undertaken their bold move because the United States was, at the time, engaged in its own Civil War, and not in any condition to attend to its foreign affairs.

That is the history of Cinco de Mayo, celebrated modestly in Mexico, reflecting the victory of a single battle which was followed by the loss of the war. Certainly, it was a moral victory, signifying the superiority in battle, at least this one, of the peasant class against the troops of an empire. The day is certainly less significant than the 16th of September (1810) when Mexico's true revolutionary war against the Spanish colonial power began. The 16th is equivalent to our 4th of July. Why then, do Mexican-Americans, Chicanos, and now, even the broader Latino community celebrate the day with such ceremony in the U.S.?

Some years ago, when I served as Director of Minority Recruitment for the U.S. Peace Corps in Washington D.C., I was invited to Minneapolis/St. Paul by our regional office to participate in Cinco de Mayo festivities. I remember flying into Minneapolis curious as to what I would find so far north and so far removed from the Southwestern part of the country where I had grown up. I smiled at the thought of a few taco stands and some Corona beer in a few *puestos* that might greet me at the promised celebration. Much to my surprise, and a complete revelation as to how much I had been missing of the American Diaspora, I was greeted by 60,000 Latinos and friends in parade, celebrating with colorful floats and food stands, Latin music and dance. While there were certainly many participants of Mexican origin there, Central and South Americans, Puerto Ricans, Dominicans were also there in large numbers as well. Everybody, including the always friendly Minnesotans, was celebrating the day. Most of them were totally oblivious as to the meaning of the historical event. In fact, it is even safe to say that most Chicano/Latinos are unfamiliar with the historical meaning of the date in the history of Mexico. They might be able to say that it commemorates the victory of the Mexicans over the French way back when. But it really doesn't matter too much that the history of the event is almost forgotten, because the day has taken on new meaning. What it really commemorates in a sense is the birth of the Chicano student movement, if not the birth, at least its legitimacy among the halls of academia as well as high schools and grade schools, and now among the general public.

In the late 60s, as a professor at several universities in California, I was among the early teachers of Chicano history. At Cal State Long Beach where I taught in the first Chicano Studies Department and later, teaching the first Chicano history course at the new Cal State Bakersfield, I was witness to the emergence of the fledgling Chicano student groups, first MAYO, the Mexican American Youth Organization, then UMAS, the United Mexican American Students, and then finally, the Movimiento Estudiantil Chicanos de Aztlán (MEChA, meaning the Chicano Student Movement of Aztlán). The last, MEChA, finally made the bold move of dropping Mexican-American the hyphenated term given to them by government entities, and proclaiming themselves Chicanos of Aztlán (the Southwestern U.S. believed to be the land of origin of the Aztecs before their migration south into Mexico in the twelfth century A.D.).

These were the 60s and as the Blacks had dropped Negro to describe themselves and proudly proclaimed Langston Hughes' term "Black is beautiful," Chicanos on college campuses all over the Southwest were exerting their political presence on American college campuses.

In an effort to publicly celebrate their heritage and burst out from the cocoon of assimilation, the Chicano students began to celebrate their presence with festivals of song and dance, and more importantly, with an academic political agenda, such as the Plan de Santa Barbara and the Plan de Aztlán which demanded cultural and historical courses reflecting their presence in the colleges and public schools of America. One way to bring attention to their goals was to plan festivities with heritage speakers and programs around a day that the school authorities would recognize as their day. Thus, Cinco de Mayo became that day. Why was it chosen over the more significant 16th of September? The answer has little to do with historical meaning after all, the Spaniards and the French were both defeated European powers. The reason is a simple matter of the school calendar. The 16th of September falls in the beginning of the school year. In fact, on some campuses school hasn't even begun by that date. In others, classes have just started. Consequently, student groups wanting to plan big festivities, invite speakers, secure venues, would be hard pressed to do it just as classes begin for the year

Cinco de Mayo falls in the springtime. An entire year of planning can go on, and in some cases does, before the week of events takes place. There is something about the spring as well. New life, rebirth, *renaissance*, romance is in the air, and I speak here of the romanticism that has inspired revolutionaries over the centuries. Thus, the Chicano students have led their elders, and the country as a whole, to celebrate the rebirth of cultural pride and self-assertion, educational reform and self-worth. We owe much to those young people on America's campuses back in the Sixties and early Seventies who, at great risk, confronted intransigent administrations, chained themselves to the pillars of academia and brought about meaningful changes in how we teach our students about the real America. Education took a major turn in the right and honorable direction, thanks to those young people who gave new meaning to the Cinco de Mayo.

Hispanic Heritage Month

Latino Encyclopedia, **Scholastic Press, 2005**

I n 1968, responding to the growing demands of Hispanic groups in the United States, led by thousands of Hispanic students on college and high school campuses, the Congress of the United States passed Joint Resolution (H.J. Res. 1299) on September 17 which established Hispanic Heritage Week. The resolution read in part:

> *Resolved by the Senate and House of Representatives of the United States in Congress assembled, that the President is herby authorized and requested to issue annually a proclamation designating the week including September 15 and 16 as "National Hispanic Heritage Week" and calling upon the people of the United States, especially the educational community, to observe such week with appropriate ceremonies and activities."*
> *(Public Law 90-498*

The impetus for this action was clearly the growing demand in the decade of the Sixties by students seeking a grater role for themselves in designing their own education. The Civil Rights Movement, the Free Speech Movement at U.C. Berkeley, and on other campuses, the college sit-ins and demonstrations, all had as one theme the growing concern that higher education in the United States was not reflecting the entire truth of American History. Black students, Asians, Latinos, Native Americans were all demanding that college curricula reflect their history in America as well as the Anglo-Saxon and Western European story in this country. Minority student groups were successful on many college and high school campuses in getting faculty and administration to begin including the histories of the non-white Americans in courses and lesson plans.

It was therefore not accidental that the Joint Resolution approved by Congress and signed by the president specifically noted that "especially the education community," observe the week with appropriate ceremonies and activities. The timing for this week, however, coming in September, just at the beginning of the school year, made it difficult for educators to plan relevant activities as most schools were in the process of getting the schools organized for the arrival of students for the new semester. In fact, in many campuses in the country, the semester may not have even begun by the authorized dates for recognition and celebrations.

For that reason, and because the Hispanic Heritage Week was becoming more popular as a significant recognition of the ever increasing Hispanic population in the U.S., (now the largest ethnic group in the U.S.) the Congress amended its original resolution on August 17 of 1988 and approved Public Law 100-402 which expanded the week to Hispanic Heritage Month beginning September 15 and ending on October 15. This new 31-day period gave to educational establishments, government offices and community groups ample time to prepare appropriate activities as suggested by the law. On September 13, 1988, President Ronald Reagan, in Proclamation 5859, established the first Hispanic Heritage Month in the United States.

The dates selected by the Congress of September 15 and October 15 are significant because of their importance to Latin American countries as they are intimately tied to the history of most of the countries of Central and South America. September 15, 1810 commemorates the beginning of the struggle by Latin American patriots to gain their independence from the Spanish Empire. Napoleon Bonaparte, in his quest for empire had invaded Spain and placed his brother José on the Throne of Spain, sending the Spanish King Ferdinand VII into exile. The Latin American Creoles, initially fighting to free themselves from French rule, ultimately asserted their independence from Spain as well.

In Mexico, two parish priests José María Morelos and Miguel Hidalgo also led the revolt against the French ruler imposed on Spain. After nearly 10 years of struggle, independence was won in 1821 in the former Spanish territories from the Oregon border in North America to the Tierra del Fuego at the tip of Argentina. Not only was independence won for the *mestizo* nations (mixed Indian and white blood), but also for all of the Indians and the slaves of the former colonies, as they were given their freedom, forty-five years before the U.S. Civil War and the Emancipation Proclamation ultimately gave the American slaves their freedom. Thus, September 15 is the official Independence Day for the countries of Costa

Rica, el Salvador, Guatemala, Honduras, and Nicaragua while September 16 is Independence Day in Mexico.

The second day which comes at the end of Hispanic Heritage Month and reflects what we have considered as Columbus Day, October 12 in the United States. This day, in Latin America, does not glorify Columbus, since the very advanced indigenous cultures of the two continents, which included the Incas, the Mayans and Aztecs, among others, had already established significantly advanced cultures. Consequently, instead of calling October 12 Columbus Day, Latin Americans call this day, *el día de la raza,* the day of the race or the people, which signifies the birth of the *mestizo* and mulatto, a mixture of indigenous, Asian, European, and African peoples. *El dia de la raza,* October 12, is culturally significant in Latin American, and by extension has become significant in the U.S. as well as it has become the anchor of Hispanic Heritage Month.

Today there are over 36 million Hispanics living in the United States. They have come from Mexico, Spain, Central America, South America and the Caribbean. As a group, they are white, Black, Indian, Asian and mixes of all these groups. The immigrants to the U.S. from Spanish America have blended in with some millions of Hispanics that have been in the continental United States as early as 1539 when the Spanish explorer Hernando de Soto led a band of Spanish soldiers and Mexican Indians and Black slaves in a year long journey of exploration of the Mississippi Valley. This troop of 600 soldiers and porters had landed in the present day Tampa, Florida in that year and begun the extraordinary adventure nearly three centuries before the Lewis and Clark expedition occurred.

Spaniards and Mexicans on the other side of the continent began establishing colonies in New Mexico, Texas and California. From the missions and pueblos of the Southwest have come millions of Hispanic descendants of the early explorers and settlers over the years. But, prior to the social movement of the 1960s, which have had major impact on our educational institutions, the story of the Hispanic historical presence in the U.S. was not reflected in most textbooks to any great degree. The historical interaction of the indigenous, Black and Hispanic populations of the U.S. with the white population was not generally told or was portrayed in a negative manner. Most textbooks, even at the university level, glossed over the period of Spanish colonization, preferring to focus on the history, formation and development of the Anglo-Saxon/European settlement of the United States.

Because of the impact of the Congressional Resolutions creating Hispanic Heritage Month and the annual Proclamation by the President of the United States, in announcing the beginning of Hispanic Heritage Month, and the specific call to educators to observe the month with activities and celebrations, significant strides have been made to tell the story of the Hispanic citizens of the U.S., their history and their culture.

President George Bush in 1989 inaugurated Hispanic Heritage Month with the statement that:

> "*Perhaps no single ethnic group has had as profound an impact upon our Nation as Hispanic Americans. From the days of the first explorers in what is now Florida, Texas, and California, Hispanic people have played a major role in taming this vast country and developing its abundant resources . . . The values passed from generation to generation in Hispanic American families are values central to the American experience . . . While our Nation's history bears ample evidence of our Hispanic heritage, we cannot view that great heritage solely in terms of the past. Rather, it is a living legacy.*" (President George Bush's message on the Observance of National Hispanic Heritage Month. Sept. 11, 1989

Today, every President announces the beginning of Hispanic Heritage Month with similar pomp and oratory. This focus on the period between September 15 and October 15 gives educators, students, and the public in general, ample time to plan significant events of both a celebratory nature and educational relevance. Numerous books and pamphlets, poster, videos, CDs and recordings are available, focusing on some aspect of Hispanic history and culture. Foods are prepared, fiestas and parades are held and a truly national focus occurs on the Hispanic community from Washington, D.C. to San Diego, California during this month.

In communities throughout the United States and especially in the Southwest, activities are planned to commemorate Hispanic Heritage Month every year. Colleges and universities plan special programs such as symposia on Hispanic topics. Fiestas of traditional dance and music are planed. School districts present programs that feature speakers and cultural activities. The Federal Government annually authorizes a variety of Hispanic Heritage programs during this period in many of its agencies. The Department of Justice, for example, in past years planned a week of activities culminating with a Hispanic lunch of traditional food for employees and guest, and featured a speech by well know actor Edward James Olmos and other activities.

Newspapers, television, and radio also devote programs of Hispanic cultural content during this period. Latin music is featured and programs with historical content such as the Life of César Chávez or biographical sketches of Hispanic notables like New Mexico Governor Bill Richardson or actor Andy Garcia might be presented. The country as a whole now devotes considerable attention to recognizing the historical and cultural contribution of the 36 million Hispanics who live in the United States.

While there is a certain degree of celebration accompanying the period, the reality is that because of the Congressional action in creating Hispanic Heritage Month and the President's annual focus on the period, significant scholarly work has also emerged as a result of this recognition. And just as this event marks the beginning of the academic year at most schools, another, now National Day of recognition of our Hispanic past takes place when *Cinco de Mayo* (the Fifth of May) occurs, commemorating the Mexican defeat of the French armies in 1862 at the Battle of Puebla. The celebration of these two events in the U.S. is significant evidence that the contributions of Hispanic Americans is fully recognized and celebrated in the United States today.

Bibliography

Humphrys, R.A. & Lynch, John, Ed. *The Origins of the Latin American Revolutions, 1808-1826*. New York, A.Knopf, 1965.

Langley, Lester D. *MexAmerica: Two Countries, One Future*. New York. Crown Publishers, 1988.

McWilliams, Carey. *North from Mexico*. Philadelphia: J.P. Lippincott, 1949.

Samora, John & Simon, Patricia. *History of the Mexican-American People*. South Bend, University of Notre Dame Press, 1977.

http://www.mcpsk12.md.us/curriculum/socialstd/Hispanic.html
http://www.rnha.org/issues.heritage.whyheritagemonth.html

Vasconcelos' Cosmic Race Shifts to the North . . . Forging the World's First Multicultural Society

Hispanic Link, **April 3, 1995**

T he odds are that the new Republican Congress will pass some sort of Proposition 187 legislation aimed at immigrants of color, legal or illegal. In addition, the House leadership appears to be fulfilling its "Contract with America" plank denying certain benefits even to legal immigrants. The attack on legal U.S.-citizen children of the undocumented in this country has begun. The hysteria and broad-brush strokes used in the debate will undoubtedly affect anyone with a foreign accent and a darker complexion. But the xenophobic Prop. 187 fanatics have always been with us.

In another era immigrants were also attacked: "They are an invasion of venomous reptiles . . . long-haired, wild-eyed, bad-smelling, atheistic, reckless foreign wretches . . . Crunch snakes before they have time to bite. They are a danger that threatens the destruction of our national edifice by erosions of its moral foundations."

GOP Is Historically Anti-immigrant

These words were not uttered by supporters of California's Prop. 187 in the heat of the campaign to pass the 1990's version of the Alien and Sedition Act or the National Origins Act. They were in fact, spoken by a preacher of Christian doctrine, the Rev. Josiah Strong, from his pulpit and in his writings (Our Country) in 1885. The attack then was not against Latinos, Southeast Asians or Haitians.

Rather, it was against the Italians, Irish Jews, Polish—Europeans streaming into the United States to become ultimately the backbone of our Industrial Revolution. These immigrants were attacked because of their Jewish or Catholic faiths, their foreign languages, their impoverished condition, and their willingness to do the jobs more established residents would not.

The Republican Party in the 19th century was already the "anti-immigrant" party, the party of the Daughters of the American Revolution and the rich industrialists of the Northeast. Meanwhile, the Democratic Party of Jacksonian populism took the ragtag immigrants of Europe who fulfilled the Lady's call to, "Give me your tired, your poor, your huddled masses, yearning to breath free."

Sen. Henry Cabot Lodge of Massachusetts epitomized the Republican animus towards the "mass of the unwashed" by passing the Immigrant Literacy Bill aimed at stopping the influx of those "twisted, unassimilable, filthy, un-American immigrants."

In the 1894 congressional elections, Republicans won an overwhelming victory. Buoyed by it, the nativists continued their immigrant bashing, which culminated in Cabot Lodge's legislation. Fortunately it was vetoed by Democratic President Grover Cleveland.

Exactly 100 years later, Republicans won another overwhelming victory in the congressional elections of 1994—and guess what? The nativists have reappeared. Anti-immigration legislation is being drafted in the nation's capital and in many state legislatures.

Racial Purity Is Elusive

On the eve of the 21st century, however, even with the Republican operatives in control of Washington and a majority of the state houses, no amount of doomsdayism will be able to stem the impact of immigration nor maintain what the early nativists called the "racial purity of the predominantly Anglo-Saxon American nation."

In the past, this "American nation" had accepted such philosophical, political policies as Manifest Destiny, Social Darwinism and the White Man's Burden, which nearly caused the extermination of the Native American population and resulted in the illegal deportation of millions of legal residents and citizens among Chinese, Filipinos, Italians and Mexicans in this country.

In 1925, the Mexican philosopher and educator Jose Vasconcelos published his essay on futuristic demographics, *La Raza Cósmica*. Vasconcelos' work was controversial from the start, challenging the European Social Darwinism that had motivated Mexican intellectuals to reject the Indian portions of their own heritage.

Politicians of the wealthy class pressured the French government to sign a treaty with Mexico over some disputed islands, in which the French government officially recognized Mexico as a "Caucasian Nation." It relegated the 80% of the population, which was either *mestizo* (Indian and White mixture) or Indian, to the status of non-Mexican.

Radically, Vasconcelos postulated in his essay that a new race would be born in the Americas which would combine all of the best qualities of the black, white, red and yellow races. He concluded this fifth race would emerge in the Amazon Valley of South America where African blacks, Amazon Indians and white Spaniards, French, British and Portuguese were already mixing their racial lines: "We will reach in America, before any other part of the globe, the creation of a race created with the treasures of all the previous races, the final, universal race, the cosmic race."

What Vasconcelos predicted for the Amazon Valley may become a reality there in another century. But what he anticipated—the emergence of a cosmic race—is in fact occurring in the United States today. This is perhaps what frightens the fans of Prop. 187, the English-only crowd and those descendants of 19th century nativists who believed in maintaining "the single Anglo-Saxon stock."

Hybrid Households Become the Norm

Vasconcelos' theme was revisited in a 1993 edition of *Time* magazine, devoted entirely to the "browning of America" or "How Immigrants Are Shaping the World's First Multi-Cultural Society."

In that issue, *Time* presented significant evolving demographic facts affecting the population of the United States. It cited the notion that "intermarriage is as old as the Bible. But during the past two decades, America has produced the greatest variety of hybrid households in the history of the world."

The incidence of births to mixed-race couples has increased 26 times as fast as that of any other group, according to *Time*. Japanese Americans, for example, marry non-Japanese 65% of the time. Among Native Americans, the figure is 70%. Of individuals contacted in a national poll by *Time*, 72% indicated they were acquainted with interracial couples.

In New York, Los Angeles, Chicago, and Fairfax County, VA., more than 100 languages are spoken in the public schools of each city. By the year 2040, California, presently 55% white, will be 32% white In cities as distinct and as geographically separated as Miami, Union City, N.J., and Santa Ana, Calif., more than half of the population is foreign-born.

Time cited the case of 29-year-old Cindy Mills, the daughter of Black and Native American parents, married to a White European immigrant, who believes that her two Native American, Black-White-Hungarian-French-

Catholic-Jewish-American children may lead the way to an unhyphenated, whole U.S. society.

Multiculturalism Flourishes in U.S.

This new American "whole" is what Vasconcelos was envisioning in his essay on the Cosmic Race. He, of course, uses America to speak of the Western Hemisphere, while we, erroneously, refer only to the United States. Nevertheless, as hard as legislators may try, as high as emotions may run, and as unlikely as it may seem in Davenport, Iowa, or Little Rock, Ark., the Cosmic Race is being born in United States.

The Jewish delicatessen in Brooklyn has become an Arab sub shop, and the Portuguese crab stand on Fisherman's Wharf has become a Vietnamese establishment. All across the land, the migrant worker stream has dropped Gonzaleses, Martinezes, and Garcias in Chicago, Portland, Saginaw and Saint Paul. And for more than 200 years, from the days of slavery, the black and white races have been mixing creating the Creole and mulatto populations scattered throughout the country.

No Set of Laws Can Stop It

Today 84% of all the school children in Los Angeles are non-white. In New York City, 85% are "minorities," or more correctly, now the majorities in both cities. These children will grow up in a more racially tolerant society than their parents or grandparents did, despite the politicians, the fearful nativists, and any efforts to self-segregate.

The challenge will be to maintain those "beautiful treasures" of each race that Vasconcelos wrote about, thus maintaining diversity while living harmoniously together. Hopefully, the children of the 21st century will be free to follow their hearts and become the proud parents of the Cosmic Race. It will happen; no set of laws or efforts by shortsighted politicians can stop it now.

The California Farmworker: Forgotten Man In the History Of Agribusiness

Sacramento Bee, March 7, 1973

It is commonly proclaimed that California is the No.1 agricultural producer in the nation. Because of the natural gifts of fertile soil, variety of climates and abundant water, the state is ideally suited for the production of a wide variety of crops

In addition, such human contributions as the state and federally funded water projects have converted the semi desert areas of California into verdant farmlands. The tax-supported programs of the University of California and the state colleges also have given the farmers of the state the benefits of free research in crop production, pest control, and the development of innovative farm machinery.

California farmers, too, have traditionally united against problems affecting the industry. The California Farm Bureau, the Council of California Growers and the State Grange, among others, have contributed to the excellence of agriculture in California, making it the leading agricultural state in the nation.

But one segment in the history of California agriculture that traditionally has been overlooked has been the farm labor force. It is this failure of recognition which has led to many of the agricultural disputes that have plagued the industry in the past. A true history of California agriculture would indicate that the development of agribusiness in California runs parallel with the importation of cheap agricultural labor into the state. In fact, the success of California farming can easily be traced to the various histories of the California Indians, the Chinese, the Mexicans, the Japanese, the Oklahoma's, the Blacks and more recently the Filipinos, Arabs and Puerto Ricans in California farming. The availability of a cheap migratory labor force is perhaps the most significant factor contributing to the undisputed excellence of California agriculture in our recent past.

The early white settlers who came from Mexico and established the California missions did more than just introduce cattle, horses, alfalfa, grapes, oranges and cotton to California. They established a *patrón* system that depended exclusively on the labor of local Indians and imported Mexican-Indians. The Spanish and Mexican dons were not noted for their love of manual labor. It was the Indian who provided the manpower for the first California farms and *ranchos*.

When gold was discovered—and some would say, because gold was discovered—California passed from Mexican hands to Yankee control. It was the gold rush of 1848 that originally enticed the Chinese to come to the United States. Stanford M. Lyman points out that "the credit-ticket system, as it has been called, enabled an impoverished Chinese worker to come across the ocean, find lodging and food in San Francisco and be assisted to going to work in the mines, on the railroads . . . . or as strikebreakers, without putting up any cash."

When the transcontinental railroad was completed in the 1860s, a severe depression hit the United States. The Chinese found themselves accused of taking jobs from whites and the anti-Chinese agitation that had begun in California culminated with the Chinese Exclusion Law passed by Congress in 1882. By this time, however, California agriculture was so dependent on a large labor force that "cheap labor was brought from many parts of the world to keep the system going."

The Japanese Tragedy

Next in line were the Japanese. John Modell in his study of Japanese-Americas indicates that, "the same explicitly racial reasoning that had denied the privilege of naturalization to the Chinese was extended to the Japanese and jobs were offered the new arrivals in the old Chinese lines of gang labor on railroads and farms."

The Japanese, however, were not content to remain in the large pools of the hand-labor force. Their enterprise and extreme personal frugality led them to prosperity in their own venturing into farming. "The Japanese rented small parcels of close-in lands, held by white absentees, who anticipated future residential subdivisions . . . meticulous farming methods made it possible for the Japanese to produce superlative fruits and vegetables, a small beginning, but one which grew to a near monopoly of many agricultural products."

The story of the Japanese Americans is one of the most tragic in American agriculture, for not only did the racially motivated Alien Land Law of 1930, passed by the California Legislature, forbid non-citizens from purchasing farm land, World War II signaled the end of Japanese American eminence in agriculture. Forced into relocation centers, their lands in many instances fraudulently confiscated or sold, the Japanese Americans returned to California after the war to find that a new class of farmers had profited at the Japanese farmers' expense, and had no intention of sharing their good fortune.

Mexican Migrants

Another group, perhaps the most significant in terms of numbers, which has contributed to agribusiness in California, has been the Mexican and the Mexican-American population. Although only 15 percent of the population of Chicanos currently is employed in agriculture, that 15 percent constitutes more than 80 percent of the entire farm labor force in California.

The contribution of the Mexican population to the agricultural industry of the Southwest, of course, goes back to the early mission days when the Mexican *vaqueros* were the first cowboys on the Western scene. In the 20th century, however, the participation of Mexican-Americans in agriculture has been less romantic. "By 1919 many California growers already had become dependent on Mexican labor. This dependency increased during the 1920s for Mexico now proved to be as good a source for cheap labor as China and Japan had been in the 19th century."

It was the federal government that served as the greatest labor contractor for the American farmer. During World War II, the *Bracero* Program was initiated. This program supplied the California farmer with hundreds of thousands of laborers at a time that the nation was sending its young men off to fight a war. It is estimated that during the years of the *Bracero* program as many as half a million Mexicans a year were imported to the United States and the largest percentage of these were destined for California farms.

The Mexican workers proved to be such a good source. of labor that the federal government extended the program in 1951 under the title of Public Law 78. In addition to the legal *Braceros*, the so-called illegal "wetbacks" also numbered as many as half a million workers a year who found jobs on American farms. These workers proved to be ideal, for as one Farm Bureau representative told a government official. "We just want workers here to do the work, then leave. We don't want to build good housing for them because this will encourage farmworkers to stay."

It was never the intention of the *Bracero* Program to encourage the workers to stay. In fact, Mexican workers just prior to World War II had been encouraged to leave. During the Depression of the 1930s, the Mexicans found themselves in competition with the "Okies" and the "Arkies," as they were called, who had been thrown off the lands in the Midwest as a result of the Depression and the draught that produced the "dust bowel" that swept across Middle America. As they moved into California by the hundreds of thousands, many Mexicans were forced to return to Mexico or they left of their own initiative. As long as the cheap labor pool was maintained, it made little difference to the farmers who filled it.

But when the war began, the citizens from Oklahoma and Arkansas found work in the oilfields and defense plants and left the farmlands to the Mexicans, Filipinos and Blacks who had arrived in considerable numbers during the war years.

Even today, the contribution of various ethnic and minority groups constitutes a major component in agribusiness in California. Puerto Ricans and Arabs join the Mexican-Americans and Filipinos in harvesting most of California's crops. The sheep industry is highly dependent on the importation of Basque shepherds who are inexpensively brought in from France and Spain and who are now being joined by shepherds from Bolivia and Peru.

There is no question California farmers are the most productive in the world, producing more than 200 crops and leading the nation in 41 of these. Yet, there is no way that one can dispute the contribution of an inexpensive and dependable labor force in the industry for more than 100 years. This labor force has continued to work at some of the most difficult jobs in the country and without the protection of the National Labor Relations Act that covers all other workers in American commerce.

Some Came to Praise César, While Others Stood Far Away

Hispanic Link, May 10, 1993

A s I neared Forty Acres, I heard the shouts: "Long Live César! *Que viva César Chávez!*" The staccato hand-clapping that had characterized the union for 30 years emanated from the large circus type tents set up to shelter the crowd. Under one of them, César Chávez's body lay at rest in the pine-wood coffin made by his brother Richard.

It was ironic that the world press had gathered—more than 300 reporters and photographers, news crews from every conceivable outlet—to record the story of the untimely death of the United Farm Workers' president. Sadly ironic, because the Kern County Board of Supervisors, the five Republicans who would have traditionally been put in office by the money of growers, land developers and oil companies, the supervisors had not bothered to recognize the death of their county's most famous national leader.

Even California's Republican governor had ordered that flags on state buildings be flown at half mast. But in Kern County, home of the grapes of wrath, and in later years *la huelga*, the political pawns of the vested interests of the Southern San Joaquin Valley had not even acknowledged the passing of the great leader, while the Pope, the President, and numerous foreign leaders had sent envoys or their condolences. (Chávez' funeral was the largest funeral for a labor leader in the history of the nation.)

To the Growers, He Was the Enemy

To the county supervisors, César had been the enemy. As the enemy of the growers—DiGiorgio, Schenley, Guimmara—he was also their enemy.

But at Forty Acres on this day of mourning for César Chávez, the pure greatness of the man and inspirational qualities of his leadership were everywhere visible. Thousands upon thousands of farm workers from across the Southwest had gathered at this, the original home of the union. They had come from throughout the state. And From Arizona, Texas, and Florida; they gathered to pay homage to the man who had emerged as one of the most significant leaders of the civil rights movement of the '60s.

Chávez had taken his place alongside Martin Luther King and Robert Kennedy. His name had become synonymous with the rights of farm laborers across the land. In the San Joaquin Valley, where nearly all the table grapes in the nation are produced, he had joined with the Filipino workers on that day in 1965 to shout *Huelga! Huelga!*, and the strike was on.

Now he was dead. The tribute to him was being paid, not so much by the Kennedys, not so much by Jesse Jackson, nor Jerry Brown, nor Martin Sheen, nor Edward James Olmos and other celebrated names present to deliver their respects. Rather, the tribute was being paid by the thousands of farmworkers, hats held in hand, with wives holding rosary beads in theirs, who prayed to their God for the happy repose of César's soul.

Story after story is being told now by countless people of how César and his movement, *La Causa*, had inspired them to stay in school, to go to college, to study the law. César's own children had become lawyers and doctors and leaders. Now, because of his efforts to raise the sights of the farm workers with his constant encouragement *Sí se puede*, the maligned "sleeping giant" was on the move.

A Horizon of Opportunity

The old theory holds that revolutions do not occur when a man's face is the mud; they occur, instead, when he begins to lift his eyes towards the horizon. And César had helped them see the horizon. He had lifted them tenderly by the chin and said, "Look up, see the horizon, see the endless possibilities for you and for your children. This world is ours as well. You and I may be destined to a lifetime of labor with dignity in the fields, but our children can aspire to other things."

This was the message he brought to the farm workers in the fields, a message sprayed with non-violence, dusted with courage and with pride. Beneath a banner of *la Virgen de Guadalupe*, supported by that spirit of rebellion of Emiliano

Zapata, and with organizing tools of Saul Alinsky, and the temperament of Gandhi, the farm workers movement became so much more than just a labor effort.

It had a mystical life of its own that no other civil rights movement had. It sought to meet the spiritual as well as the bodily needs of the workers and to meet them continuously, as Dolores Huerta had assured in her eulogy. "César's spirit is alive. It is alive. It is a million times stronger in death than in life. César, in dying, has ensured the farm workers union will live on."

On this spring day, in the yet mild temperature of the San Joaquin Valley, thousands came to mourn the beloved leader. I regret that it was not until my own advancing years that I, also a product of the Valley, recognized the greatness of the man and the movement he spawned. As I trekked along the dusty road to Forty Acres, between the vineyards and orchards where I too had worked as a young man, I prayed that César would forgive those of us from the Valley who had not always seen the greatness and constancy of his leadership, his extreme personal sacrifice and that of his family.

It was all very clear to me now as the thousands walked in procession along the Padre Garces road toward the place in Delano where his movement had been born and where he would now be laid to rest. *Que viva César Chávez, y que descanse en paz!*

... and the Strawberry Pickers Shall Lead

Hispanic Link News Service, **April 1997**

They were all there, Baptist ministers, Jewish rabbis, nuns and priests, students, as well as teachers, and union, after union, after union—all those under the AFL-CIO umbrella, and the Teamsters too. And of course liberals and Democrats, Jesse Jackson, Dolores Huerta, Martin Sheen, young and old, Latinos, Anglos, blacks, Asians, Native Americans, straights and gays, all there, in Watsonville, California, on a Sunday in April.

In a peaceful gathering reminiscent of the 1960s marches of social protest and civil rights crusades, the United Farm Workers Union (UFW) had successfully organized, perhaps, the largest pro-labor rally in this country in several years in support of the strawberry workers of California. The event was an unqualified success if one's intention was to mobilize thousands, capture a lead spot on national news, and garner support for the 20,000 strawberry pickers in the state, who stoop the lowest of any laborers to harvest agriculture's lowest (to the ground) crop.

But beyond the immediate success of the well-organized and peaceful march along the main streets of this Santa Cruz county agricultural community of Watsonville nestled in perhaps the richest farmland in the nation, three significant events and harbingers of things to come were taking place:

1. The UFW, the only union in the country whose workers have historically been excluded from the protection of the National Labor Relations Act (the right of workers to organize into a union and bargain collectively)

157

emerged as the moral leader of the beleaguered labor movement in the United States.

2. The cause of the strawberry pickers, who earn an average of $720 a month for a 10 hour day, six day work-week, has become the rallying cry for numerous other groups concerned with social issues confronting the country, such as cuts in social and education spending, attacks on immigrant rights and affirmative action, and resurgent racism and hate crimes.

3. The old coalition of the 60s is coming back together again as a result of the "mean-spirited" legislation and attitudes which have affected Latinos, Blacks, immigrant groups, women's organizations, environmentalists, and of course, labor unions.

UFW as Leader

The United Farm Workers Union, which itself had reached a low point at the time of founder César Chávez' death in 1993, has regrouped under its second president Arturo Rodríguez and the inspirational leadership of founding Vice-President Dolores Huerta. Rodríguez has skillfully targeted strawberry workers, certainly one of the least protected groups in the country, as the focus of organizing efforts. Why the strawberry workers? Because, like the "grape-pickers" of the 60s, strawberry workers harvest a labor-intensive crop, which cannot be mechanically harvested, and is a "luxury crop" like grapes are. No one has to eat strawberries. If push comes to shove between the UFW and the strawberry growers, the Union could conceivably begin a strawberry consumers' boycott like the successful world-wide boycott of California table grapes in the 60s and 70s which ultimately brought the growers to the bargaining table. Ironically, because the farm workers' union is still not covered by the National Labor Relations Act, as are all other unions, it is not prohibited from conducting a secondary consumer boycott. Other unions would by charged by the NLR Board with an unfair labor practice.

Rodríguez recently suggested the possibility of using consumers in the struggle when he stated, "Only the public can force the strawberry industry to bargain in good faith." The growers are also aware of this possibility. Gary Caloroso, a spokesman for a growers alliance, in commenting on the Watsonville march, noted, "If union supporters were to picket grocery stores and exaggerate the problems strawberry workers face in the fields, they could put a dent in the demand for strawberries, even without waging a formal boycott."

The Watsonville rally was the largest union-sponsored rally in the country in the last few years. As a result, the UFW appears to have emerged as the moral leader of the U.S. union movement which has been declining significantly in recent years, down to a low of 15% of the labor force from nearly 50% just after W.W.II. The AFL-CIO totally supported the rally and its member unions from the building trades to teacher unions were on hand. The Teamsters, who in other times, were foes of both the UFW and the AFL-CIO were also present, with president of the union, Ron Carey, pledging continued support to the farm workers. "Never again will the growers be able to divide us. We are united in this struggle." National presidents of the United Auto Workers, the SEIU, AFSME, the Mine Workers were all present.

John Sweeney, President of the AFL-CIO, perhaps summed up the attitude of organized labor in his address to the thousands of Latinos and immigrants whose initial entry into the labor movement for many has been through the UFW. "You are the future of the labor movement. You will determine whether we succeed or fail." Obviously, he is aware of the changing demographics in the country and in California. Twenty-five percent of the state's population is foreign-born, and service unions such as the SEIU are the growth unions in the country. The service unions are heavily Latino and immigrant, just as the early industrial unions were made up primarily of European immigrants, the Irish, Italians, Poles and Jews. So on this sunny Sunday in April, the fourth anniversary of Chavez' death, the UFW brought the union heavy-weights from Washington, D.C., New York, Chicago, Detroit . . . to Watsonville in support of the strawberry workers, and perhaps, in search of labor's future.

Strawberry Workers' Cause as Social Galvanizer

The cause of the strawberry workers—no right to organize and bargain collectively, exposure to pesticides, and the nature of the back-breaking work for the purpose of providing garnish for banquet tables and toppings for ice-cream sundaes, appears to have not only pricked the conscience of organized labor, but of those many citizens who have traditionally stood for social justice and fair play. The image of a Latino worker (and they are the only ones who do this work) bent over to harvest such a luxury food for ten hours a day in the hot sun, seems to epitomize the growing disparity between the rich and the poor. Recent legislation such as welfare reform, passed by a Republican congress and signed by a Democratic president underlines the gap between the haves and the have-nots. To those gathered in Watsonville, the image of the socially abused strawberry picker was certainly more real than that of a "welfare queen." Similarly, corporate welfare was more of an issue than food stamps to those gathered.

California's Propositions 187 and 209 have also led to immigrant bashing and a perceived retreat from equal access for minorities and women in education, the workplace and in government contracts. NAFTA, corporate downsizing, and the transfer to offshore sites by U.S. manufacturers have had the cumulative effect of lowering the strength and earning power of the American worker, according to rally speakers. All of this has led many to conclude that both government and the private sector are retreating from the social commitment the country has had to its citizens since the New Deal, and has resulted in this growing disparity between rich and poor, which many speakers correctly noted, is the largest disparity of all the industrialized nations of the world.

The Old Coalition of the 60s

One could observe that, though the march was in support of Latino strawberry workers, at least half of the 30 thousand were not Latinos. Reminiscent of the civil rights marches of the 60s, white America was present and accounted for. Blacks, Asians, Native Americans were present in significant numbers too. Union members from all the industrial and trade unions were there. Religious leaders from Franciscan friars to Baptist ministers, to Jewish and Muslims leaders were on hand. And students by the thousands were everywhere, some with pierced noses and lips, others looking like sorority and fraternity pledges, but all carrying banners and chanting the slogans of the day. The regulars like NOW, the Sierra Club, MEChA and even some groups thought to have disappeared like the Brown Berets, the Black Panthers, and the Socialist Workers Union were present and marching. And of course, figures who had spoken at similar rallies in the past were as eloquent three decades later. Jesse Jackson, "we will not retreat because our cause is fair, our cause is just, our cause is right." The tireless Dolores Huerta, "*Sí se puede, Cesar está con nosotros.*" Arturo Rodrígues, "we are on the march, *El pueblo es el poder.* The people are the power." Luis Valdez, screenwriter and producer, and founder of the farmworkers' Teatro Campesino, now a professor at Cal State Monterey Bay, was the Master of Ceremonies. It seemed like old times.

To many participants, the greatest result of the march, the benefit of this struggle for strawberry workers' rights, was the gathering of liberals, who for several decades have been intimidated to the point of not showing their heads, shying away form social issues. As one participant commented, "The mean-spirited nature of people like Gingrich and Wilson and Props 187, and 209 and the so-called welfare reform have inspired me to get involved again. I'll be damned if I'm going to let those guys recreate my country into their image." Perhaps the 60s are back, and California's strawberry workers are carrying the banner for all the rejuvenated marchers.

Labor Unions in the 70s in the U. S.

The 1970s Almanac, **Salem Press, 2005**

Unions in the United States

L abor unions in the United States had reached their peak of 35% of the labor force in the years immediately following WW II. By the end of the 1970's they would be down to a low of 25%. The decade and decades to follow would produce an even more precipitous decline as American industrial realities began to transform from a localized industrial model to one that featured globalization, outsourcing, a shift to a service oriented workforce, and a decline in domestic manufacturing. Severe economic conditions during the 1970s, such as the Arab Oil embargos and accompanying inflation, unemployment, and social dislocation all combined to usher in a period of declining union membership and a decline in the political clout of organized labor. The Viet Nam War that still raged at the beginning of the decade also had an effect within the Democratic Party family by pitting George Meany the President of the AFL-CIO against George McGovern the Democratic Party's anti-war candidate in the elections of 1972.

The first major blow to the growth and strength of organized labor after WW II was the growth of foreign competition in manufacturing during the 1960s and 1970s. Japan and Germany and the rest of Europe, now back on their industrial feet, thanks to U.S. financial support, such as the Marshal Plan, were again becoming competitors with the U.S. in the world marketplace. The auto, steel, electrical, textile, rubber and other industries in the U.S., in order to maintain their high levels of profit, were forced into critical restructuring because of the competition from abroad. Plants began to close in the industrial Northeast and Midwest, ushering in the phrase "rust belt" to describe the effect that was occurring in states like Pennsylvania, Ohio, Michigan as plant closures became a very common phenomenon. As major steel plants and other manufacturing plants closed, industrialists scrambled to find a way to survive in the ever-increasing global economy.

World Financial Institutions Make Globalization a reality

During the decade, U.S. corporations began to develop a new ability to move capital to various parts of the world without regard to national boundaries. This, in turn, allowed them to move their production operations to locations around the world to take advantage of significantly lower labor costs. They were aided in this effort by global economic institutions such as the World Trade Organization, International Monetary Fund, and the World Bank. This globalization had horrendous effects on organized labor in the U.S. and the workforces in other industrialized nations. It allowed business to pit workers in Third World countries against workers in the industrial countries. Some believed that many corporations had effectively created a "global hiring hall" which allowed them to move their operations to countries offering the lowest labor costs. Initially, some industries like the textile industry, in order to take advantage of non-union labor, had moved to the American Deep South where organized labor had never fully penetrated. As union organizers followed these industries to the South, the companies then moved their operations offshore to avoid unions, eventually, even fleeing locations like Mexico and the Caribbean to seek even lower labor costs in Bangladesh or India.

The response to the economic crisis in the early part of the decade and as a response to increased competition from abroad, corporations began to reject the "class compromise" that had existed between them and labor since the end of WW II and the beginning of the 1970s. Douglas Fraser, head of the United Auto Workers put it this way, during the decade; "The leaders of industry, commerce and finance in the U.S. have broken and discarded the fragile, unwritten compact previously existing during a past period of growth and progress . . . . leaders of the business community with few exceptions have chosen to wage a one-sided class war." There was some truth to Fraser's words as during the decade there was a hiring of as many as 10,000 permanent replacement workers a year for fired workers attempting to organize unions at various U.S. plants.

As the U.S. population shifts, new jobs emerge

One of the other elements affecting labor in America during the decade was the population shift that accompanied the emergence of the rustbelt in the Northeast and Midwest. The 1980 census showed the dramatic population shift from the rustbelt region, which had actually not increased population, to the Sunbelt area, notably California, Florida, Texas and Arizona. The population shift also reflected significant economic realities. The growth of high-tech industries, computer, microchip, and electronic companies located in the Sunbelt, attracted more highly educated blue-collar workers and college graduates. While massive unemployment was occurring in the East and Midwest, new, primarily non-union jobs were being created in the Sunbelt. The net effect of the population shift to the Sunbelt and to suburban areas around major cites was to divide the working class along geographic, racial, and economic lines. The low-paid, minimum wage earners, were now centered in the inner cities—barrios and ghettos with astronomical unemployment rates while those with significantly higher paying jobs relocated to the suburbs and to the Sunbelt. At the same time that this population shift was occurring with the accompanying shift to high-tech jobs, there was a shift from manufacturing jobs to service employment taking place across the land. Positions as insurance agents, real estate brokers, sales personnel, consultant specialists in everything from advertising to personal fitness, along with numerous other service occupations were replacing the traditional manufacturing jobs.

Pubic Sector jobs the only bright spot for Labor

The only significant growth for labor unions during the decade was in the public sector. Teachers, firefighters, prison guards, highway patrol troopers, nurses and other healthcare workers, and other government employees were beginning to organize into unions, sometimes into preexisting ones like SEIU and AFSME or into new ones like the teachers unions and municipal employee unions. Many states like California and Massachusetts, during the decade, passed public sector labor laws modeled on the National Labor Relations Act, allowing for public employees to organize into unions and bargain collectively. Traditional industrial unions like the Teamsters, Auto Workers and Chemical Workers got into the act as well, vying to represent various bargaining units in the public sector as they sought to organize under the new laws. Public sector union growth was the only bright spot for labor during the decade as membership in industrial unions continued to decline.

The growth in these new public sector unions was accompanied by an increase in union membership by women and minorities. The previous model of industrial unions and skilled craft unions was decidedly weak on the notion of affirmative action. The leadership of all of the industrial and craft unions was almost universally white, with many of the leaders coming from white European ethnic backgrounds. Certainly, blacks, Hispanics and women were in no way represented in union membership or leadership positions commensurate with their percentage of the labor force. Traditionally, only the unskilled laborers' unions were where minorities found a spot. Women fared better in the new teacher unions and hospital workers unions as they represented a significant percentage of the labor force in these occupations. From this group of female union leaders in the service industries would eventually come many of the women union leaders of subsequent decades.

The only other high spot for labor during the decade was the success of union organizer César Chávez to get governor Jerry Brown of California and the legislature to enact the Agricultural Labor Relations Act in 1976, allowing for California farm workers to legally organize themselves into unions. California is to date the only state in the nation to have passed such a law. While it has produced significant benefits for California farm workers by putting the spotlight on California growers who cleaned up working conditions in the industry, the law had limited impact on the labor scene overall. Chávez' efforts to have similar legislation passed in other agricultural states met with no success. While the AFL-CIO brought Chávez' United Farmworkers' Union under the AFL-CIO umbrella, the federation has never made an effort to have agricultural workers included under the National Labor Relations Act. This would be a monumental task for the labor federation, which has seen its political clout diminish significantly over the years.

Labor loses political clout as membership slips

Early in the decade, AFL-CIO president George Meany embroiled the labor federation in the first of many political confrontations with the Democratic Party where labor had found its political home since its inception. In the midst of the Viet Nam War and as a prelude to the Watergate scandals, the McGovern-Fraser Commission of the Democratic Party enacted new rules for the Party's nominating procedures for national conventions. Instead of backroom deals, the Commission instituted reforms that would guarantee delegation spots for women and minorities at nominating conventions. Angered by these new rules that diminished labor's role in the nominating process, Meany's AFL-CIO boycotted the 1972 presidential election and refused to endorse the Party nominee George McGovern. Labor's support of the Viet Nam War was in sharp contrast to much of the Democratic Party membership's position. The War served to create a significant wedge between liberal Democrats and union members. Internationally as well, organized labor's support of national policy to support dictators in various parts of the world so long as they professed to be anti-communists, alienated labor from much of the Democratic Party. The AFL-CIO through its four international bureaus supported labor movements in Third World countries with funds provided by the U.S. government, leading to speculation that these institutes were working closely with the CIA in respective Third World countries.

The aftermath of this conflict within the Democratic Party on the part of labor may have had something to do with labor's failure to pass any significant legislation during the decade. Even though labor had persuaded Congress in 1975 to overturn a 1951 Supreme Court ruling limiting picketing at construction sites, the bill was nevertheless, vetoed by President Ford. Later, with Carter as president, labor confidently attempted to pass the legislation again only to come up a few votes short in the Democratically controlled House of Representatives. In 1978 labor again moved a comprehensive Labor Law Reform Bill, endorsed by President Carter, but it was blocked by a Republican filibuster in the Senate. The bill had been designed to reverse labor defeats in the workforce by simplifying procedures for representation elections under the NLRB, by increasing the number of members of the Labor Board to speed up the processing of unfair labor charges, and by increasing penalties against employers found guilty of unfair labor practices.

These legislative labor defeats came as union membership was also declining in the country. In order to stem the diminishing clout, labor chose to increase political activity at the expense of increasing union membership. The size of labor's political lobbying force increased, as did political action committee activities (PACs). This new aggressiveness at the end of the decade ushered in a period of instability and conflict for labor unions. The notion of unions collecting dues from members and then using much of these funds for political activities rather than on member support alienated not only some union members, but business executives as well. Already citing low-wage foreign labor competition, corporations felt emboldened in rolling back wages and opposing unions at home, as well as shipping jobs overseas. With the election of Ronald Reagan in 1980 labor would be faced with the wave of conservatism that would increase the rate of decline for unions in America. In addition to firing thousand of airline traffic controllers who went on strike early in his Administration, Reagan appointed an unsympathetic NLR Board which, within the first two years, reversed twenty-nine NLRB precedential decisions which had favored labor. It was clear that business had been given the green light to "bash unions," according to a *Business Week* report of the time. The heydays of American Labor were clearly coming to an end.

Impact

The realities of global competition, with the ability for manufacturers to relocate factories to countries with significantly lower labor costs because of global access to finances, brought about a significant decline in union membership in the U.S., dropping from 35% to 25% of the labor force during the decade. As factories began closing in the newly termed "rustbelt" region of the country, both increased population and non-union high tech jobs in computers and electronics began to emerge in the Sunbelt and suburban regions of some major cities. The only area to see union growth was in public sector jobs. Beginning in the McGovern era, labor also began to see its political clout diminish within the Democratic Party. By the time Ronald Reagan was elected, unions were clearly on the ropes and the decline continued.

Further Reading

Breecher, Jeremy and Costello, Tim. "Labor's Day: The Challenge Ahead," *The Nation, Sept. 21, 1998*

Brody, David, ed. *The American Labor Movement.* New York, Harper and Row, 1971.

Crenson, Matthew A. and Ginsberg, *Benjamin. Downsizing Democracy.* Baltimore, John Hopkins University Press, 2002.

Divine, Robert, et. al. *America Past and Present.* Scott, Foresman, Illinois, 1990.

Gershman, Carl. *The Foreign Policy of American Labor.* Beverly Hills, Sage Publications, 1975.

Lopez, Steven Henry. *Reorganizing the Rust Belt.* Berkeley, University of California Press, 2004.

Smith, Jim. "The AFL-CIO's Last Cold Warrior," *Z Magazine*, July, 1995.

Hispanic Growth Will Have Enormous Effects

The Sacramento Bee, **Dec. 2, 1979**

I f the predictions of many prestigious organizations come true—and there is every reason to believe they will—then the "sleeping Hispanic American giant" will arise, shake himself off, and demand his share of the economic and political pie during the 1980s

It is expected that Hispanics will be the most numerous group in Los Angeles County by the end of the decade. The United States Census Bureau calculates that Hispanics will likely be the largest minority group, surpassing Blacks in the U.S. by 1990

These predictions of the growth of the Hispanic community in the nation—and most specifically in California—will have enormous effects in the '80s and beyond. This accelerated population increase among Hispanics will result in significant movement in economic development, education, and political participation of Hispanic Americans as well.

It is generally agreed that the 1970 census seriously under-counted the minority community. The Census Bureau concludes that it missed at least 5.3 million blacks and Hispanics. In California alone, 643.000 persons of Spanish surnames were not counted in 1970. This is approximately 20 percent of the State's Hispanic population.

Hispanic groups such as the Mexican American Legal Defense and Education Fund are determined not to let this happen again. These organizations have pressured the Congress and the Carter administration to implement an active program that will guarantee an accurate head count of Hispanics. They correctly see higher numbers as a prerequisite to more Federal dollars into the Hispanic community and hopefully more political clout.

Census officials have agreed to make a special effort to get an accurate count for the 1980 Census, which will begin in April. Thus, many community service specialists such as Ellie Enriquez Peck of Sacramento have been assigned by the bureau to the task of making the minority community aware of how important the census is. "On the whole," says Peck, "most minority groups are concerned more about the services that come back to the community as a result of the taxes they pay than they are about political clout."

If Ms. Enriquez Peck is correct, the Hispanic community is not likely to allow another under-count. As Carmela Lacayo, head of a community service group in Los Angeles, concludes. "It's a numbers game. We have to be counted." Ms. Lacayo points out that 42 percent of the Hispanic community is below the age of 20. This means that during the decade of the '80s Hispanics will be the most conspicuous group in the child-bearing group, between the age of 20 and 40 years. Currently the Hispanic median age is 19.2 as compared to 29.2 for the total population. This is a significant figure for it means that, the baby boom of the '80s will be led by Hispanics.

This expected baby boom and low median age of Hispanic coupled with the high immigration rate, estimated at one million a year of both legal and illegal entrants, will raise the current 19 million figure beyond 12 percent of total U.S. population, thus going ahead of the Black population by the mid-1980s. This new status as the most populace minority group in the U.S. will carry with it as many opportunities as it will obligations.

It is of obvious significance that Hispanics constitute 15 percent of California public school enrollment. But even more important is the fact that they represent 50 percent of kindergarten children in the Los Angeles Unified School District—the second largest district in the nation. And in such typical San Joaquin Valley farming communities as Parlier, Arvin and Delano, Hispanics constitute well over 90 percent of the entire school enrollment.

What is important about these figures is the impact they are having on the entire educational programs throughout California. Currently both state and federal funds total $134 million in support to bilingual-bicultural programs in California. And $245 million is used to support migrant education.

It is difficult to gauge the immediate success of such categorical aid programs. Nevertheless, it is significant that from 1960 to 1970, the numbers of Hispanics in the 14-to-17 age group enrolled in school increased from 83 percent to 91 percent. The 1980 census figures are expected to show as high an enrollment figure for Hispanics as for Anglo students.

Remarkably, while Hispanics still have one of the highest high school drop-out rates, over 54 percent of Hispanic that graduate from high school do enroll in colleges. And in spite of the Bakke decision against Affirmative Action admissions, Hispanics are enrolling in professional schools at an increasing rare. Ralph Ochoa, former chief aide to Assembly Speaker Leo McCarthy, recalls being the only Chicano to graduate from an accredited law school in Los Angeles just 10 years ago in 1969. Today, Ochoa a successful attorney with offices in both Sacramento and Los Angeles believes that "Hispanics have to continue their efforts to get college educations and get into professional schools. In order to have an impact on economic issues, politics, and such areas as ecology and agriculture, we need leadership and that traditionally comes from our institutions of higher learning."

Ochoa will no doubt have company in the field of law. From the days when he was the only law school graduate in the entire University of California system, he will see that the U.C. Davis campus alone will graduate 12 Hispanics in 1980.

But Ochoa and other Hispanic leaders believe that while the role models will likely come from the university campuses as lawyers, physicians and educators, real success depends on the emergence of a true middle class in the Hispanic community.

George Pla, Deputy Director of the State Office of Economic and Business Development, for one, believes that the Hispanic community should shy away from dependence on government programs. "I am advocating for Hispanics to get into business and economic development instead of waiting for government to always supply the jobs."

Figures supplied by Pla's office indeed suggest that Hispanics are primarily blue-collar workers, but rapidly developing some entrepreneurial avenues. The insurance and real estate industries rank as the fifth largest employer of Hispanics in California. Manufacturing work is the number one employer, while service employment is the fastest growing sector.

This is significant since the services represent a tremendous leap from agricultural work, which ranks fourth with 12 percent, because individuals employed in hotels, restaurants, hospitals, etc. are more able to see to the education of their children and develop such other middle-class traits as establishing credit and getting into debt. This group, too, tends to eventually become urbanized as occurred with the Irish and Italian immigrants when they occupied this lower rung of the labor force ladder in the U.S.

As Hispanics continue to move farther away from the farm (85 percent of the population now urbanized) they will likely develop the political interest that often dominated the life of other immigrant groups to this country. And even though 75 percent of all Hispanics in California are native born U.S. citizens, their introduction into mainstream American life has been delayed by a series of obstacles.

Hispanics, despite the fact that a small number have always been here, are in reality late arrivals as an immigrant group. Their political education has been to a large degree influenced by less than democratic systems of government in their countries of origin. Their preoccupation with church, family and barrio affairs has tended to keep them isolated from the dominant political issues of the country. But most significant as a reason for the poor showing of the Hispanics in the social life of the country, up to his time, has been their failure to register and to vote. Only 31 percent of the potential voters are registered as compared to 66.7 percent of the population as a whole. And in California, despite their near 20 percent of the population less than 5 percent usually turns out to vote in general elections.

This is a fact well known to Hispanic leaders and Anglo politicians. Because "votes are power" Hispanics are beginning to mobilize in efforts to get their share of the American dream, such as it is at the end of the '70s. Assemblyman Art Torres of Los Angeles believes that the '80s will hold a brighter picture for Hispanics, "Well probably see a Hispanic named to a presidential Cabinet and successful candidates for statewide offices by the end of the decade."

Torres, as does Joe Serna, political science professor at Sacramento State and former aide to Lt. Governor Mervin Dymally, believes that coalition politics is the answer for Hispanics.

"By ourselves we couldn't win a dogcatcher's race," states Serna. "Success means coalition with groups outside of our community."

Torres predicts that Hispanics will form a coalition with Asian and Pacific peoples because of common goals such as bilingualism and population growth. He feels that Blacks will see the value of joining this coalition once initial suspicion disappears.

There is no question that things can only go up politically for Hispanics in California and the country as a whole. The number of Hispanics in the California Legislature has remained at six for the last 10 years, while at the national level, there are only five Hispanics in the house of Representatives as compared to 16 blacks and 22 Jews. But it appears that Hispanics are on the verge of making the most dramatic gains of any minority group in the country.

Politics of Trade and Empowerment

New Reality in California, April 2004
Latin American Pacific Trade Association Publication

C onservative political science professor from Harvard University Samuel Huntington is publishing his second controversial book, again bashing the non-white, non-protestant citizens of the world. After his first controversial book, the *Clash of Civilization* in which he attacked the middle eastern societies, in his new book *Who Are We?* he goes after Latin Americans, especially the Mexicans. Huntington states: "In this new era, the single most immediate and most serous challenge to America's traditional identity comes from the immense and continuing immigration from Latin America, especially Mexico." He argues that these new immigrants are not like earlier immigrants. Most have no interest in assimilation. He accuses these new immigrants of being slow to learn English, acquire good educations, become successful business-persons, and a host of other shortcomings that other immigrants have overcome. Most critically, Huntington accuses these immigrants of failing to buy into the American Dream. He states that, "There is not American dream; theirs is only the American dream created by an Anglo-Protestant society. Mexican-Americans will share in that dream and in that society only if they dream in English."

Huntington is not only incorrect with respect to the facts that he presents to support his arguments, he is also guilty of an extreme nativism that we hoped had disappeared in the last century, that same nativism that had produced the fallacies of Manifest Destiny. He fails to recognize that Latinos in America are the fastest growing number of entrepreneurs, that 68 percent of those who have lived in this country 30 years or more own their own home, that by the third generation, most Latino children do not speak Spanish, that Latino parents are the most interested parents in the country with respect to their children's education, that Latinos represent a much higher percentage of their national population as members of the armed services, and have earned as a group the highest number of Congressional Medals of Honor. Huntington is not only wrong, he is seriously wrong. Instead of lamenting the fact that American culture might be receiving a bit of new blood, he discounts the contributions of African Americans, Asian Americans and especially the Native Americans to the creation of the American image. He would have us believe that America is and should be Anglo and Protestant and that all newcomers should eventually conform to this description, at least in spirit if not in color.

The difference today with respect to what Huntington would like American society to be has been the angry response by Latinos to the immigrant, and by extension, "Latino-bashing" that has come from some academics like Professor Huntington and politicians in both Sacramento and Washington, D.C. Additionally, the political groundwork done by the United Farmworkers' Union over the years, and the increased stability of the once, very mobile, farm labor force, has begun to pay-off. The growing civic-minded-ness of this very large labor force has become ever apparent. New educational opportunities for the children of these workers are also beginning to pay dividends as many college graduates return to take up professions in their rural communities.

Clearly, the sheer growth in the Latino population of California since the early 80s has been phenomenal. Today the Latino population in the state is approaching 12 million, a 48.8% increase in this last decade. In the next fifty years this same population will experience an astronomical growth rate of 125%, reaching 31.5 million. By contrast, the present majority white, non-Latino population will grow by only 19%, from 17.1 million to 20.5 million, and cease to be the majority in the state by the year 2005.

Latinos will become the plurality in the state by the year 2020 and the majority by 2040. But sheer numbers are not the only changes taking place. The 1996 presidential elections showed a 20% increase in the Latino vote nationwide. Latinos in the U.S. are taking their rightful place in American society, in politics, business, education and social life, just as so many other groups have in the past, the Irish, the Italians, the Poles, the Jews. Not all of them were Anglo or Protestant. Instead of diminishing the American cultural bloodline as some suggest, they have added to it. So to will the immigrants from Mexico and the rest of Latin America.

The 'Pachuco' Character Searches For Identity and Recognition

The Sacramento Bee, **Feb. 11, 1979**

In 1978, one of the West Coast's most successful theatrical hits was a musical production with a substantial dosage of social commentary called "Zoot Suit." In a dramatic sense it recaptures that Damon Runyon quality of "Guys and Dolls," but instead of Nathan Detroit, Harry the Horse and Sky Masterson, the characters of this Chicano-morality musical are such Runyonesque semi-good-guys as Smiley Torres, Swabbie, Chucka and Ragman.

Ironically, playwright Luis Valdez is having such success with his musical re-creation of the historical Sleepy Lagoon case of the 1940s at the same time that CBS' "Sixty Minutes" presents a chilling and all too graphic documentary segment on Pachuco gangs flourishing in Los Angeles and other areas of the Southwest.

What makes the current success of "Zoot Suit" all the more bizarre is the truth to the comment made by CBS' Mike Wallace that unlike any other musical melodramas about gang warfare such as "West Side Story," this activity has been continuous among a certain segment of the Chicano community.

Wallace suggests that, "On the West Coast, gang warfare has never stopped. Today, it is more violent than ever. Who is fighting whom? Americans of Mexican heritage are fighting each other, and embarrassed community leaders have been unable to stop it. What's more, it is spreading throughout the Southwest."

The phenomenon Wallace describes is by no means new. As early as the 1940s, Octavio Paz, Mexico's greatest living poet, attempted to explain the *"razón de ser"* of this character known as the Pachuco or Zoot Suiter. This character, despite his negative and somewhat sinister behavior was eventually made popular by such Hollywood types as Frank Sinatra and Gene Kelly.

But, there was much more than clothing to his personality. Paz, the poet-philosopher, saw as early as the 1940s an underlying conflict in attempting to explain this character who was at once Mexican and American and at the same time neither. "(This) spiritual condition, or lack of a spirit, has given birth to a type known as the Pachuco. They are youths, for the most part of Mexican origin, who form gangs in Southern cities; they can be identified by their language and behavior as well as by the clothing they affect."

In his book, *The Labyrinth of Solitude*, the Mexican poet attempted to find the soul, the essence of the Mexican character; instead, he stumbled on the essence of a "misfit" in North American society, as it were.

In the '40s and even today into the '70s, the Pachuco persists in the Chicano community as almost a caricature, an exaggeration of a type that has led to imitation and stereotyping as distinguishable as the Black pimp whose outlandish dress and behavior have made him a popular prop in current television and motion picture productions.

The Pachuco as a gang member is, of course, more real and more dangerous than the basically independent Black entrepreneur. As stated before, even in the 1940s, Octavio Paz recognized the essence of his character which was formed as much by history as he was by psychology. "The Pachuco has lost his whole inheritance: language, religion, customs, beliefs. He is left with only a body and soul with which to confront the elements, defenseless against the stares of everyone. His disguise is a protection, but it also differentiates and isolates him; it both hides him and points him out."

Paz recognized even then the potentially dangerous ingredient in the Pachuco's character. "(He) is an impassive and sinister clown whose purpose is to cause terror instead of laughter." And he often did.

Paz felt that there was no desire then and perhaps it is as true today for the Pachuco to vindicate his race or the nationality of his fathers, no real socio-political affirmation. Rather, "their attitude reveals an obstinate, almost fanatical will-to-be . . . but not to be like those around them."

Today, the Pachuco or a miniature version of him exists in virtually every Chicano community in the Southwest. In the '40s, the Pachuco carried the impracticality of clothing to an extreme. Its novelty existed in its exaggeration, the pegged high-waisted pants, gold chains hanging down to the knees, pointed shoes, aesthetic colors, and tattooed crosses between thumb and index finger.

Today, the Pachuco or *Vatos Locos*, as they are also called, can be seen in loose-fitting jeans or khakis, sometimes wearing neatly folded handkerchiefs around the head or wool caps pulled down below the ears. T-shirts or wool Pendleton-style shirts hanging outside of the pants and buttoned at the neck are also common. This latest style appears to reflect an influence of the prison apparel worn by the *Pintos*, or Chicano inmates. The clothing is always clean and neat, though obviously a badge, a symbol.

In the '40s Paz believed that the Pachuco reflected a suicidal tendency, almost an "exasperated will-not-to-be." The Mexican poet was sure that the Pachuco was aware that in North American society it was dangerous to stand out, thus the tremendous desire to assimilate on the part of European immigrants, which led thousands of Italians, Poles, and others to change their names. Not so for the Pachuco.

The Pachuco, unable to change his color, did just the opposite. He appeared to seek and attract persecution and scandal. Paz concluded "it is the only way he can establish a more vital relationship with the society he is antagonizing. As a victim, he can occupy a place in the world that previously had ignored him; as a delinquent he can become one of its wicked heroes."

Paz was prophetic. In the 1970s the Pachuco has become a hero. The theatrical production of "Zoot Suit" is virtually sold out at the Aquarius Theater in Los Angeles until March, when it will likely move on to Broadway. Hollywood, too, is just completing two "Mexploitation" films about Pachuco gangs, "Boulevard Nights," and "Gang."

Romanticism aside, however, the resurgence and glorification of Chicano gangs belies the reality of their significance and potential danger for the Chicano community as a whole. As Paz pointed out, even today "the Pachuco is the prey of society, but instead of hiding, he adorns himself to attract the hunter's attention." The entire Chicano community may find itself the hunted.

It is perhaps possible today to trace the U.S. Civil Rights Commission's documented increase in the incidents of police brutality against Chicanos throughout the Southwest to the resurgence of the Pachuco's conspicuous dress and his defiant desire to be different.

Even in such a place as Sacramento, a less than teeming urban community, there are evidences of the dress and activities sometimes likened to the Pachuco (the girls known as Pachucas also stand out because of their dress accented with an abundance of white eyeliner).

In cities such as San Jose, complaints have been lodged against the Chicano youth who prefer to cruise streets and shopping-mall parking lots with their easily recognizable "low-rider" cars, activity which is really no different, in a cultural sense, than families traveling together in recreational vehicles for a Sunday outing.

One Chicano youth responding to a reporter's inquiry about youths in Sacramento answered what Octavio Paz might have predicted. "Why do people make such a big deal about the way we dress? Don't we have a right to wear whatever we want? Can't we be what we want to?"

The will to be or perhaps not to be is obviously manifest. One wonders if there isn't present in this conspicuous attire and seemingly pointless gathering a defiance that almost shouts out in a still gentle silence among some "come and get us *cabrones!*" One wonders if confrontation, not necessarily violent, is ultimately the goal.

As "Sixty Minutes" so vividly pointed out, sometimes the confrontation occurs merely because a member of one gang crosses over into the territory of another. One young Chicano still in his teens proclaimed, "you have to fight for your barrio. Sometimes you have to kill for your barrio just to keep your reputation."

In other situations where the gang situation has not reached the extreme of the larger urban areas, authorities for their part seem to be making martyrs out of the Chicano youths even before any major incidents.

In Sacramento, various respected Chicano organizations in the community such as MAPA and La Raza Lawyers Association have come to the defense of the Chicano youth, perhaps feeling the potential for seeing the entire Chicano community used as scapegoats for the business establishment and city authorities, especially in view of the fact that the Chicano youths seemed to be suffering harassment without being guilty of anything.

Sadly, however, the situation seems to put everyone on a soapbox. The youths proclaim their right to be. The merchants protest the effects on business. The Chicano organizations demand "freedom of assembly." And one obviously enlightened and clever young Chicana proclaimed, "We don't have any place else to go. Proposition 13 knocked out a lot of cultural programs that used to keep us occupied. We like to do things with our culture and we can't do a lot of those things anymore since so many programs have been cut."

The tragedy of the situation is not whether the young lady's comments were true or simply convenient exaggerations, but that this obviously bright young lady would blame her own idleness on Proposition 13. The tragedy is that neither the neo-Pachucos, nor the merchants, nor the Chicano organizations, not the city fathers, can come up with enough creative resources to find a way to interest young people in an existence that would reflect a bit more direction and a bit more joy in being.

Perhaps there has always been a penchant among the youth of any group for just "hanging out." These young people, however, seem to be imprisoned by their own idleness while adults scurry about as their jail-keepers lacking the mental capacity to deal with the problem. What we must lament is both the idleness of youth and the idleness of the so-called wiser generation.

The Barrio—the Third World in the US, Cries Out for "Human Rights"

Speech To the National Council for Social Studies
November 23, 1979, Portland, Oregon

Kawlesa mama, Kawlesa, Kawlesa mama, Kawlesa. Kawlesa is a South African song. It comes from the townships, reservations, locations near Johannesburg. The children shout from the streets when they see police cars coming to raid their homes for one thing or another. They say "Kawlesa mama," which means simply "hurry up mama and hide. Please don't let them catch you." Kawlesa mama, Kawlesa, Kawlesa mama . . .

I n the early sixties, the African songstress, Miriam Makeba chanted the lyrics of this ballad along with many other songs of Black Africa's anger, despair and revolution. Today, the African continent is reaping the whirlwind of repression that colonial powers had sown over the centuries.

Today, if I were a balladeer, I might intone similar words as Makeba's song of anguish.

Cuidado mamá, Cuidado, Cuidado mamá, Cuidado
Escóndete, Hay viene la migra.

Which means "Be careful mama, be careful, be careful mama. Hide yourself mama, there comes the immigration."

In early November of this year, Leo McCarthy, the Speaker of the California Assembly, sent a letter to Joe D. Howerton, District Director of the Immigration and Naturalization Services in Los Angeles, and to Senator Edward Kennedy and Representative Peter Rodino, respective chairmen of the Senate and House Judiciary Committees. He requested that the INS put an end to its current policy of raiding Mexican-American homes in the Barrios of East Los Angeles and Orange County for the purpose of rounding up supposed illegal aliens.

Said the Speaker:

> I am concerned that the actions taken in carrying out this policy violates the civil rights of Hispanics and discriminates against persons of Mexican Heritage. Newspaper accounts and my own staff inquiries reveal incidents that smack of Nazi Germany in the 1930's. Let me cite some examples:

> The wife of a Huntington Park apartment house manager, as quoted in the Los Angeles Herald Examiner: 'They (INS agents) knocked on the doors and asked for papers. When they knocked on doors, and nobody answered, they broke the doors down and took out all the people inside.'

> Kawlesa mama, *Cuidado mamá.*

When President Jimmy Carter nominated Benjamin Civiletti to replace Griffen Bell as US Attorney General, the Hispanic community of the Southwest almost universally opposed this nomination. Why? Because in 1978, after Civiletti was dispatched to tour the Southwest for the purpose of investigating the "epidemic of alleged brutality by law enforcement officers against Hispanic citizens," little resulted from the Justice Department's good will tour.

What has so enraged the Hispanics in the Southwest and other parts of the country? Documented cases such as the well-publicized Joe Campos Torres case in Houston, Texas.

Torres, a U.S.-born Mexican-American and Vietnam war veteran, was brutally beaten by three Houston police officers. After the precinct sergeant refused to book him because of his battered condition, advising that he be taken to a hospital, the three officers dumped Torres into a canal jeering, "See if the wetback can swim." Torres could not swim, and because of his condition, he drowned.

The Texas court ruled that the death was the result of negligent homicide, only a misdemeanor in Texas. No sentence was imposed on the police officers.

Incensed by this action on the part of the Texas Court, Chicanos and human rights activists throughout the Southwest pressured the U.S. Justice Department to prosecute the three policeman for having violated Torres' civil rights.

The Justice Department finally did prosecute and the three policemen were found guilty. But when it came time for sentencing, US District Judge Ross N. Sterling merely fixed a one year term and granted the three officers immediate probation. Once again enraged by the token sentence, Chicanos and civil rights activists persuaded the Justice Department to file an appeal with the U.S. Court of Appeals for the 5th Circuit asking for a more appropriate sentence. The appellate court then ordered Judge Sterling to impose prison terms on the three defendants.

The Texas judge, demonstrating his obvious contempt for the higher court, sentenced the policemen to a one year and one day sentence to run concurrently with his previous sentence, thus adding only a single day to his previous sentence.

Now the Chicano community cries for impeachment of the Judge as a last resort. This is hardly likely since their political clout is no stronger than their legal clout in West Texas.

In the past few months, there have been more than 15 killings of Hispanics and over 150 alleged incidents of police brutality against Hispanics. The Justice Department seems either unwilling or unable to do much about this situation. Consequently, cases like the Campos Torres killing and the Larry Lozano incident remain as symbols of repression against a powerless community. The 27-year-old Lozano was found dead in an Odessa, Texas jail cell with 100 cuts and bruises on his body. The Justice of the Peace initially ruled that Lozano had committed suicide. The case is on appeal.

And in Arizona, three ranchers tortured and shot three Mexican immigrants who had wandered onto the ranchers' property. The ranchers were acquitted of felonious assault. This case, too, was appealed.

The list could go on. We could add a list of incidents involving Blacks, Asians, Native Americans and even white Americans, the poor, but there is no great value to a mere list. The value, if one could say there is a value to be derived from such inhuman treatment, is that there is a lesson to be learned.

We must understand that human rights is an issue and as a true right is not just some abstract concept that is applied with a modicum of *noblesse oblige* to unfortunate peoples of Third World Countries. For us as Americans, it must begin in our own land. The true value of complying with a UNESCO instrument on International Human Rights, or any such other proposal, is so that we can practice what we preach abroad in our own country.

It is my firm belief that no other issue is of more direct relevance to ethnic minorities in the United States than the Human Rights cause that is being debated in the world forum today. While we may discuss man and his biosphere, the world of the creative arts, oil and ecology, nothing is more directly tied to the ghettos and barrios of our country than police brutality in South Africa or Rhodesia, Nicaragua or Argentina, or Iran before and after the Shah.

The release of only the Black males from the American Embassy in Iran just this week is a message from the fanatical forces in Iran to black Americans. The Sandinista overthrow of the Somoza dictatorship in Nicaragua was almost universally endorsed by the Hispanic community of this country.

Can the U.S., now that it supports the downfall of tyrannical and cruel dictators who violated every human right imaginable, claim absolution for its past support of these regimes? Can the citizens of this country claim with clear conscience that a Rhodesian government is any less onerous than the Ku Klux Klan that was spawned in our own waters and gunned down dissidents in the streets of our cities in full view of the world press?

Surely, we must make a distinction between the deplorable acts of individual lunatic groups in our country and a policy established by our government. But we cannot deny that some of our past practices by government officials, as well as those that continue to the present, such as the midnight raids that continue in East Los Angeles, make it exceedingly difficult for our President to be the champion of human rights abroad while there are serious violations here at home.

As charity begins at home, so should human rights. Kawlesa mama, *Cuidado mamá.*

The Other Migrant Workers

Hispanic Link News Service, **July 2005**

Several weeks ago, Lionel Martinez, in his weekly column in *the Bakersfield Californian*, wrote about my pending travels in my new RV as I planned to tour America and continue writing on several projects I have started. My first stop was at the Grand Canyon in Arizona.

The first thing I noticed when I arrived at the RV park at Tusayan near the South Rim of the Grand Canyon was that many of the clerks working in the shops and stores were foreigners. They were not Mexicans as one might expect, but white Europeans. They were young men and women from the Ukraine, Romania, the Czech Republic and other former Eastern Bloc countries. Certainly there were Mexicans, but they were busboys and waiters and cooks in the restaurants, and also working as grounds keepers and janitors in the RV parks and grocery stores.

I spoke to both Europeans and the Mexicans during the seven days I spent in the area. The Europeans were in the country on summer work visas. Many were students who would be returning to their home countries in the fall, or going off to schools somewhere in the U.S. Their English was on the way to becoming very good as they spoke daily to customers that came into the stores where these foreigners worked. With the Mexicans, I spoke Spanish to put them at ease, but I often overheard them speaking in developing English to their young fellow European employees or store and shop managers.

I must say that I was shocked by the number of young Europeans I saw working in this tourist resort area. In appearance, they looked like white American teenagers. The Mexicans, on the other hand, were easily identifiable as Mexican migrants, and did not look or speak even like Mexican-Americans who had been born here or had been in the U.S. for many years.

Shortly after I arrived in the area I also heard a report on the local National Public Radio station that related the phenomenon of these Eastern Europeans in the thousands working in resort areas all over the U.S. There were interviews with Ukrainians. Czechs, Romanians working in Atlantic City, Rehoboth Beach Delaware, The Catskills, Yosemite, Washington D.C. The young Europeans told about the great experience they were having in our country. "Jobs are easy to get here, not so easy in my country," said one Romanian girl. This was her second summer working in the U.S. Others told about how easy it was to get a work visa for the summer, and they were amazed at the variety of work sites they could choose from, Niagara Falls to Fishermen's Warf.

I am happy for these youngsters. What a great experience they are having getting to know the U.S. and its people. I recall the year I spent in Spain as a student when I worked at various locations teaching English. I really got to know Spain and the Spaniards and I hope they learned a little of the U.S. from me.

But I am troubled by one thing, and that is the fact that I have heard no complaints from Americans about these foreigners taking jobs from Americans. Hannity and O'Reilly have not pontificated on these former communist citizens doing jobs that young Americans might be doing for the summer. I have heard of no vigilante movement afoot to seek and apprehend these foreigners who are invading our country, using our services and paying little in taxes. Most are legal, but I suspect that there are others who have overstayed their visas or who have no visas at all.

The treatment of these European workers is much different than the treatment of Mexican workers. First of all, none of these young and healthy Europeans are working in American agriculture to harvest America's food in the heat of the summer. Most work indoors and at better than minimum wage jobs. One Mexican worker that I spoke to who supervised several of the young Europeans noted they were pretty lazy and not skilled. He commented that they liked to party a lot. This was confirmed on the NPR program as well where the young Romanian indicated that, "we go out a lot to clubs. We party a lot."

Of course I am generalizing here, but the point is this. As Americans we should get our priorities straight. Do we value hard work? Do we appreciate the work done by those who put food on our tables, slaughter our beef, clean our houses, at least as much as those who sell us trinkets and curios in tourist shops? In our American past, we respected the man and woman who worked hard and sometimes got dirty. We respected those who did what they had to do to feed their families, sometimes with two and three jobs.

Unfortunately, today we seem to be offended by the fact that job seeking Latinos are coming into the country to do the work that we as Americans will no longer do. I ask myself why is it that these European youngsters find work to do here that most of our own children are not willing to do. I respect both the

Romanian and the Mexican who are coming to our country to keep our economy buzzing. As a people we need to look in the mirror and ask ourselves what has become of that old Protestant ethic we so valued in the past that held that any honest work was good. If we still believe this, let us applaud the foreigners who are helping us out, all of them, instead of picking on one group or another to attack and ridicule.

Habitat for Humanity:
As Much for Me as for the Poor.

(From an upcoming book: *Travels with Carlitos*)

I actually retired from teaching at Cal State, Monterey Bay in 2004 but agreed to teach in the fall semesters as a retired annuitant. So in December of 2005, after I finished the fall semester, I headed down to Bakersfield to spend the holidays with my family. It was indeed a great time, making tamales, buying and wrapping presents, and having the Christmas Eve gathering with son and daughter, grandchildren, brothers and sisters, nieces and nephews, and more cousins than I can count.

But after the holidays, what? Though I had great plans to travel around the country in my new RV (Coachman Class C, 23 footer) and do a lot of writing, after the Katrina catastrophe and the continuing news coverage of the ongoing disaster, I felt a need to do something. So, thanks to a family friend, Christine Aronhalt, who works for the Bakersfield branch of Habitat for Humanity, and who hooked me up with the Habitat for Humanity RV Care-A-Vanners' program, I was able to jump in my RV and head to Louisiana. This would allow me to fulfill my goal of traveling and writing and also let me attempt to do a little something in the way of good works for my fellow brothers and sisters who had suffered so tragically as a result of both Hurricanes Katrina and Rita. As I drove towards New Orleans on February first 2006, I thought of how the ancient Caribe Indians of the Caribbean had been correct in depicting *Huracán*, the god of ocean storms, as a fierce deity.

Habitat the Organization

Habitat for Humanity was started by Milard and Linda Fuller, outside of Americus, Georgia in 1976. "The Fullers having recently left a successful business in Montgomery, Alabama, and all the trappings of an affluent lifestyle to begin a new life of Christian service, developed the concept of "partnership housing"—where those in need of adequate shelter would work side by side with volunteers to build simple, decent houses." In 1984, former President Jimmy Carter and his wife Rosalyn took their first Habitat work trip to New York City. Their personal annual involvement in Habitat's ministry has brought the organization national visibility and sparked interest in Habitat's work across the nation. Since that time, Habitat has built hundreds of thousands of houses in the U.S. and around the world.

The Habitat Mission Statement reads: *Habitat for Humanity works in partnership with God and people everywhere, from all walks of life, to develop communities with people in need by building and renovating houses so that there are decent houses in decent communities in which every person can experience God's love and can live and grow into all that God intends.*

The RV Care-A-Vanner program offers those who travel in RVs an opportunity to make a difference by working on Habitat build projects around the country and have fun doing it. The program generally involves eight-to-20 RVing volunteers in two-week programs at building sites. More than 600 people are involved. Builds are spread out from Oneonta, New York to Laramie, Wyoming, to Indian Wells Valley, California throughout the year.

Hurricane Rebuilding

Because of the magnitude of the hurricane disasters in the gulf coast this season, Habitat for Humanity has stepped up its efforts in the region. The Bayou Habitat for Humanity Branch in Thibodaux, La. has purchased a large tract of land and has begun the Operation Home Delivery project to build 86 homes for hurricane victims in this year.

This is the project that I am working with in Grey, Louisiana, just forty-five minutes from New Orleans. In addition to the 20 Care-A-Vanners in our group, people come from across the country, New York, Michigan, Arizona, Illinois, Wisconsin. There are also about a dozen youngsters, recent high school or college graduates in the AmeriCorps program, and volunteers from the Global Village organization all working together at the site. At 67, I am by no means the oldest person on the job. The Steinburgs, Phil and Gloria from New York City, are 75 and 74 respectively. We all put in a full day's work, hammering, sawing, roofing, siding, and enjoying one another's company. In the evenings we might sit around a campfire, drink a few beers and swap tales as we rest our sore muscles. Lunches are provided for us by local churches, that do their best at sharing with us their Cajun cuisine, gumbo, fried catfish, and jambalaya. For one lunch the Knights of Columbus even brought out a portable kitchen and cooked and entire pig on a spit for us.

As much as doing good works for those in need of help after the hurricane disasters, I feel that so much more is being done for me. I am grateful for this opportunity to help, to make new friends, and to share in the good things the people of Louisiana have to share with us. While I work, I like to chant the local slogan that makes the rounds at Mardi Gras time in these parts: *laissez les bons temps rouller*, or for the non-locals, Let the good-times roll.

A National Disgrace Continues

I arrived in Louisiana in early February, not knowing what to expect. I had seen continuing news coverage of how New Orleans and the entire gulf cost that had been devastated by both Katrina and Rita was slow to recover, but I was shocked when I finally entered New Orleans and saw for myself the destruction of the Ninth Ward and other parts of the city. Estimates are that 70% of the city is still uninhabitable. Hundreds of thousands of former residents of the devastated area are still scattered throughout the country, with lingering doubts as to how many will ever return. What I saw made me think of pictures I had seen of Berlin after the end of WWII. In the Ninth Ward, only the streets had been plowed clean with the rubble piled high on the sides of the streets with the rest of the destroyed houses and businesses. Six months after the hurricanes, I had to conclude that our Nation is not presently capable of dealing with a large disaster of these proportions. This is a scary thought as the next hurricane season that lasts for 5 months is only three months away.

John Biguenet, a novelist and resident of New Orleans talks about the tale of two cities that is now the tale of New Orleans: "New Orleans has become two cities. The French Quarter, the Garden District, the university section, the business district, the West Bank will soon be as beautiful as ever, throbbing with the intense life we live down here. But the areas devastated by the flooding are another city, a ghost town." Biguenet describes the second city as an area strewn with abandoned cars, shattered windows gape, un-repaired from walls stained white by the salty flood. There are still holes punched through the roofs where families trapped by the flood, awaited, sometimes for days, to be rescued. On the walls of those houses still standing were the grim painted reminders of the tally of those living or dead found by rescuers as the floods subsided.

The physical devastation is overwhelming, but just as horrific to me is the response by government at all levels, national and local. On Valentines Day it was announced from Baton Rouge, the state capital, that FEMA (the Federal Emergency Management Agency) had decided not to extend the time for victims who were staying in hotels and motels in the state, paid for by FEMA. They would be evicted immediately. These were basically the poor people of the city that had nowhere else to go after the disaster. Now they were being put out into the street with the national government's FEMA program having made no further provisions for them. Church groups again are having to step up to provide temporary shelters for these people, half a year after the disaster.

Another remarkable example of the government's ineptitude is the fact that 10 thousand empty trailers remain in Arkansas, while FEMA tries to untangle its administrative problems so that these portable dwelling places can be set up in Louisiana and Mississippi. And here, a sorry vision of humanity has reared its ugly head. One of the problems FEMA is having results from local jurisdictions and some of Louisiana's own citizens. Some city councils, mayors and local citizens of communities not seriously affected by the storms and flooding are refusing to accept any temporary trailer parks in their areas. Politicians and residents, alike, protest that the criminal element will be housed in their neighborhoods. They claim that drug dealers, child molesters, and gangs will move in next door. Much of this is a very thin disguise for the fact that their new neighbors will in actuality be the poor and African American, but not exclusively Black citizens affected by the hurricanes. There are also whites among the poor and some of the mayors and city councilmen are actually Black. More than a racial issue it appears to be a class issue.

It is sad to note that after such a horrific event in our nation's history, that brought out such good works by volunteers in the Red Cross, Catholic Relief Services, Habitat for Humanity and many other groups and volunteers from across the country, we are still dealing with the insensitivity of both government and some citizens towards other human beings.

New Orleans is trying to put on a good face during its Mardi Gras celebrations, Good Morning America originates in the Crescent City on this day, showing New Orleanian Emeril Lagasse preparing his gumbo dishes and Louisiana native Britney Spears taking four teens on a shopping spree. But the fact is that it is Fat Tuesday, which is the day before Ash Wednesday, and which begins the Lenten season by the symbolic Biblical notion that "dust thou art and into dust thou shalt return." Hopefully, by the end of the solemn Lenten season both governments and citizens alike will learn to deal realistically and compassionately with the human suffering that goes on and we might look forward to the resurrection of the old New Orleans.

Ray working with Habitat for Humanity, Louisiana 2006

New Orleans' 9th Ward, Six Months after Katrina

Rodeo, A Latino Contribution
to the American West

Latino Encyclopedia, Scholastic Press, 2004

T he **Rodeo** is a public competition in which contestants participate in standardized events such as bareback bronco and bull riding, team roping, steer wrestling, and calf roping. Female competition in barrel racing on horseback also often takes place. The word *rodeo* comes from the Spanish verb *rodear,* to surround or round up.

The origin of the Rodeo began in the early days of the Spanish/Mexican period in the Southwestern part of the United States. During the late 1700s and early 1800s when the missions and *ranchos* were established throughout the Southwest, cattle raising flourished as the region supplied beef and leather to the Spanish territories. There was a great need for skilled horsemen to handle the herds as they made their way to markets. In the early days, especially before the U.S. War with Mexico in 1847, most of the horsemen were *vaqueros,* Spanish or Mexican cowboys, who brought to the Southwest the various breeds of horses that had been introduced to the Americas by the Spanish. Among these breeds were the Andalucians that had been introduced in Spain during the Arab occupation of Spain. In the Southwest, many of these horses escaped into the wild, transforming American Indian culture and eventually becoming the working horse of the American cowboy.

After the Mexican territories, which included most of the present Southwestern United States, became part of the U.S. at the end of the War in 1848, American cowboys began to work along side the *vaqueros* in the large *ranchos* of the West.

There they learned many of the techniques and traditions of Spanish/Mexican horsemanship.

Much of the language that is associated with the American cowboy and the folklore of the West has its origins in the Spanish language and the Spanish/Mexican traditions of horsemanship. In addition to rodeo, the *rancho* became ranch; lasso and lariat come from Spanish *laso* and *la reata*. The leather chaps worn by cowboys came from the Spanish *chaparreras*. The cowboy's horse was the mustang from the Spanish *mestengo* (a stray or wild) and he had to tame the *bronco* from the Spanish meaning wild or rough. If the cowboy got into trouble with the law, he was sent to the hoosegow, from *juzgado*, a tribunal, or to the calaboose from *calabozo*, jail.

The names of many towns, states, land formations, and animals identified in the West also came from the Spanish. Colorado means "reddish," Montana from *montaña* mountainous, Nevada "snow covered." California was named for an exotic land that appeared in a Spanish novel of chivalry of the 15th century. *Mesa, chaparral, las vegas, arroyo,* are all Spanish words which described the western landscape. *Coyote, armadillo, puma, burro* are Spanish as well. City names like Santa Fe, Amarillo, Sacramento, Los Angeles, El Paso, San Antonio and its Alamo and hundreds of others in the Southwest are Spanish in origin. The influence of both the Spanish/Mexican language and culture became part of the cowboys' everyday life on the cattle ranches of the West.

It was, however, after the end of the U.S. Civil War in the 1860s that the cattle ranches spread throughout the West and the ranks of the cowboys grew. Many of these American *vaqueros* worked for the large cattle barons, driving herds across the western plains to the stockyards in the growing cities of the West. But with the advent of the railroads, the open rangelands were fenced off and cattle cars began to carry beef to markets in the East. This reduced the demand for labor and many cowboys eventually saw their life style undergoing significant change.

There had always been competition among cowboys and *vaqueros* in the skills used in ranching like roping cattle and breaking broncos. As employment decreased for the cowboy, a more formal form of competition began to emerge in towns throughout the West. This friendly competition between cowboys was sometimes called a rodeo and it provided an opportunity for cowboys to supplement their income by winning prize money at rodeo event.

In the early years of the 20th century those cowboys who had, in essence, become professional rodeo performers began to see a need to establish rules and regulations for their own safety and to guarantee fair competition. The formation of the Professional Rodeo Cowboy's Association (PRCA) was believed to have occurred in 1936 when competing cowboys at a rodeo in the Boston Gardens staged a walkout over a dispute about prize money. They had originally called themselves the Turtle Association for having stuck their necks out. In 1945 they formally adopted the PRCA name.

Today, rodeos enjoy great popularity, and are sanctioned by PRCA. There were 170,000 fans attending the National Finals Rodeo in Las Vegas in recent years. ESPN television broadcasts rodeo finals regularly to as many as 13 million viewers. Cowboys from Australia, Canada, Brazil, Mexico, join American cowboys in high stakes competition at events throughout the country. Many communities host annual rodeos as significant events in their community's cultural calendars, usually accompanied with large parades during their *fiesta* days. Also alive and well in the Southwest are the *Charriadas*, the Mexican version of the rodeo in which *charros*, elegant *vaqueros*, compete in a variety of events where their horsemanship is on display.

Today many more Latino *vaqueros* are participating in modern rodeos as many of them continue to work on today's modern cattle ranches. While helicopters, jeeps and pickup trucks are in common use on many of today's ranches, the cowboy or *vaquero* on horseback continues to be a crucial part of ranching. Anglo and Latino cowboys together learn the skills of ranching, and usually the best of them compete against one another in modern rodeos.

The success of rodeos today, however, is accompanied with a significant degree of controversy as animal rights groups have protested what they consider the cruel treatment of the rodeo stock used in these events. These critics claim that while the rodeo is promoted as the "rough and tough" display of human skill and courage in dominating wild animals in the tradition of the Old West, the facts are that the shows are displays of the cruel treatment of animals for "greed and profit."

Animal rights groups note that rodeo animals are not aggressive by nature but are provoked into displays of wildness by the use of electric prods, caustic oils and other devices such as cinched straps on horses and bulls to make them buck. Every year dozens of animals die as a result of injuries suffered in the rodeo arena. While cowboys also suffer many injuries, critics note that the cowboy volunteers for the competition while the animals have no choice. Because of the popularity of rodeos today and the attention focused on rodeos by animal rights groups, government officials have stepped up their efforts to make sure that animals are protected as much as possible.

Bibliography

Bannon, John Francis. *The Spanish Borderlands Frontier 1513-1821*. Albuquerque. University of New Mexico Press, 1974.

Billington, Ray Allen. *America's Frontier Heritage*. Albuquerque. University of New Mexico Press, 1974.

Fredriksson, Kristine. *American Rodeos: From Buffalo Bill to big Business.* Portland, Reed Business Reports, 1994.

Pitt, Leonard. *The Decline of the Californios: A Social History of the Spanish-speaking Californians, 1846-1890.* Los Angeles. University of California Press.

Wooden, Wyne S. & Ehringer, Gavin. *Rodeo in America: Wranglers, Roughstock and Paydirt.* 1996.

An Answer for Mr. Raspberry
on Official English

Hispanic Link News Service, **Feb. 1998**

¿*C ual es el pleito?* What's the fight about? asks columnist William Raspberry recently in the Washington Post. Raspberry notes, "I've been trying to follow the debate over making English the "official" language of the United States. Now I'm asking for help. Will someone please tell me, in plain English, just what the argument is about?"

Well, Mr. Raspberry, thank you for asking. Your confusion on the issue is no greater than that of most Americans, and that includes most of the nation's educators, lawmakers, and ordinary citizens. It is a complicated issue fraught with controversy over pedagogy, American history, race relations, ethnocentrism, and out and out bigotry on all sides. Let me give you my explanation for what it's worth.

One cannot discuss the "English Only or English First" issue without some acknowledgment of American history relative to the topic. I, too, agree with Senator Dole's comments you referred to when he spotlighted the issue recently in referring to English as "the glue of language to help hold us together." But the Senator went on to say that one motivation of opponents to his position was "elitist guilt over a culture built on the traditions of the West." By "West" we must assume that Senator Dole was speaking of European/Anglo culture upon which presumably American culture was built. For the Senator to refer to the reaction of some as "elitist guilt" does little to bring us to an understanding of the issue.

In the past, the American nation had accepted such philosophical/political policies as Manifest Destiny, Social Darwinism, and the White Man's Burden as the way things were or should be, even if these policies nearly caused the extermination of the native Indian population and resulted in the illegal deportation of millions of legal residents and even citizens among Chinese, Filipinos, Italians and Mexicans from this country. The reality is not so much "elitist guilt" as it is a sorry chapter in American history.

Ironically, the drive to make English the only official language of the United States is occurring almost exactly one hundred years from another period in American history when xenophobic forces attempted to blame immigrants for all the evils afflicting the country. "They are an invasion of venomous reptiles . . . long haired, wild-eyed, bad-smelling, atheistic, reckless foreign wretches . . . They are a danger that threatens the destruction of our national edifice by erosion of its moral foundations." Such were the words hurled at immigrants by preachers and politicians at the end of the 19th century.

In the 1894 congressional elections, the Republican Party won an overwhelming victory. Buoyed by it, the Republican Senator from Massachusetts, Henry Cabot Lodge, advanced the nativists agenda by passing the Immigrant Literacy Bill, aimed at stopping the influx of those "twisted, unassimilable, filthy, un-American immigrants." The Bill which was vetoed by President Cleveland, would have required all prospective immigrants to the country to learn English even before leaving their homelands. In those days, however, the law was aimed at Italians, Jews, Polish, Greeks and other non-English speaking Europeans, while currently it is Latinos, Asians, Haitians and Middle-easterners that are targeted.

Today, after the centennial anniversary of that Republican victory in the Congress during the 19th century, the organized nativists and Republican majority are at it again. Anti-immigrant and "English Only" bills are wending their way through the Congress. But the rationale is lacking. Those who bring up the issue of Quebec as an example of how language divides a country, conveniently forget about Switzerland which has three official languages (French, German and Italian) and has long been recognized as perhaps the most stable country in Europe. And Belgium with its official French and Flemish speaking populations has become the capital of Europe, hosting NATO and the European Union.

And with respect to that "frequent argument of the English-first crowd . . . that bilingual education doesn't work very well—that it may even retard the development of fluency in English," one can only say "get real!" There are just as many educators, legislators, parents, students, and studies that cite the value of such programs. What is at issue here is that opponents fail to see the broader picture, the benefits that bilingual education offers this country in a modern world. While they haggle over achievement gains or whether the data is accurate in assessing programs, critics refuse to recognize this country's need for bilingual individuals.

The world is getting smaller. We speak now of global villages, the internet, and common markets. Europeans have created a common Union. They will have a common currency, and they may eventually even communicate with a common language, which will more than likely be English, as is the case now with NATO and the EU. But the French will continue to be and speak French, the Italians will never give up their language. In this country we have over 57 million people who can communicate in a language other than English, with French, German and Italian more common than Chinese, Vietnamese or Tagalong. These individuals don't have to be told how important English is for them and for their children's future in this country. They know and accept this fact.

It does not appear to make much sense to force a language to be lost after an immigrant or even a citizen already has fluency in it, just so we can teach it to them again later as we, as a country, recognize the value of doing business abroad, practicing diplomacy and chatting on the internet in another language. What a tragic waste it will be if we let these languages wither away while at the same time we spend millions of dollars trying to teach our foreign service employees, border patrol agents, and international business folks, and military personnel another language. And as we continue offering high school, college, and adult extension classes in foreign languages, sometimes to many citizens who are unfortunately already past their prime language learning years, how can we justify forcing others to forget a foreign language?

Bilingualism is not just a good idea for giving Asian and Latino children and others an equal opportunity to survive in our schools. Certainly it makes more sense to allow a child to continue learning, for a time, in whatever language that he or she can use, rather than to wait a few years until fluency allows the child to join the rest of the class. Arithmetic is neither English nor Spanish.

An old saying in Spanish suggests that *Hombre que sabe dos lenguas, vale por dos.* A person who knows two languages is worth two people. So Mr. Raspberry, in answer to your question as to *¿Cual es el pleito?* There should be no fight. English is our language. No one disputes that. But those who want to write this fact in concrete are dishonest in their motives. They would have us believe that anything else is un-American, when in fact, that which makes us Americans is not the language, but the richness of our diversity. No other country in the world has within its borders so many cultural beauties brought to it by millions and millions of immigrants who have, over the centuries, come to these shores "yearning to breathe free."

III

International Issues

Summary of Articles

Most of the pieces in this section on global issues were written in the late 1970s and 80s when the Cold War antagonists, the U.S. and the Soviet Union, were conducting their cold war in many unfortunate countries of the Third World. Latin America was the setting of much of this conflict; thus, a series of articles that appeared in the McClatchy Bee newspapers, "Somoza's Land . . . , Costa Rica Can Show Nicaragua . . . , Two Big U.S. Mexico Problems . . ." are reflective. The article dealing with U.S.—Mexico issues of immigration is instructive, given today's lingering concern over the issue. In this section I also present several SECRET cables that I drafted while serving as a political officer at U.S. Embassies in Latin America and the Caribbean. "The Church in Guatemala" was an in-depth reporting cable on the plight of foreign missionaries in the violent Guatemala of the early 1980s. The piece on "The Death of Father Francisco" is my own personal memoir of one of the most heinous violations of human rights I had to deal with during my tour of duty in Guatemala (1980-82). A more recent piece "Wars and Rumors of Wars," was written just days before George W. Bush's ill-conceived invasion of Iraq, which is still on-going as this book goes into print.

Wars and Rumors of Wars, and Manifest Destiny Revisited

Latino Vote, **January 17, 2003**

There seems to be no question that there will be a war in Iraq, even if the U.S. has to go it alone. The build-up is like a locomotive careening down a Sierra mountain with no way to stop. President Bush seems crazed with the idea of making his mark on history like a Teddy Roosevelt who carried "a big stick" and thought that it was his destiny to be the policeman for the world. Bush may also be attempting to salvage his father's legacy as many credit the elder Bush for the mess we are in now because of his failure to dispose of Saddam Hussein at the end of Persian Gulf War a decade ago.

George W. is aided in his drumming for war by much of the press, especially the electronic media. The major networks and the news channels like CNN, MSNBC, and Fox News fill their hours by stoking the fires of war. With such programs as "Showdown Iraq," "Iraq Watch," "Road to Iraq," "On the Front Line," one wonders how these broadcasters ever filled airtime before Bush got it into his head that he had to make the Middle East safe for Democracy. Commentators like Chris Mathews, Geraldo Rivera . . . , as well as the Sunday morning news programs, *Meet the Press, This Week, Face the Nation, Late Edition . . .* seem to consider the war and rumors of war the only thing worth exposing the American public to. The gun is cocked and it appears that one of the Administration's arguments for war is that we have the troops there now. We would appear weak at this point if we did not use them. What a poor argument this is to pull the trigger.

As in other times in our history, the combination of Napoleon-minded U.S. presidents and "yellow" journalism have led our country down the precarious road of imperialism. When William Randolph Hearst was disappointed that a sketch artist for his New York Journal reported back that there was little happening in Cuba just prior to the Spanish-American War of 1898, Hearst shot back: "You furnish the pictures, I'll furnish the war." So too, the American press, not so much the newspapers as the Television Networks, seem to have bought into Bush's war. The Administration has even run media reporters through combat survival training at Fort Benning, Georgia so that they can land with the troops in order to send home the expected glorious accomplishments of the "greatest fighting machine any country has ever assembled," 300,000 strong at latest count, ready to pounce.

Unfortunately for the American public, neither Bush nor the major broadcasters seem to have read much of American history. If they had, they would be less willing to plunge us into a war in the Middle East that escapes reason and has left our European Allies in NATO, the EC and the United Nations attacking our motives and questioning our integrity. For the U.S., a country so devastated after 9-11, a country that had gained the honest sympathy of most, if not all the rational nations of the world, to now become the world's pariah, is lamentable. It now appears that instead of sympathy we are called warmongers, imperialists and bullies. We have squandered much good will. As the only nation to have ever used the ultimate weapon of mass destruction on another county, we should indeed walk softly, but put away the big stick. Instead, Bush admonishes our former allies, "anyone who is not with us, is against us."

If we are honest and examine our own history, we can list numerous occasions where we have acted the bully and the imperialist. Let us begin with the 1848 War with Mexico, a war that was trumped up from the start by President James K. Polk, "frankly an unjust war which completely exposed the aggressiveness of United States policy and the violent character of its territorial expansion," notes one prominent historian. The westward movement and the "Manifest Destiny" which declared that the white, Anglo-Saxon character should dominate the continent as befitting a God-fearing Christian nation, nearly caused us to exterminate the Native American. Surely, no scattered Mexican colonies north of the Rio Grande were going to stop us in our effort to possess all the territory from sea to shinning sea.

President Polk provoked Mexico into a war. Pushed by businessmen and farmers alike, he declared a war on the pretext that American soldiers had been fired upon, despite the fact that they had crossed into Mexican territory. General Winfield Scott swooped down to Vera Cruz with ships carrying American Marines who took the same route as Cortez into Mexico City. The bloody battle of Chapultepec is commemorated on the Marines' dress blue uniforms by the red stripe along the pant legs and in the Marine hymn, . . . from the Halls of Montezuma . . . . General Zachary Taylor headed south with his army into Chihuahua, while General Kearny joined forces with the uncontrollable John C.

Freemont and Admiral Sloat in California. After it was over, the United States possessed one third of Mexican territory from the Rio Grand north to the Oregon border and as far east as Kansas.

This was the first of the United States very unpopular wars of aggression. Many in the Congress were vociferous in their opposition. Senator Corwin of Ohio declared: "a war against an unoffending people without adequate or just cause, for the purpose of conquest . . . . I will lend it no aid, no support whatever. I will not bathe my hands in the blood of the people of Mexico, nor will I participate in the guilt of those murders which have been and will hereafter be committed by our army there." Abraham Lincoln also protested against the war, considering it unconstitutional and unnecessary and wrote that, "the blood of Abel, cries out against it." General and President Ulysses S. Grant wrote many years later: "I do not think there was ever a more wicked war than that waged by the United States in Mexico."

Perhaps one of the most notable criticisms of the War with Mexico was that of Henry David Thoreau. In his enduring essay on Civil Disobedience which became the guiding torch for peaceful, political dissidents Mahatma Gandhi, Martin Luther King, César Chávez and others, he proclaimed: "The government itself, which is only the mode which the people have chosen to execute their will, is equally liable to be abused and perverted before the people can act through it. Witness the present Mexican war, the work of comparatively a few individuals using the standing government as their tool; for, in the outset, the people would not have consented to this measure . . . I quarrel not with far-off foes, but with those who, near at home, co-operate with, and do the bidding of those far away, and without whom the latter would be harmless."

Thoreau, of course, eventually spent time in a Massachusetts jail because he refused to pay taxes to support the war. "It is not a man's duty, as a matter of course, to devote himself to the eradication of any, even the most enormous wrong . . . but it is his duty, at least, to wash his hands of it, and, if he gives it no thought longer, not to give it practically his support."

The Spanish-American War of 1898 is another classic example of the "my country, right or wrong" philosophy that has caused us to blindly set off on murderous adventures over the centuries, not the least of which was the Vietnam War. In the case of the Spanish-American War, with the depression of 1893-97 coming to an end, Americans felt another surge of that "Manifest Destiny" which had caused us to look beyond our own shores. The rebellion on the Spanish Island of Cuba seemed an appropriate pretext to flex our expansionist muscles. "The chauvinist New York governor Theodore Roosevelt, believed President McKinley was as spineless 'as a chocolate éclair." Goaded by Roosevelt and Hearst's newspapers, McKinley eventually got us into a war, using the still mysterious explosion of the U.S.S. Maine in Havana harbor as the cause. On April 11, 1898, the President sent a war message to Congress: "the United States must protect the lives and property of American citizens and put an end to the barbarities, bloodshed, starvation, and horrible miseries right at our door." Intervention was justified, the president claimed, "by the wanton destruction of property and devastation of the island." The Teller amendment to the peace treaty declared, "U.S. military occupation in order to pacify the island of Cuba." When it was all over, the United States ended up with the islands of Cuba and Puerto Rico in the Caribbean and the Philippine Islands in the Far East, thus ushering in the years of "Big Stick" and "Gunboat" diplomacy that we would be known for during most of the first half of the Twentieth Century." (*Quest for Our Past,* Unger)

It was nothing for Roosevelt to push even harder now that as President, the big stick was in his hand. In 1904 Roosevelt had the Congress amend the Monroe Doctrine declaring that, "the lack of order in any country called for the intervention of civilized states . . . ." Under this new formula known as the Roosevelt Corollary to the Monroe Doctrine, the president assumed the new "divine mandate" that had derived from the "Manifest Destiny" of the previous century. During his tenure then, Teddy Roosevelt fomented revolution in Colombia for the sole purpose of causing the breakaway of the Panamanian isthmus so that the United State could have the sole right to build the canal across that newly independent nation, leaving the French stuck with their canal efforts in Nicaragua.

Intervention in Latin American and in Far Eastern affairs became the pattern of the United States with its developing and powerful navy, which surpassed the English at this point in history. Ships heavy with American Marines landed here and there, proclaiming themselves rulers of any unfortunate country that possessed something that America's greed needed, be it bananas, bauxite, oil, mahogany, or other raw materials for American industry and American consumers. The venerable Commandant of the U.S. Marine Corps, General Smedly Butler, proclaimed in his memoirs that after four decades in the Marine Corps during this period, "I finally realized that I had been little more than a policeman for Wall Street."

The Marines served as occupying forces and governors in the Dominican Republic, Nicaragua, Panama, the Philippines and other countries. My own Ray Gonzales corollary of American intervention holds that one need only recognize that all the countries of the world that play baseball as a national sport have been occupied by American forces at one point in their history. Most recently, we have seen footage of American service men showing youngsters in Afghanistan how to pitch and hit the ball, and round the bases. How long will it be before Iraqi children are handed a baseball and mitt as their first steps towards democracy?

The American public may be moving very slowly away from Bush's build up to war towards a consciousness that Thoreau would have been proud of, and this is no thanks to the electronic media that seems to be in a frenzy to gain and retain viewers. As we watch our TVs, we see ourselves aboard American aircraft carriers, in the desert with helmeted Marines and Army troops, in Pentagon briefing rooms. We are a nation being led towards another war that will stain our American history in this new century. What a sad way to begin this new millennium. We have learned little about questioning the motives of our leaders. We seem to be like sheep allowing our government to lead our lambs to war. Perhaps when the body bags begin returning home, and the devastation of war, including our own dead solders and the children of Iraq become the nightly news as we eat our dinners, will we say "enough."

We hear the constant refrain that the war is being promoted to safeguard our American security, a security that was shattered in Manhattan, not in Iraq. We are told that we must save the people of Iraq from the despotism of Saddam Hussein, a man who has used weapons of mass destruction against his own people and his neighbors. We should remember that we gave him the formula and ingredients for much of the devastation when we supported him against Iran, which was then our hated despotic government of the month. This should cause us to recall the devastation we perpetrated against the Native Americans when we purposely contaminated blankets with small pox that were distributed to them so as to hurry their decimation.

Our American President and his generals should remember all of the despots we have put in power and sustained over the years, before we declare we are fighting a war to save a people from a dictatorial leader. Wasn't it an American president who said: "He may be a son-of-a-bitch, but he's our son-of-a-bitch" in reference to the despotic allies we supported in the past. And many of those SOBs are well know in our history of intervention. Generalitos like Batista, Trujillo, Pinochet, Samoza (father, brother and son), Noriega (when it suited us), Marcos and wife, Diem, Rojas Pinilla, Castillo Armas, Papa Doc and Baby Doc, the Shah, and on and on, with most of them having had the aid of the CIA in gaining power. Whenever popular national elections resulted in a left-of-center government, we engineered a coup from behind the scenes.

While President Bush stretches credibility to give reasons why we are about to invade Iraq, to safeguard our security, to topple a bad regime, to do some nation-building and establish democracy, and of course, the word oil never drips from the President's lips, nor Condolezza Rice's, nor Collin Powell's lips, we must remember that his father had little excuse to invade Panama, except that he was offended by the presence of a disobedient general who had possession of the Panamanian controlled canal. And Ronald Reagan had invaded Grenada ostensibly to rescue American medical students, who were never in any danger, but while we were at it, we should force the Cubans, who had been invited to the island by the Grenada government, off the island, as an effort to protect our national security.

History will record the events that are about to take place, which in our time may have all the hallmarks of a tremendous show of arrogance and military vanity. Fire the gun now; after all, it is loaded with bullets. I remember the Gung

Ho feeling we Marines experienced as we got out of boot camp. The training was superb. I could get a perfect score of twenty bulls' eyes at 500 yards with my trusty M-1 rifle; I could hike 20 miles with a forty-pound pack on my back; I could wield my bayonet with the efficiency of a Samurai warrior, and above all, I thought I was brave. But we were all so disappointed, we brave and well-trained leathernecks, disappointed that there was no war for us to fight, anywhere in the world at that time. We had been trained to be the lean, mean, fighting machine. We of the *esprit de corps* and the *semper fi* mentality. It would not be long, however, before many of those same young men who signed up for another hitch would lose their lives in a pointless and devastating war for both Americans and Southeast Asians in the jungles and hamlets of Vietnam. The protest came too late for them. Hopefully, history will not be so cruel to us this time as our President contemplates sending young men and women off to fight the old men's war. Hopefully, the protests will come sooner than they did for so many young Americans who lost their lives in a pointless war and for hundreds of thousands of Vietnamese who also perished.

U.S. Policy In Nicaragua and Central America

A Dissent Channel Cable From U.S. Embassy, Bridgetown, Barbados
June 1986

Confidential

Introduction: U.S. policy in Central America continues to loom as one of the country's biggest disasters. In El Salvador we cannot assume that one presidential election makes a democracy. Sixty thousand young lives have been lost there. Half a million Salvadorans live as refugees or as illegal aliens in the U.S. The sad truth is that the military is still the power in that unfortunate country. In Honduras, our policy has turned that former banana plantation into a U.S. military base, sustained by nearly $100 million of military assistance annually. In Guatemala, two military coups have occurred during the Reagan Administration's "watch." Panama is certainly no democracy by any stretch of the imagination. Costa Rica fears that it will be militarized by the rampant paranoia of both the far left and the far right in the neighboring countries. And Nicaragua, of course, is undergoing a third U.S. intervention in this century.

It would appear that no one at the highest levels of the Reagan Administration has ever read the history of this region. Certainly there is some truth to the notion of a collective Latin American "macho" as relates to relations with the "colossus of the north." Now, however, it appears that this Administration is attempting to respond in its own "macho" fashion.

President Reagan's May First statement to Congress announcing economic sanctions against Nicaragua cannot be based on any well thought out policy plan.

World reaction has, I am sure, even surprised Administration advisors, including my own Department of State.

It is the weakest of arguments to suggest that the sanctions were invoked because of the emergency situation crafted by the Nicaraguan government's aggressive activities in Central America. This "emergency situation," if it can be termed that, has existed for five years. It would be more honest to say that the President took this action because of the failure of his policies in the region thus far.

It should be clear to us by now that we have been part of the problem in Latin America not part of a solution. The area has been in our sphere of influence for over two hundred years. The Soviets just arrived in the 1950s. We must drastically change our perspective on Latin America if, in our own national security interest, we wish to keep these countries from falling into the Soviet/Cuban camp. We should recall here the words of General Smedly Butler, the venerable Commandant of the Marine Corps in the early years of the 20th Century, who noted in his memoirs that he had come to the conclusion after fifty years of service, that he had been nothing more than the policeman in the world for Wall Street interests.

A New Policy: The following points are offered as a suggestion for a new beginning for a more realistic, honest, and honorable policy towards Latin America.

Our continued support of military governments in Latin America only encourages them as political entities. As long as we continue to accept their veto power over the electoral process, nothing will change. Instead of encouraging militarism we must attempt to aid the other legitimate sectors of society. Economic and social aid should be our primary aid. The notion that we can defeat Marxism in the region by military assistance only indicates that we have learned nothing from the fiasco of Vietnam. We continue to confuse nationalistic movements aimed at recovering from years of outside domination and internal elitism with true Marxists revolutions. The former, while it may be anti-Yankee, is only by necessity pro-Moscow; the latter is an ideology that is not even remotely understood by a majority of the masses in Latin America. If, for example, we continue to militarize Honduras so that it can serve as our proxy against Nicaragua, we will only guarantee that the military will, in due course, feel it can handle things more efficiently than its own civilian government and assume power. On the other hand, significant economic aid to Honduras would strengthen the civilian government's hand and be a more effective counter balance to the Nicaraguan threat. Ambassador Negroponte in Honduras should be instructed to direct economic aid to that country, not assist in making Honduras the military training camp for Contra rebels that the Congress has specifically prohibited.

We should understand that Nicaragua is in the midst of severe growing pains, in great part inspired by our many years of support of the despotic

Somoza family. That the Sandinista government is not our dearest friend should not surprise us. Instead of attempting to isolate Nicaragua, we should initiate meaningful discussions with the leadership. We should desist in attempting to instigate another Bay of Pigs. Any association on our part with former Somoza national guardsmen is in reality an association with the offspring of a despot. To equate the Contras with our "Founding Fathers," and "Freedom Fighters" is to equate soldiers of fortune with the Salvation Army. We can in no way justify any effort to reestablish the rule of the radical right wing as the lesser of two evils.

We should realize that even in Nicaraguan, Marxists have a love-hate relationship with us, as do most Latin Americans. All things being equal, Nicaraguans and even Cubans are more disposed to our way of life than they are to the Soviet's. We sometimes overlook our own virtues. Nicaraguans are presently toying with Marxism. Despite nearly three decades of Castro in the Western Hemisphere, it is not surprising that Marxism has not been more successful. The reason for this is not the vigilance of military governments. They, in fact, encourage subversion. The reason is that Latin America is fundamentally conservative; it is Catholic, and it is underdeveloped. Marxism will only succeed in Latin America if the free enterprise system or a modification of it fails. We must always keep in mind the fundamental nature of a country or a region and not be put off by temporary spokesmen.

We must encourage alternatives to the military control of political systems in Latin America. Free trade unionism should be dramatically encouraged. The American Institute For Free Labor Development (AIFLD) should be greatly expanded so that democratic unions can serve as viable alternatives to subversive organizations

By the same token, political education of the business sector should accompany economic aid to this sector. The notion that the business sector as well as unions should stay out of the political sphere, or that politics is a "dirty game," only encourages the military to fill the vacuum. Both labor and business must become relevant parts of the political life of the region. Grants, loans, scholarships, exchange programs should be greatly expanded for the political education of the business sector and trade unions.

Political parties should be openly encouraged and supported rather than aided in covert manners. In this area, scholarships, exchanges and grants can be useful if done above-board. Aiding the evolution of a relevant political party system should not be viewed as any more meddlesome than supporting the military, which in most Latin American countries is, in reality, the strongest of political parties. We have traditionally supported the military establishment at the expense of other institutions in these countries because of our blind adherence to a Cold War mentality.

Conclusion: Finally, we should realize that democratic governments, within our definition of the term and in our own image may not be what will or should necessarily emerge in Latin America. We should not reject the possibility of the emergence of a more socialistic form of government in some of these countries. Certainly we have tolerated them in countries like Sweden and Spain. We should develop a rational policy of promoting peaceful social, economic, and political reform in the region. We should understand that the extreme poverty of the region and the division of many of those societies between the very wealthy and the very poor may not be conducive to an American style economic system. We should reject, once and for all, the notion that military governments, which claim to be anti-Communist, are *per se* preferable to all forms of socialism

Somoza's Land: Military Elite Made In The U.S. of A.

The Sacramento Bee, **Nov. 12, 1978**

Aside from the fact that Anastacio Somoza Debayle received his military training at West Point, he is today perhaps the most real and vivid manifestation of the fiasco of U.S. foreign policy in Latin America.

His presence in Nicaragua and the bloody effort in that tiny nation to overthrow a tyrannical dynasty is a bleak reminder of the past that haunts the State Department and the Carter administration. Though President Carter cannot be blamed for the situation in Nicaragua today, he is saddled with 100 years of shoddy if not outrageous U.S. intervention in the destiny of that small Central American nation.

Of all the original Central American Republics, Nicaragua perhaps has been most affected by U.S. intervention. Nicaragua's first notorious dictator was in fact an American citizen, William Walker, who with a small army of "filibusters" had invaded the country in 1855 and had himself elected president.

He was encouraged and partially supported in his efforts by the slave-holding Southern states in the United States and by the Accessory Transit Co., which was in the business of transporting passengers between New York and San Francisco by steamship and an overland route across Nicaragua.

Walker's dictatorship was short-lived however because he was soon attacked by the other Central American Republics who were, in turn, supported in their efforts by Cornelius Vanderbilt. He desired the control of travel across the isthmus for his own company. Walker surrendered to superior forces on May 1, 1857.

In 1893, civil war broke out again in Nicaragua, resulting in the assumption of power by Jose Santos Zelaya, a brutal and unscrupulous tyrant who exploited the country for his own personal profit. He surrendered his country to foreign investors, principally American businessmen; he completely abrogated civil liberties, imprisoned and murdered his opponents, and fomented revolutions in all of the other Central American countries.

As in the case of Walker, the United States played a significant role in the dictatorship of Zelaya. While it was profitable, the U.S. supported Zelaya, but President Taft broke off diplomatic relations with Zelaya after his troops executed two reprobate American soldiers of fortune. The United States then financially aided the revolutionary forces that toppled the tyrant in 1909.

The emergence of Nicaragua's next and perhaps most durable dictator, Gen. Anastasio Somoza Garcia, also was an obvious result of U.S. intervention in Nicaragua affairs. From 1912 to 1925 and from 1927 to 1933, Nicaragua was under occupation of American Marines. Even though the real reason for the occupations was economic, the U.S. mission did attempt to establish some form of democratic government, which was to be protected by a well trained and U.S. equipped National Guard. But Somoza took over control of the National Guard, destroying the constitutional government the United States had attempted to establish.

During his long reign, from 1937 until he was assassinated in 1956, civil liberties were drastically curtailed. During his dictatorship the country prospered somewhat but it was perhaps Somoza, himself, who enjoyed the greatest success. His private commercial interests included distilleries, sugar mills, cotton gins, lumber mills, a steamship line and much more.

Somoza had placed his two sons and other members of his family in key positions. Thus, his son Luis Somoza Debayle served as president from 1957 to 1963, after the father's assassination, while brother Anestasio Somoza Debayle was chief of the Guardia National, having been well trained for the post at West Point. Anestasio then was elected president in a mockery of the democratic process in 1967.

Anastasio Somoza Debayle remains in power by the use of that very efficient and U.S. equipped National Guard that also kept his father in power for 20 years.

Somoza's most critical job now is to keep that military unit of only 8,000 troops loyal to him. One way of doing this is by treating them not only as an elite corps but also as elite citizens.

At the same time, he attempts to have the world believe that there is a Communist conspiracy reaching to Cuba and even Moscow behind the civil war in his country. In the past, this has been an appealing enough reason to guarantee U.S. sympathy and even intervention in Latin America.

After World War II, the U.S. policy in Latin America was so motivated by the fear of communism that little distinction was made between dictatorial and democratic governments. In many respects, U.S. intervention in Latin American affairs has been a colossal failure if its intention was to ensure democracy and has actually resulted in the perpetuation of many dictatorships up to now.

Even the Kennedy administration, despite its attempts at furthering democracy in Latin America through the Alliance for Progress, failed miserably in its attempt to encourage representative governments. The Kennedy policies were inconsistent. On the one hand, the administration sought to encourage the growth of political establishments to enhance the chances of democracy. Yet in order to isolate Castro's Cuba from the rest of the Latin American nations, the administration did not hesitate to make political use of the military against the civilian governments of Frondizi in Argentina and Arosemena in Ecuador. It appeared that the Kennedy administration was compromising democratic principles for the sake of expediency.

In 1963, the civilian governments of Juan Bosch in the Dominican Republic, Villeda Moreales in Honduras and Joao Goulart in Brazil were overthrown by the military. In most instances, the military forces that replaced the civilian regimes had received the tacit approval of the United States simply by implying that they were anti-Communist.

What has become apparent in the last few years of Latin American history is that the nations in this part of the world have not moved any closer to democracy than they were at the end of the 19th century. Traditional dictators such as Anestasio Somoza have been joined by right or left-wing military governments, none of which seem to be the least bit interested in the establishment of democratic countries.

The recent events in Nicaragua, which show no signs of coming to a peaceful resolution, once again tie the destiny of that small, and seemingly insignificant nation of 3 million inhabitants, to the destiny of the United States. At a time when President Carter has reached an accord over the Panama Canal and has come down from Camp David with a plan for peace in the Middle East, he must deal with despotism and human suffering in his own backyard.

Ironically, those very Latin American countries controlled by military dictatorships and recognized and militarily supplied by the United States have just recently voted in a block to defeat a U.S. supported proposal presented to the Organization of American States criticized the cruelty and bloodshed caused by the Somoza regime in Nicaragua. In essence what these countries were saying to the United States was, "Now that we have your guns, your tanks and your planes, don't talk to us about human rights."

Costa Rica Can Show War-Weary Nicaragua Path to Stable Democracy

The Sacramento Bee, **July 29, 1979**

"I have to be true to my people," asserted Anastasio Somoza Debayle in a recent statement to newsmen as the world anticipated the crumbling of a family fortune and a political dynasty that has lasted some 46 years. "When and if I leave, I'll tell my people about it."

The use of the possessive phrase "my people" perhaps best characterizes the tenor of the Somoza family rule over the tiny Central American republic since 1937 when Somoza's father, Anastasio Somoza Garcia, took control of the U.S. trained national guard and established himself as dictator. A U.S. president might use terms like "the voters," "the electorate" or "the citizens" in referring to the inhabitants of the United States. Even a communist country head of state would use such terms as "the people" or "the state." Only in a true dictatorship of the Latin American or African variety would the head of state use and intend the concept of "my people" for the term embodies not only the aspects of possession, but even a modicum of divinity that the leader often ascribes to himself.

Curiously, Nicaragua's neighbor, Costa Rica, which was drawn reluctantly into the conflict in Nicaragua, represents the opposite of the political system embodied by the Somoza family dictatorship. At the same time that the Somoza family was establishing a private family fortune of over $500 million by filling Nicaragua with sugar mills, distilleries, cotton gins, and steamship lines that it controlled, Costa Rica was emerging as the most democratic, the most stable, the most educated, and the most peaceful nation in all of Latin America.

The reasons for the Costa Rican success are primarily due to the fortuitous conditions of demography and historical events. Though this process began as early as the 1500s with the arrival of the Spaniards, it is nevertheless very relevant in today's turmoil in Nicaragua. The Sandinista rebels' success in toppling Somoza will likely result in a new form of government emerging from a war-torn country, and this new form of government will be based on either a Costa Rican or Cuban model. Somoza's charges that Cuban communism was responsible for his situation were feeble outcries of a tyrant whose end was near. Although it is true that Cuba played some role in the events in Nicaragua, as did the United States, it is also true that the provisional Nicaraguan government, while located in Costa Rica, made no commitments to any form of government except for a united effort to overthrow the dictator.

The fact that the provisional junta had its headquarters in Costa Rica is very significant. Somoza made clear his displeasure at this and the two small "banana republics" broke off diplomatic relations. The two countries, in spite of their proximity, have long reflected the most obvious contrasts in forms of government. While U.S. intervention in Nicaraguan politics is a historical fact, and to a degree responsible for the current situation in that country, it is curious that Costa Rica, never having suffered from the U.S. government's well-intentioned intervention, has emerged as the Latin-American country most reflective of the U.S. form of democratic government.

The country's democratic tradition has evolved over centuries and has been the result of certain specific factors. Many of these elements have been geographical, social, and economic in nature and not too unlike the factors that produced the democratic tradition in colonial New England.

Ethnically, Costa Rica is considered one of the three white nations of Latin America (the other two being Uruguay and Argentina). Fewer than 3,000 Indians remain in the country. There were few to begin with when the Spaniards arrived, and those that were there either were killed off in merciless wars, such as occurred in the American West, or were shipped off to work in the gold and silver mines of Peru and Bolivia.

The fact that there was never much intermarriage has resulted in a fairly homogenous population that has not had to deal with the impoverished Indian groups such as in Guatemala, Ecuador and Peru. This homogeneity, despite its dubious origin, has resulted in a unique class structure for Costa Rica. While it cannot be said that it is a classless society, the small wealthy class is not offensively ostentatious and in most cases has been productive instead of parasitic and has harbored little class contempt. At the other end, the most impoverished group identifies with a large middle class and generally members of this group own their homes and have some education.

Widespread land ownership primarily accounts for this pattern. The fact that the country had neither gold nor silver guaranteed that the early Spanish explorers paid little attention to this area. This resulted in few large grants being passed out to the soldiers by the Spanish king, which was generally a tradition during the Spanish conquest of the Americas. Add to this the fact that there were few Indians and Blacks to work the land. What resulted was the emergence of a family farm system rather than the hacienda (plantation) system that emerged in most of Latin America. The Costa Rican settlers discovered that they had to do the work themselves or perish and Costa Rican historians point out that from this poverty was born a sort of rough egalitarianism.

This egalitarianism has resulted in a country that produces more teachers than soldiers. In fact, Costa Rica has no standing army, choosing instead to spend its national funds on schools instead of planes, tanks, and cannons. The population of the country has more than an 80 percent literacy rate. The availability of education has also resulted in a strong political party system that except for a brief civil war in 1948 has established an exemplary democratic form of government.

Now, however, the fortunes, or misfortunes, of Nicaragua are spilling over into Costa Rica. The country stands in the middle of a virtual powder keg that can set off explosives in all parts of Central America. The other four countries are controlled by military dictatorships that on the right are represented by the repressive regimes of Guatemala and El Salvador, and on the left, the military regime of Torillos in Panama, and in a neutral posture because of its own recent civil war is Honduras. While it is a false assumption to believe that Central America is a battleground in the war between world communism and Western capitalism, it is quite likely that the nationalistic desire for freedom from tyrannical leaders will lead the revolutionaries like the Nicaraguan Sandinistas to accept support from wherever it is offered.

In the meantime, Costa Rica, even more than the United States, serves as the best example of what is possible in terms of the establishment of a democratic form of government in countries with a Hispanic tradition. It is hoped the Costa Rican government's position, in support of the provisional Nicaraguan junta, will have some influence on the form of government that emerges in Nicaragua now that the Somoza dynasty has fallen.

It is also hoped that the new Nicaraguan government will heed the advice of Jose Figueres, president of Costa Rica from 1953 to 1958. Figueres speculated on the future of Latin America in a 1965 article, "Political and Economic Forces in the Hemisphere," in which he outlined the choices between communism and capitalism.

"Can democracy do the job of development?" Figueres asked. "Can we meet this challenge democratically? No matter what our difficulties are . . . this is the system attuned to our way of thinking, the system, which we have in our veins. This is the political conception we share with the United States as common heirs of European culture.

The Panama Canal—
A Last Ditch Effort?

International Technical Service, **Publication, Sept. 1978**

C uba and Panama have much in common. They were both created by
the United States. They both emerged as countries during that period of
"Manifest Destiny" that had decreed that the United States should supervise the
welfare of the hemisphere. In 1898 Congress passed a resolution declaring Cuba
to be independent from Spain. In 1903, when the Colombian Congress refused to
lease to the United States the strip of land that was required across the isthmus for
the building of the Canal, the United States recognized the Panamanian isthmus
as an independent nation. In both instances U.S. Military Forces guaranteed the
independence.

In both instances the egomania of Teddy Roosevelt was also a factor. In the
case of Cuba, he had valiantly led his Rough Riders up San Juan Hill during the
Spanish American War; in the case of Panama, as President of the United States,
he ordered U.S. warships to obstruct the landing of the Colombian troops sent
in to suppress the "insurrection." "I took Panama! While the Congress debated,"
he later declared.

The creation of both Cuba and Panama has been intertwined in other ways
as well. The United States' Latin American policy required that before work
could begin on the canal, it would be essential to control "the outworks"—those
strategic islands in the Caribbean that faced toward the isthmus. Thus, Cuba and
Puerto Rico were first wrested from Spain in a somewhat suspicious war. And
shortly thereafter, Panama was created to satisfy the U.S. expansionist appetite
after its own West had been won.

Ironically, today the destiny of Cuba, Panama and the United States are inextricably tied together again, for if the U.S. Senate fails to ratify some sort of treaty with the Panamanians over the canal, it may be the "Manifest Destiny" of all the Latin American nations to bring the "Colossus of the North" to its knees as the black-pajama armies did in Southeast Asia. The Cuban Liberator, Jose Martí, in 1898 predicted the confrontation that ironically exists today. He noted: "Spanish America was able to save itself from the tyranny of Spain; and now . . . it must be said because it is true, that the time has come for Spanish America to declare its second independence."

Most foreign policy experts concede that the canal today is nothing more than a symbol of another age, an age of a youthful, exuberant America. Now, however, less than 4% of U.S. shipping goes through the Canal. It is almost of no military value. The most modern U.S. aircraft carriers do not fit through the locks. The whereabouts of nuclear submarines is supposed to be top secret, so it is unlikely that they would be ordered to spend hours bottled-up and plainly visible in the old waterway.

What then is the practical value to the U.S. for the continued possession of the Canal? There appears to be very little, except pride, patriotism and our national need for political non-issues at election time. Paul Wyrick, one of the chief election strategists for the Committee for the Survival of a Free Congress, gave this advice recently to a group of potential conservative Congressional candidates: "The politics of the Panama Canal issue is something you ought to keep in mind because whether the proponents of the give-away like it or not, this issue is going to be with us all the way through the 1978 elections. So it's a golden opportunity for conservatives . . . . If you can't take advantage of that opportunity, then I think your campaign is in fact going to be defensive."

The arguments for keeping the Canal are indeed nebulous. Ronald Reagan, who is credited with first making a political issue of the Canal during the last presidential election, actually began with little substantive argument when he declared in a primary campaign speech in Florida that, "When it comes to the Canal, we bought it, we paid for it; it's ours and we should tell Torrijos and company that we're going to keep it." The slogans and the depths of the debate have not changed much since then. The issue has found its ultimate expression in billboards springing up across the country depicting Uncle Sam in his typical posture, pointing his finger at you, but with a new twist. The other hand is cupped to the ear and a slogan reads: "Honk! If you want to keep *our* Canal at Panama."

At this point in the debate, the question really is not whether the Canal is ours. It might very well be, just as a Sumitomo Bank building in San Francisco might belong to a Japanese corporation. Ownership of the Canal is really not the issue. Nor is who built it of any real significance. The French constructed the Statue of Liberty. The real issue is whether or not we, as a country, will once again allow old men to get us into another war that young men will have to fight. As the crusty old senator from South Carolina, Strom Thurmand, put it: "There *is* no Panama Canal; there is an *American* Canal in Panama." Thurmand of course, is the chairman of the American Conservatives Union's Canal Fund Raising Drive. If his attitude prevails, there is no doubt that the U.S. would commit troops to defend the Canal Zone. Even President Carter, sensing the emotionalism of the issue, declared he would commit 200,000 troops to the defense of the Canal.

The grave error the U.S. may commit is in mistaking the significance of the symbolism of the Canal to all of the countries of Latin America. To the U.S. it is a symbol of its ingenuity, its enterprise and its resolve. To the Latin Americans, it is a symbol of U.S. imperialism, of the "Big Stick," and of "ugly Americanism."

Those sentiments expressed almost a century ago by the Cuban Liberator, Martí, are echoed today by leading Latin American scholars. Historian Saenez Peña has declared that the U.S. must listen to "the voice of Latin America, its thirst for freedom and independence and its demand for respect from a domineering and arrogant power whose expansion is violating the rights of other nations." Martí is echoed again in the words of contemporary Mexican scholar Enrique José Varona: "We believe that our people face an inexorable dilemma: either submissive surrender and praise of the Pan American Union (America for North Americans), or joining together to prepare to defend their independence by laying the foundations of a Latin American Union (Latin America for the Latin Americans). We are aware that the latter task is a long and difficult one . . . but to be discouraged beforehand by its magnitude is tantamount to surrender."

These are the words of Latin American scholars, of intellectuals not guerrilla leaders. A Panamanian student recently responded to a CBS reporter's query as to how far he would go to gain control of the Canal for his country: "I would give my life," was his response. On the same broadcast, an American, obviously in his fifties and a veteran of WWII, indicated he would be willing to fight to retain the Canal. Curiously enough, no twenty-year-old Americans were asked if they would be willing to give their lives for the waterway. In the case of the Panamanian student, one can assume his single voice reflected the voice of many, for as recently as 1964, 21 Panamanian students gave their lives for much less than is offered today in the proposed treaties. They were killed by U.S. soldiers while they were attempting to raise the Panamanian flag in the U.S. controlled Canal Zone.

In addition to the prevailing attitudes in Panama as demonstrated in the recent election to ratify the treaties, this attitude of Latin America for the Latin Americans is felt throughout much of the Western Hemisphere. It exists, without much doubt, in Cuba. Though some say "we built it," the reality is that the U.S. engineered the Canal. Much of the manual labor force that built the Canal came from Jamaica, Trinidad, Haiti and other Caribbean countries. Many of those laborers and their descendants are now the Panamanians. As a result, Panama is one of five mulatto countries of Latin America (the others are Cuba, Brazil, the Dominican Republic and the territory of Puerto Rico).

The significance of these Afro-Latino cultural factors is often overlooked or not even recognized by modern political strategists in the United States. It was noted merely coincidental that Cuban military forces succeeded so well recently by intervening in African Angola, for Angola had been for several hundred years a Portuguese colony, just as Cuba had been a Spanish colony. For over a hundred of those years they had been ruled by the same Hapsburg-Spanish monarchy. Their history as colonies and their history as third-world nations are not dissimilar. They have had to shake off the yoke of imperialism of both a political and economic nature. Castro's forces succeeded in Angola because they were, by and large, a black army; because they spoke a similar romance language and because they were identified a sister nation within the third world of ex-colonies. Ironically, Cuba, which gained its independence as a result of the questionable intervention of the United States in the Spanish American War, now assists Angola in the maintenance of its recently achieved independence.

The above-mentioned factors make Panama a country built to order for Latin Americans. It is a romance-language nation; it is a third-world nation seeking to rid itself from foreign domination; and most significantly, it is a mulatto nation. Whether its leader is a dictator or not should be of little relevance to the U.S. since we currently have ties with dictatorial regimes throughout the world.

The question facing the United States now is whether it is prepared to ask its young men to defend a fairly obsolete ditch and whether the Latinos, the Blacks, the students, "the doves" and the other disillusioned Americans that finally saw the futility of the Vietnam War are willing to go through all of that again? The Panamanians certainly are, for they feel they have everything to gain and very little to lose.

SECRET CABLE

FROM: AMEMBASSY GUATEMALA   DATE: June 18, 1981

To: DEPARTMENT OF STATE, NATIONAL SECURITY AGENCEY

INFO: Dept. PASS TO ROME FOR VATICAN OFFICE

SUBJECT: (S) THE ROMAN CATHOLIC CHURCH AS A FACTOR IN GUATEMALAN POLITICS

REF: (80 STATE 277913 (REPORTING REQUIREMENTS)

EXIDIS (Executive Distribution)

(U) *Summary:*

T his report on the Roman Catholic Church in Guatemala includes a short historical introduction; a discussion of the 1968 Medellín and 1979 Puebla Conferences of Latin American Bishops; a discussion of the precepts and impacts of "liberation theolotgy" in Latin America and Guatemala; the evolution of the Guatemalan Church since Medellín; the influence of foreign clergy; the impact of political violence on the Guatemalan Church; the Guatemalan clergy's influence or lack of same over the Government, the military, and the business sector; and finally, the social reformist trends growing within the Guatemalan Church. End of Summary

(C) *Introduction:*

Over the last 10 months relations between the Catholic Church on the one hand and the GOG (Government of Guatemala) and extreme right on the other have reached a point of high tension. The killing of six priests and a large number of catechists; the removal of all religious from the diocese of El Quiché by the Bishop; the Papal letter attacking the government for its failure to guarantee the safety of churchmen and its inability to control the extreme violence in the country; the failure of the GOG to accept a Papal Nuncio nominee; and finally, the refusal by Guatemalan authorities to allow the reentry to the country of Guatemalan citizen Msgr. Juan Gerardi Conedera, Bishop of El Quiché and head of the Bishop's Conference, have bred tension in Church-State relations. Add to this the growing evidence of a number of clergymen now roaming the highlands as guerilla collaborators and we have the formula for a major confrontation between a military government, perceived to be the defender of the centuries old oligarchy of rich landowners, and what is viewed as the emerging new church in Latin America. In consonance with the Church's positions in other Central American countries such as El Salvador and Nicaragua, the Guatemalan clergy may find itself pushed into a radical posture because of events and pressures coming from outside.

(U) *Historical Perspective*

The role of the Catholic Church in the conquest and colonization of Latin America is well known. The tyranny of the Inquisition and the *Santa Hermandad,* the extremist Catholic views of Ferdinand and Isabel and their descendents Carlos V and Phillip II, all guaranteed that nearly 500 years later Catholicism would continue to be the dominant religion in Latin America. Throughout the colonial period the Church solidified its position by accumulating large estates and some religious orders even exploited the indigenous population, forcing them to work on church lands in a manner not unlike the plantation system in the pre-bellum period of the Deep South in the United States.

After Independence, in Latin American countries where revolutions of the magnitude of the Mexican rebellion of 1910 did not occur, and where the land tenure system perpetuated control by the small groups of wealthy landowners and foreigners, the Church prospered. In countries such as Guatemala, Nicaragua, El Salvador, Cuba and the Dominican Republic, coalitions were formed between the church, the landed gentry, and ruthless despots. Whether it was Trujillo, the Somozas, Batista, Rafael Carrera, or other dictators, the Church always seemed to fare quite well.

In Guatemala, for example, although church land was expropriated in 1829 after independence from Spain, this event caused such continuous upheaval in the country that the conservative Rafael Carrera (1847-1865) was swept into power with the promise of restoring church lands, which he promptly did. Dictator Carrera remained in power for 18 years, enjoying the continued support of the Catholic Church. In the ensuing years the fate of the Church continued to rest in the hands of other Guatemalan dictators such as Manuel Estrada Cabrera (1898-1920) and Jorge Ubico (1931-1944).

From the beginning Latin American Catholicism had as its cornerstone the concept of *"resignacion a la vida,"* resigning oneself to a state in Life; "One's position in society was the will of God." Catholicism gave the landowners on a religious level the justification they needed for perpetuating the socio-economic system that existed during the colonial period in most of the Latin American countries with large indigenous populations, and which exists today to some degree in Guatemala and other Latin American countries.

(U) Medellín and Beyond

While for most of the first half of the twentieth century the Church continued in its ways of spiritual and economic "benign neglect" of the poor in Latin America, by mid-century the "winds of revolution" in the broader socio-political context were stirring. Castro made his move in Cuba; Trujillo was assassinated in the Dominican Republic . . . . Still, in other countries such as Guatemala and Nicaragua, the traditional power structure hung on. The attitude of the conservative Church was perhaps best expressed by Cardinal Mario Casariego in a speech to La Limonada, one of Guatemala's poorest cardboard barrios: "You the humble ones of this colony are the most cherished by me; I was born poor like you (in Spain); you live in shacks like the Bethlehem stable that housed the Infant God, but you are happy because where there is poverty, there is happiness." (El Imparcial, Feb. 2, 1967).

But while such churchmen as Casariego, who was then and is presently the leading prelate of Guatemala, were preaching the centuries-old theme of *"resignacion a la vida,"* other religious were beginning to preach a new doctrine and went so far as to back it up with a call to arms. Camilo José Torres, a priest in Colombia, was a symbol of the breaking with the past, for while Casariego touted his humble origins, Torres was from one of the wealthiest families of Colombia. His defection from the traditional church and enlistment as a guerrilla perhaps best symbolized the break with the traditional past and an awakening of social consciousness by the younger, more radical clergy.

(U) Liberation Theology: From Medellín to Revolution

The years between the Medellín (1968) and the Puebla (1979) General Conferences of Latin American Bishops were perhaps the most dynamic and controversial years experienced by the Church in Latin America in this century. Medellín had a significant impact on the hemisphere's religious community because of its strong advocacy of "social activism." In such countries as Colombia the impact was tremendous. In Guatemala, on the other hand, it was initially a bit more than minimal. It is safe to say, however, that no region escaped the theological debate that accompanied these years of political and religious evolution in the hemisphere.

The significance of Medellín cannot be underestimated. In many respects the attending bishops merely "legitimized" what was becoming a movement toward social activism since Pope John XXIII's Vatican II. They, nevertheless, put into structure and dicta a new direction for the Latin American Church. They gave encouragement to those who believed that the Church had been at the service of the elite for too long.

"Hence-forth, "they concluded, "temporal authorities claiming obedience would be obliged to justify their claims through the promotion of social justice . . . that will liberate the people of Latin American from situations of sin and oppression, internal and external, that impede their integral development." (INR. Report No. 1164)

Medellín sought to develop a "critical awareness" so that the poor could become more effective agents of their own "religious liberty," and assume their "civic and political responsibilities." From the discussion of such terms emerged the debate between the more conservative and the more radical leftist clergy. And from this debate emerged the term "Liberation Theology." Already inspired by Camilo José Torres, the liberation theologists today see a distinctly Latin American approach to the "connection between religious, social, and political liberation." ("Liberation Praxis and Christian Faith" Gustavo Gutierrez)

Foremost among the "liberation theologists" is Father Gustavo GUTIERREZ, a Peruvian theologian who has been a teacher at the Catholic University of Lima and studied philosophy with Torres in Europe. His book *A Theology of Liberation* published by the Maryknoll Press in the U.S. in 1973 is considered the classic presentation of "the theology of liberation." Summarizing from his work one sees immediately the nexus between true Christianity in his view and social reform or revolution:

"Stripped of every ideological element that falsified a cruel and conflict-ridden social situation, the gospel message not only had no quarrel with revolution but actually demanded one. Thus, around 1966 we see the appearance of a new line of biblical reflection, which was made explicit and publicized as a theology of revolution . . . . External dependence and internal domination characterize the social structure of Latin America . . . . Seeing politics as a dimension that embraces all of human life, entails conflict, and demands a scientific line of reasoning; and rediscovering evangelical poverty as fellowship with the poor and protest against their poverty—lead us to a wholly different way of perceiving ourselves as human beings and Christians . . . . To begin with, we come to a radical question of the prevailing social order. The poverty and injustice experienced in Latin America are too deeply rooted to allow for half measures . . . . Only by getting beyond a society divided into classes, only by establishing a form of political power designed to serve the vast majority of our people, and only by eliminating private ownership of wealth created by human labor will we be able to lay the foundation of a more just society . . . .

It is not difficult to see how Father Gutierrez's meshing of the Gospel and the teachings of Christ with political science and international relation led other Latin American theologians to go even further than he in their proclamation of "liberation or revolutionary theology." Father Raul Vidales of Mexico proclaims, "liberative evangelization stems from solidarity with the exploited classes from a decision to take their side actively in the struggle for life. "Reverend Segundo Galilea of Chili believes that the new theology "presupposes a clear-eyed awareness of reality, of the exploitation, injustice, underdevelopment, and frustrated hope that scar our continent." He goes on to call this a "sinful situation" and institutionalized violence by those in power.

Whatever the path the new theologians have taken, they all seem to reach the same point: The Church can no longer form a part of the old oligarchy that had "its foot upon the neck of the masses," and even more, the Church cannot remain a silent and passive witness to the "social injustices" endemic in Latin America, they argued.

Boiled down to its essence, then, the new concept of "liberation theology" in its Latin American context concludes that: (1) most Latin Americans live in a state of underdevelopment and unjust dependence; (2) seen in Christian terms this is a "sinful" situation; (3) thus, it is the duty of every Christian of conscience and the Church in its pastoral activity to commit itself by whatever means necessary in good conscience, to end this situation.

Ten years after Medellín, the Puebla conference in 1979 at which Pope John Paul II presided was merely a reaffirmation of Medellín, though perhaps in a more pragmatic approach by the Latin Bishops. In the intervening years there had been much tension within the Latin American Church. The theological debate between progressives and conservatives raged. Finally, it was Pope John Paul II who set the tone of the Puebla conference; and though he disappointed extreme "liberationists" he nevertheless continued the Church's course in that set by the Medellín conference. His strong commitment to the cause of the poor, his over-riding emphasis on human dignity, his criticism of human rights abuses and structural inequities that permit and even encourage such abuses, and his call for social justice were all issued in the spirit of Medellín (INR Report No. 1164).

Today because of Vatican II, Medellín, Puebla and the political evolution taking place in Latin America, the Catholic Church has, in the words of Tad SZULC, "marched on to the battlefield of social revolution." While for centuries the Church had been a key element in preserving the power structure, it has now moved to the forefront of reform movements.

This change in the attitude and activity of the Church is perhaps the most significant institutional evolution in Latin America in this century; the Church has been shaken to its very foundations by the conflict between its traditional and more radical elements. While there may still persist aging conservative cardinals and bishops in some countries, the tendency is for the Vatican to consecrate younger and more liberal bishops. They in turn give encouragement to the young liberal priests and nuns who are profoundly altering the character of the Church in Latin American and who by their commitment to the poor and to social reforms inevitably come into conflict with authoritarian governments. **Such is the case in Guatemala.**

(C) The *Guatemalan Evolution*

The reform movement occurring within the Catholic Church during the early sixties in Europe, the United States, and some parts of Latin America went initially almost unnoticed in Guatemala. While in the U.S., priests and nuns joined in freedom marches in the Deep South, along with their Protestant brothers and sisters in the early sixties, the high clergy of Guatemala was content to continue its old ways and stay out of the political struggles that continued between the right and the left.

What was occurring rapidly in the Universal Church began as a gradual transformation of the Church in Guatemala. A church that had since the end of the XVI Century survived as an independent ecclesiastical institution was becoming again—as it had during the Spanish Conquest—a mission church. In 1872 there were 119 priests in Guatemala; in 1940 there was the same number. There could not be great change in the Church without change in the political structure of government.

Several events occurred that began the movement towards the missionary church. In 1937 the anti-clerical liberal politics was broken, with President Ubico suspending government prohibition against religious orders being allowed into the country. Several Jesuits were allowed to enter and teach in the local seminaries. And in 1943 several U.S. Maryknoll priests established themselves in Huehuetenango Department after China became closed to the Order as a result of the Second World War.

During the Arevalo and Arbenz leftist governments, the Church and state were more or less at peace as long as the Church was not involved in any anti-reform movements. Even after the coup of 1954, the 1956 Constitution of Castillo Armas repealed many prohibitions against the Church, such as the use of foreign priests. This did not set well with Archbishop Mariano Rossell y Castillo, who as head of the Guatemala Church at that time feared a takeover by foreign priests. The Vatican exerted great pressure on Archbishop Rossell, as did the U.S. Government which was very interested in the use of U.S. missionaries to counter the growing influence of the Castro Revolution in Cuba. Rossell was finally convinced by the Vatican. The Pope later called for a 10 percent voluntary group of U.S diocesan priests as well as regular missionaries to go into Latin America.

Archbishop Rossell's fears were soon realized. By 1966, 85 percent of the Guatemalan clergy and religious were foreigners. In that year there was a total of 197 native Guatemalan priests, nuns and brothers as compared to 1,235 foreigners. The success of the foreign clergy in Guatemala is directly attributable to the very fact that they were foreign. For one, they received financial support from their liberal friends and religious communities at home. Additionally, they were better educated and imbued with a missionary zeal which brought to the country the more adventuresome and progressive spirits. Since the mid-sixties, then, the influence of foreign missionaries would begin to have a profound effect on the Guatemalan Church, which if not so visible externally would indeed cause an internal struggle, both theological and political, from which it has not yet emerged.

It has been stated above that the Guatemalan Church was not quick to accept change. The conservatism of the high clergy, the control of the land and the masses by the few, and the political dominance of the military had all contributed to slow liberalization of the Guatemalan clergy. But as it has also been noted, the arrival of foreign religious workers who were as much social workers as they were religious began to have an impact in the sixties.

It might be said that the expulsion of two Maryknoll priests, the Brothers Melville in 1967, along with other foreign clergy during the same period, is a point of demarcation in the slow process of liberalization of the Guatemalan clergy. Thomas Melville, after his forced exodus form Guatemala for participating in guerrilla activities, collaborated in a book with his wife Marjorie who had served as a Maryknoll nun in Guatemala for ten years. The book, *Guatemala: The Politics of Land Tenure*, aptly describes the thinking of the more radical foreign clergy working in Guatemala at that time. The book has often been quoted in religious magazines and newspapers. "The military and political administration of Guatemala is placed in power and maintained there by the oligarchy, which is also aided by United States political, economic, and military interest. These forces, along with the Catholic Church, are silent partners in the arrangements, and land owners reign supreme."

With this attitude expressed by former religious who worked for many years in Guatemala, it is not surprising that dozens of priests and nuns . . . not only left Guatemala, but left their religious duties as well. Faced with the conservatism of the high clergy in Guatemala, and many having come from countries where political systems were at least more democratic than authoritarian, these liberal clergy-men and women found it difficult to accept the perceived injustices perpetuated by the military regime and the silence of their own Church leaders.

Today such former American priests and nuns as the Melvilles, Blais Bonpane, Gail Phares and others continue to be active in such groups as the Council on Hemispheric Affairs, Friend in Solidarity with Guatemala, and other human rights-oriented organizations that lobby both on Capital Hill and in international arenas for the eradication of what they consider "repressive" military regimes such as the GOG. Many religious who have served in the mission fields of Central and South America and returned to their own countries also carry back a vision of the oppressed masses of the countries in which they have served and have effectively swung a great deal of the popular sentiment in the western world in favor of the "have nots" and against authoritarian military regimes, often supported by the U.S. in the past.

Today in Guatemala the dominance of foreign religious still exists and these religious can be said to be the impetus for the liberalization of the Guatemalan

Church. Of the 556 priests in the country, 496 of them are foreigners. Then, too, many of the 62 Guatemalan priests are members of religious orders such as the Jesuits and Salesians, and have received their education out of the country. None of these orders have seminaries in Guatemala. A similar situation exists with nuns. Of the 989 nuns in the country, only 271 are Guatemalans, many of whom have been trained outside of the country. The totals, then, for religious working in Guatemala is 1,710, with 333 of these being Guatemalan and 1,377 being foreigners (as per the publication of Confederation of Religious in Guatemala, 1979). The only senior seminary in Guatemala ordained a total of only nine seminarians. The instruction of philosophy and theology tends to be in the hands of Dominican priests of foreign backgrounds rather than local Guatemalan clergy.

(S) Politics, Violence and the Guatemalan Church

Last September 7, 1980, President Romeo LUCAS Garcia, while addressing an anti-Communist rally in front of the National Palace, dedicated one chilling line to the clergy: "If the priests and clerics do not attend to the business of saving souls, we will throw them out." It would appear that violence continues against elements of the Church. Clear evidenced of this was the killing of the fifth foreign priest in the last year on February 16.

The dead and kidnapped priests over the last two years are: Eugenio Hermogenes LOPEZ Coarchita, Guatemalan secular priest, assassinated in the Department of Guatemala, June 30, 1978; Walter VOORDECKERS, Belgian Immaculate Heart priest assassinated in Escuintla, May 12, 1980; José María GRAN Civera, Spanish Sacred Heart priest assassinated in El Quiché, June 5, 1980; Faustino VILLANUEVA, Spanish Sacred Heart priest assassinated in El Quiché, ALONZO Fernandez, Spanish Sacred Heart priest assassinated in El Quiché, February 16, 1981; Conrado DE LA CRUZ, Philippine Immaculate Heart priest kidnapped (assumed dead) in Guatemala City, May 1, 1980. On May 14, 1981, Guatemalan secular priest Carlos GALVEZ Galindo was machine-gunned at the entrance of his church in Tecpán, Chimaltenango Department. While this airgram is being prepared a seventh priest, Guatemalan Jesuit Luis Pellecer has been kidnapped under circumstances that do not bode well for a safe return.

Lucas's words of "throwing them out" can be interpreted as also meaning, "carrying them out." Sources indicate that Spanish priest Juan Laudino ALONZO Fernandez was machine-gunned by elements of the Army in the Department of El Quiché (Guate. 1072). As a result of the violence aimed at churchmen in that Department in the past, former Bishop of the Diocese Juan GERARDI had ordered all religious out of that Department last July (1980). The Bishop himself had escaped a reported attempt on his life and now lives in exile in Costa Rica. (80 Guate. 7789.)

Father Alonzo had gone into El Quiché with a small number of priests in what appeared to be a new attempt by the clergy to service the area since their departure in July when the 18 priests and 25 nuns had been ordered out. This latest incident and indications that rightwing pressure was also responsible for the departure from Guatemala of two American priests, Father Ronald BURKE and Father Stanley ROTHER, whose names reportedly appeared on death lists, are very recent indications that the repression continues against certain elements of the church.

As recently as mid-May 1981, the Army's spokesmen on nationwide television accused the Order of Sacred Heart of having "for years" spread "subversive ideology" among peasants in El Quiché Department.

The present paranoia on the part of the GOG cannot be separated from events in other countries in Central America. The fact that priests now serve in the leftist Government of Nicaragua must certainly be of concern to the GOG. Most prominent among the radical priests are Nicaraguan Foreign Minister Miguel D'ESCOTO, a Nicaraguan Maryknoll priest who was educated in the Maryknoll Seminary in the U.S. and for ten years was editor of the Maryknoll Magazine. A Jesuit, Fernando CARDENAL, directed the Nicaraguan literacy program and now advises the Sandinista Youth organization.

In El Salvador, too, where civil war continues, the Church has often been at odds with the supposed centrist government junta. The killing of the three American nuns and a Catholic lay worker in December, most likely by elements of the government, has also heightened tensions between church and state and has raised criticism of the Government for the attack on the Church to the international arena. Even though the new Bishop of El Salvador, Damas y Rivera, who succeeded the slain Archbishop Romero, is less radical than his predecessor, he nevertheless feels that, "there are many social issues here (El Salvador) that demand change. Otherwise, we will return to the old system of rightist rule." (*Miami Herald*, March 5, 1981.)

It is statements like these now coming from the high clergy of Central America that makes the GOG nervous. As long as it was conflict with individual priests such as Jose Maria RUIZ Furlan (better known as Father "Chemita"), during the late sixties, the GOG was confident the high clergy could control its more radical elements. Father "Chemita" was sent on "extended" retreat to El Salvador in 1967 by Cardinal Casariego, and has since made his peace with the Cardinal.

Today, however, though the Cardinal continues in his conservative ways, the Bishops' Conference and individual bishops in Guatemala are beginning to challenge the authority of both the Cardinal and the GOG. A series of events, beginning with killings in Nebaj (El Quiché) in March 1980, has begun to polarize church and government (80 Guate. 1759). Even prior to the events in Nebaj the Council of Bishops and 52 Jesuit priests had published separate criticisms of conditions in Guatemala. On February 15, 1980, the Catholic Bishops' Conference of Guatemala promulgated a message to the people of Guatemala (80 Guate. 4829). The message, reflecting the direction of the hierarchy's new leadership, condemned all forms of violence and called for social justice. Under the leadership of the moderate Bishop of El Quiché diocese Juan Gerardi:

1)   The Bishops noted the increasing polarization of Guatemalan politics and the general confusion about the role of the Church.
2)   They postulated the need for a climate of peace and unity for the resolution of Guatemalan political and economic problems and stated that peace is the result of justice and love. They quoted Pope Paul VI saying that "if you wish peace, work for justice."
3)   The Bishops acknowledged that injustices are present in Guatemala, and called upon all Guatemalans to take stock of the existing social order and to examine their own past in the creation of this society as well as their responsibilities for it improvement.
4)   They unequivocally condemned all forms of violence, "subversive and repressive", even though they stated, this "arises from a permanent situation of injustice." They quoted Pope John Paul II's January 1, 1980 message saying that the best of political motivations do not alter the nature of violent acts such as murder, torture, exploitation and oppression.
5)   They called for greater attention to be given to the poor and the resolution of the problems of poverty. They also noted that some Guatemalans have already begun to focus on this matter and that there is increasing consciousness of the human dignity of all Guatemalans.
6)   In accordance with the discussions at Puebla, they stated that the Church will defend and promote human dignity. The Bishops noted that class warfare and the encouragement of hate are excluded by Christianity.

There was no significant official reaction from the GOG to the Bishops' declarations, but there was ill feeling within the hierarchy when it was discovered that Cardinal Casariego had unilaterally blue-penciled some language in the document before it was published. This demonstrated the Cardinal's continued deviation from the more activist posture of bishops such as Gerardi, Mario Rios Montt, Garcia Urizar and then-Bishop Luis Manresa. (Note: The Cardinal has no official jurisdiction over the bishops of other diocese.)

Barely a month earlier, 52 Jesuits working in Guatemala issued a statement January 16, 1980 condemning "a system of anti-Christian power that dominates Guatemala, a system which kills life and persecutes those who struggle for this same life." The Jesuits, attacking the excess profits of the plantation owners, noted "living conditions crush the wage earners more every day . . . . In our country there are kidnappings, torture and assassinations." The priests cited alleged official documents that reported death squads had killed 3,252 people in the first 10 months of 1979 (Impacto, Nov. 14 1979). The priests said, "we feel an obligation to break our long silence in the face of the cry being raised by millions of impoverished and oppressed brothers and sisters in Guatemala because of the preferential option for the poor expressed by Latin American bishops at their 1979 assembly in Puebla, Mexico." They added that "to close our eyes before this truth under the pretext of anti-Communism is equivalent to what the Latin American church affirmed at Puebla: 'Fear of Marxism keeps many from facing up to the oppressive reality of liberal capitalism.' (*Origins*, U.S. Bishops Council, March 13, 1980.)

For their public statements the 52 Jesuits received as a group a death threat from the Secret Anti-Communist Army (ESA). The GOG responded with a statement threatening to expel the priests, calling the Jesuits "political clergy" and indicating that they were subject to trial for misuse of their freedom and for "making irresponsible accusations." The GOG also pointed out that there were certain constitutional limitations on the role of the clergy.

(S) *Clergy Condemns the Violence*

In addition to the general criticism of violence and injustice in the country cited above, Church entities have been more specific in their challenge of the government. On March 11, 1980, the "Bishops, Priests and religious" of Quiché Diocese, issued a statement that put the blame squarely on the Army for the killing of *campesinos* in Nebaj. At least eight Indians died in the incident which the Army claimed was a leftist-inspired attack, but which the church people claimed was a wanton massacre of women and children.

The church bulletin concluded with denunciations of the military for "this massacre," for the use of arms against "defenseless *campesinos*," for the arrest and bad treatment of *campesinos*, and for the arbitrary requirement for identification papers "which discriminates against the Guatemalans of Nebaj."

Following this pronouncement, the churchmen in Quiché continued to have strained relations with the GOG. Two priests were killed in San Juan, Cotzal and Joyabaj, El Quiché, and a car belonging to a group of Canadian nuns was riddled with sub-machinegun bullets (80 Guate. 4829). One of the nuns reportedly saw a person presumed to have been a soldier, throw a grenade into the parish house. No one was injured in the last two incidents, but, added to the threats and reported attempted ambush of Bishop Gerardi, this was enough for him to order all of the priests and religious out of the Quiché diocese in July 1980. (80 Guat. 4829)

On the 26th of July, the Guatemala Bishops Conference issued a statement to the press expressing "deep concern about the persecution of the Church, especially in the diocese of El Quiché, aggravated most recently by the killing of two priests . . . ." The bishops also called for "a dialog with the authorities to enable the church to carry out its mission in religious freedom, *a human right* (emphasis added) sanctioned by the Constitution." The Bishops further added that Bishop Gerardi would travel to Rome to explain the situation to Pope John Paul II. (80 Guat. 4829.)

Gerardi did indeed travel to Rome, where he remained several months. It is not certain how extensive his discussions were with the Pope. However, it is reasonable to assume that he was partly responsible for the November 1 Papal letter that appeared in virtually all of the Guatemalan newspapers, as a paid ad submitted by the Bishops Conference. In the letter, the Pope condemned "the many acts of violence (in Guatemala) that violate *human rights* (emphasis added), the first of which is the right to life." The Pope cited what he called "vile and treacherous" killings of clergymen in the country, asked Guatemalan authorities "to do everything possible to assure the tranquility of the citizens, and to guarantee to the church the possibility of undertaking its evangelizing mission, especially in the Quiché diocese where, because of the many criminal acts and threats of death against religious, all pastoral work to the community has ceased . . . ." (80 Guate. 7548)

It was obvious to the GOG that Bishop Gerardi had a hand in the Pope's message for upon his return to Guatemala from Rome and a day after the Papal letter appeared, Gerardi, a Guatemalan citizen, was refused entrance into the country. As a result, the remaining members of the Bishops Conference, of which Gerardi is the head, published an unusually sharp reaction to Gerardi's plight. They perhaps viewed the situation not so much as the problem of an individual, but saw Gerardi as a symbol of the Church itself. The Bishops protested in the press claiming, "there is no legal or moral reason why the borders of the country should be closed to a Guatemalan citizen." They further added that there were "grave risks involved in sending a Bishop into exile." (80 Guate. 7612)

Throughout the entire affair, Cardinal Casriego, Guatemala's leading traditionalist, continued to separate himself from the more progressive and at this point, frustrated elements of the Church. His public response to the situation was an expression of confidence to the press that the situation would work itself out and Gerardi would return to Guatemala. Typically, he concluded, "Prudence is a virtue we all must practice . . . especially Bishops."

As these events unfolded, it was discovered that the name of Bishop Mario Rios Montt of Escuitla had appeared on a "death list," as well as that of an American priest, Father Ronald Burke who worked in Parramos, Chimaltenango. Bishop Rios Montt met with an Embassy official to discuss his situation (80 Guate. 8117). He noted that the priests (all foreigners) in his area were very frightened. They had lost a Belgian priest and a Filipino who had disappeared. He placed the blame primarily on the GOG, which "simply doesn't have the will to change . . . the will to do good." Reflecting the attitude of liberation theologists, he felt "there are people in the Government who are in it for their own benefit, to fill their pockets, to better their own situation and could care less about the humble and the poor." He did not fear for his own safety, as he felt resigned to his fate. "I will continue to do my church work." In terms of the Church, he felt there was a great deal of violence, a great deal of stress and this would not change short of radical change in the form of the government's attitude towards the masses. It was clear he felt the GOG was the main source of the Church's problems.

Bishop Rios Montt, as a Guatemalan, is not alone in his criticism of the GOG. The Provincial of the Jesuit order in Central America, Father Cesar Jerez, also a native born Guatemalan citizen, has left Guatemala because of this poor relation with the GOG. He, too, appeared on a "death list" of the Secret Anti-Communist Army and has not returned to the country. Father Jerez states, "From my point of view, some of those extreme rightists are acting very much like Somoza. They are acting blindly . . . the future has to be more open in Guatemala, the distribution of wealth can't be in the hands of a few." Jerez goes on to say that the violence and the killing is directed at those who are trying "to make a more democratic country and to better distribute the wealth." The Jesuit Provicial said that the Government and the Church in the past supported the oligarchies, but that now "some of the Guatemalan Bishops are doing a fine job for the poor." (Brukdown, Vol. IV, No. 10, Belize City.)

Jerez' radical bent is well known from his activity in El Salvador. Evidence, however, supports Jerez' claim. In recent months the Bishops Conference has spoken out vigorously against some GOG action, as mentioned above, and while the Church has not involved itself in the politics of the country to the degree of the Nicaraguan and Salvadoran clergy, the religious community has become more aggressive and critical. In recent months there have been a number of visits to the Embassy by both Guatemalan and American priests and nuns who have been less reluctant than in the past to share their accounts of massacres, murders, and abductions of members of their congregations by elements of the GOG or far Right (80 Guate. 7426). The comments of one American priest who has worked in Guatemala for ten years are indicative of the general attitude of the foreign clergy. He speaks of how the Indians view the Government, "more recently as more families are directly affected by the repression—they take away our boys, now they rob our lands, massacre whole villages, molest our women, tell the world we are Communists—what option do they leave us? The laws do not protect us. We must seek arms to defend ourselves." (MemCon fr. Burke, 10/30/80.)

Many religious believe this is an ever-increasing attitude among the Indians. It is true, too, that most of the rural clergy agree with the anti-Government attitude of many Indians. One estimate is that at least 90 percent of the rural clergy, while not in sympathy with the far left, is at least opposed to the GOG's harsh methods of dealing with the left and potential Indian collaborators. They see their people as victims of the political struggle that is going on in the Indian Highlands and virtually all of the rural areas of the country.

It would not be an exaggeration to say most of the foreign religious, who constitute nearly 80 percent of those working in the rural areas of the country, are left of center. This does not mean, however, that they are Marxist or guerilla activists. All of the evidence available to us indicates that at most two to five priests are actively working with the guerillas, while perhaps 5 percent of the lower clergy is in sympathy with the far left.

As an institution, the Church appears to lean quite heavily to the left at the lowest levels, while the Bishops Conference can be considered moderate. Cardinal Casariego, Archbishop of the Central Arcdiocese, can be viewed as the leading conservative.

Of the Cardinal's assistants, auxiliary Bishops Pellecer and Fuentes seem to be a bit more moderate than he, but still in the conservative camp. Pelecer and Estrada of Izabal are Charismatics. Only four bishops—Rios Montt of Escuitla, Urizar of Quezaltenango, Martinez of Huehuetenango, and Flores of Alta

Verapaz—can be considered liberals. The others are moderate to conservative, but it would appear that the overall tendency of the Bishops Conference, composed of these prelates, is one of moderation and becoming more aggressive as they see certain abuses such as the denial of entry to Guatemala of their president, Guatemalan Bishop Gerardi.

The structure in Guatemala is that each diocese is autonomous, receiving direction from the Vatican rather than Cardinal Casariego. This situation with the Cardinal being nothing more than "first among equals" has led to a gradual estrangement from the Cardinal of a number of his colleagues. Many of the bishops, along with a majority of the lower clergy, tend to view the Cardinal as a relic of the past. The bishops and their diocese are listed below:

Archbishop of Guatemala	Cardinal Mario Casariego Acevedo
Auxiliary Bisops in Guatemala	Rafael Gonzalez Estrada
	Ramiro Pellecer Samayoa
	Eduardo Ernesto Fuentes Duarte
Quezaltenango	Oscar Garcia Urizar
Jalapa	Miguel Angel Garcia Arauz
Zacapa	Rodolfo Quezada Toruño
San Marcos	Prospero Penados Del Barrio
Sololá	Angelico Melotto Mazzardo
Huehuetenango	Victor Hugo Martinez Contreras
El Quiché	Bishop Martinez of Huehuetenango Was also named by the Pope as Administrator of El Quiche Diocese
Izabal	Luis Maria Estrada Pateau (Apostolic Administrator)
Peten	Jorge Marco Avila del Aguila (Apostolic Administrator)
Escuintla	Mario Enrique Rios Montt
Alta Verapaz	Gerardo Flores Reyes

In the opinion of one American priest who spent 15 years in Guatemala, Casariego "is a scandal, something out of the Middle Ages, ill-prepared to represent or lead the Church in these times." There is considerable evidence that this is an opinion shared by much of the clergy.

As an indication of this, even the moderate to conservative Bishops Conference has shown signs of becoming more militant. This last April in a pastoral letter the Bishops issued their latest and to this date strongest commentary on the violence in Guatemala. In a three-page newspaper ad the Bishops went as far as they have ever gone in aligning themselves with the poor and attacking "institutionalized" violence in the country. While agreeing that the mission of the Church was not "political", they nevertheless declared that it was the Church's obligation to "insert the gospel into all human endeavors." The Bishops declared that they would continue their denunciation of the injustices suffered by the poor and to call for respect for "human rights". They also recognized that their efforts on behalf of the poor led to criticism that Bishops and priests were "fomenting class struggle and serving as vehicles of Communism." Nevertheless, they declared that they would follow in the footsteps of Christ the Savior and work for a "more just social order . . . where justice and love will prevail." (La Nación, April 8, 1981, Guatemala.)

The Church's Influence on the Traditional Structures of Government and Business

Up to now, because of the absence of strong leadership in the Guatemalan Church resulting from Casariego's reticence and slight popularity, and the exile of Bishop Gerardi, President of the Bishops conference, the Church as an institution appears to have little influence over the Government, the military, or the business sector. One influential general in discussions with an Embassy official echoed the attitude of President Lucas Garcia—"They had better stick to their soul-saving or we'll take care of them." And it appears that they have, since the latest killing of the Spanish priest in El Quiché, February 16, was attributed to the military (Guate. 1072). This could have been a symbolic warning, since there is no evidence that the priest was engaged in political activity. One general told us Father Alonzo was killed by guerillas, but produce no evidence to that effect.

In recent weeks, as a result of events in El Salvador relative to the killing of several nuns and the ten-day journey of Maryknoll priest Roy Bourgeois "among the poor", Guatemalan military officials have expressed their long-held views about foreign missionaries, especially the MaryKnoll order. They are convinced that in Guatemala the Maryknollers continue to aid the guerilla movement as they feel they did in the late sixties (Guate. 3155).

Most of the business community views the Church in much the same terms as the military. "Let them stick to saving souls" comments a right-wing lawyer. "We've seen what has happened in Nicaragua where the Church was in the forefront of the revolution against Somoza, and how they make up a large part of the government." Some businessmen are convinced that "a group of Roman Catholic priests started the whole thing," referring to the guerrilla activities in the Indian Highlands. Conservative businessmen accuse priests and nuns of "teaching politics and legal rights, not religion."

The precarious situation of the Church in Guatemala is not helped a great deal when newspaper and magazine articles carry stories of priests roaming the mountains with bands of guerrillas. A purported leader of the Guerilla Army of the Poor (EGP) was recently quoted as saying, "The Catholic Church is an important part of our revolution." One Priest, Irishman Don McKenna, has even joined the fighting forces of the leftist movement in the Indian Highlands and spoken openly to the international press of his conversion to violence and Marxism. Thus, while many well-intentioned religious carry on with their work of evangelization and social welfare, their every act becomes suspect. Some food from a Church-run cooperative farm finds its way into a guerrilla camp and all those involved in the project are branded as communists by the army. Medicine from a CARITAS health clinic ends up in a dead guerilla's knapsack and everyone connected with the Church project comes under suspicion.

Governments have looked benignly at Protestantism in Guatemala, which may have, as many as a million converts, because it diluted the power of the priests and because the fundamentalist sects that dominate here tend to focus on other worldly concerns more than the Catholics, who in recent years have been moved to "bread and butter" issues by the Catholic Action Movement. In recent months, however, even Protestant groups appear to have fallen into disfavor. In one month five evangelical ministers were killed (Guat. Airgram-14, 1981). While we are unable to confirm these and other deaths of protestant lay workers as political killings, it is clear that not just the Catholic Church is suffering violent deaths. There is increasing evidence that any religious ministry, that has as a component some type of social welfare or community organization activity is being watched very closely by the GOG and the extreme right.

While some of the lower clergy is prepared to take on a more militant role, both fear and the absence of leadership keep them silent. It would appear that a majority of the clergy, both foreign and domestic, are most anxious to continue their work in the form of traditional pastoral ministry with, of course, a new emphasis on social commitment based on the doctrine of "dignity of man" set forth in Medellín. They nonetheless find it difficult to walk a middle road. They see some of the younger members of their congregations beginning to be swayed by the Marxist doctrine and pushed into the arms of the guerillas as a result of GOG overreaction on some occasions.

At the same time, the message coming from the clergy in the U.S. and other pars of the Western world is one of condemnation of military regimes in Latin America, and specifically today, condemnation of the governments of El Salvador and Guatemala. While there may be some truth to the tales told in the church newspapers and magazines, it is decidedly a one-sided story. As Father William

Mullin, Superior of the Maryknoll Order for Central America, put it, "They (the Church press) have to realize that they are either going to have missionaries in Central America or be propaganda mills. They can't have it both ways. Our guys' lives are in danger down here and all this literature doesn't help us one bit." (Guat. 3989).

Thus, while at the international level a propaganda war continues with respect to authoritarian regimes such as in Guatemala, in the country itself, the real war that exists between the extreme right and extreme left has placed the Church squarely in the middle. Nevertheless, despite the number of deaths and the continued violence that besets the country, the safest course for the Church to take is to stay in the middle and avoid taking sides. We leave it to the Department to determine whether this message should have wider distribution, End

The Death of Father Francisco

From Personal Memoirs, **2004**

When the call came from the Marine at the Embassy, I had only been asleep for about two hours after a late night of drinking. My head was bursting and my throat felt like it was full of cotton balls. The Duty Officer came on the line, "Mr. Gonzales, there's trouble at Lake Atitlán, . . . Santiago." I knew at once that it was Father Rother, the American Pastor in the remote Indian village of Guatemala's volcano region.

"An American priest has been killed," the Duty Officer continued. "The Ambassador wants you to go up there right away. We'll contact the family in the States to see what they want done with the body. By the time you get there, we'll probably have that information and you can call us from there by radio. You need to come by the Embassy to pick up the Consul and some agents. The Ambassador wants a full investigation. There may be trouble up there."

As the armored Blazer and chase car headed along the winding mountain road towards Lake Atitlán, I had forgotten about my hangover and was recalling, with some pain, memories of Father Francisco, as the Indians called him, the Oklahoma farm boy who had been sent to the Indian parish of Lake Atitlán some twenty years before the present troubles in the Guatemala of 1982. Father Stanly Francis Rother, his real name which the Indians could not pronounce, had remarked to me that though he had had such a tough time with Latin in his seminary days, he had been amazed at the ease with which he had learned Quechiquel, the local Mayan language, giving sermons in the tongue and teaching catechism. "God's will be done," he had said to me.

Father Francisco had been one of the first American clergy in country who had become friends with me after my arrival in Guatemala the year before. Prior to my coming, most of the American priests and nuns in country were suspicious of the embassy staff, considering most of them CIA agents and too friendly to the host military government. But in my favor, before I had arrived, direct from California as a new mid-level foreign service officer in my first assignment, some of my ex-Maryknoll friends had contacted their friends at Maryknoll House in Guatemala City to tell them about this former seminarian and liberal politician who had gone into the Foreign Service as a third or fourth career. They had affirmed that I certainly was not CIA, and vouched that I was a true friend of "the masses".

It was true that, I had been encouraged by the Liberation Theology movement that had been making inroads against the Medieval-minded Church in Latin America in the Sixties and Seventies. My Ph.D. dissertation in Latin American Studies had dealt with the theme of dictatorship in Latin America. I numbered many of these new clergy that had emerged after Vatican II among my friends. There was Blais Bonpane, the Maryknoll priest who had been kicked out of Guatemala and left the priesthood to pursue a career in politics and with whom I had been in the doctoral program at USC; and there were the Ruperts, former Maryknoll priest and nun out of Guatemala who had left the order and married, settling in Sacramento to do social work. And there was a Franciscan, who had returned from Central America and enlisted with the César Chávez farm labor movement. These were good people whose only political sin had been supporting the Indian masses in Central America against the oligarchy of traditional church, landowners, and military dictatorial governments. American Maryknoller, Father Miguel D'Escoto in Nicaragua, had perhaps gone a little too far, becoming Foreign Minister of the new Sandinista Government there. But my friends were still good Americans, who still had friends among the enlightened clergy in Guatemala, so when I had decided to go into the Diplomatic Service in 1980, they had communicated with friends in Guatemala that I could be trusted. I was not a "spook," they had assured there friends in country.

As the heavy bullet proof Blazer struggled up the windy mountain road, I began turning green from the excesses of the night before. The air conditioner was not functioning and the bullet proofed windows could not be lowered. Finally, I asked the driver to stop the vehicle and I climbed out to throw up on the side of the road. "*Son las curves,*" the bodyguard standing next to me with Uzi on his hip, said diplomatically. No, it wasn't the curves in the road, I tried to smile. It was a simple hangover and some guilt.

In recent days, I had been spending nearly every evening drinking late into the night because my wife and children had left the country a month earlier when I had been placed on a death list by the right wing, *Mano Blanca*, death squad. The Ambassador had recommended that I send the family home for awhile until things could be straightened out. The Agency would get word to the *Mano Blanca* that the Embassy was aware of the threat against me and had communicated its concern to the Foreign Minister. One way or another, my name would hopefully come off the death list because the Death Squad and the Foreign Ministry slept in the same bed.

In the meantime, the big, lonely house with only the maid for company was too much for me to handle every night, so I would stop off at the Shakespeare Bar after I left the Embassy to drink and hang out with other expatriates. At home, the maid would leave a plate for me, ready for the oven, but the night before, I had drunk more than usual and just fallen into bed when I got home. I thought, wiping my mouth with a Kleenex the bodyguard handed me as I got back into the car, that at the same time I had been getting plastered, at the Shakespeare Bar, someone had been assassinating Father Francisco. I felt like hell.

What a meek and decent fellow Father had been. I had met him several times when the humble priest had come into town and stayed at Maryknoll House, which served as sort of a motel for many American priests when they came in from the bush. I had promised Father more than once that I would go out to visit him at Santiago on the Lake. I had been to the lake before, but that was before I had met Father Francisco. The area had attracted tourists and newcomers to the country before the guerrilla wars of the early Eighties had heated up. This was a very pristine area, not reachable by paved road. One had to cross Lake Atitlán by boat to visit the 12 Indian villages on the far side of the Lake, each named after one of the 12 Apostles. In each village the Indian residents wore different, distinctive clothing of bright patterns that they weaved. Santiago was the largest of the villages, with the parish church. Father Francisco had said he had at least 10,000 parishioners, most of whom came down from their farms for Sunday mass from the volcanic mountains of Agua and Pacaya that surrounded the Lake.

The Consul, Ray Baily, tried to make conversation with me during the trip to the lake, but had given up after he surmised that I was not in the talking mood. As the Blazer began its decent into Panajachel where we would board the police motor launch that was to carry us across the lake, I remembered the first time Father Francisco had come to the embassy. When the Marine at post one had called up to me to tell him there were two priests waiting for me in the lobby of the embassy, a Father Rother and a Guatemalan priest, Father Bocel, I figured it must be important. Father would not come by the embassy for a social visit.

I was right. After I brought the two priests up to my office from the lobby, Father Francisco proceeded to tell me that the night before, a message had been tacked to the door of the church with a *mano blanca* on it and the note said: "Leave this country or you will die." "What do you think it means Ray?" Father asked, with some concern. "They can't be serious, probably some pranksters. I made some Indians mad because we wouldn't sell their corn in our *cooperativa*. They have not joined and paid their dues. It was not my decision, but the rule of the *compesino* council."

"It's not pranksters, Father. I am sure it is the real thing. Do you have the note with you?" Father Francisco pulled out a folded brown paper and handed it to me. I stood up and walked over to my safe and brought out a file marked "Top Secret: Mano Blanca" and laid it on the desk. Inside were a number of brown sheets with a white hand stenciled on them.

"You see Father, your note is the same as these, and these are real. Several of these were found next to bodies that have been discovered in recent weeks. It's real, alright. It's real and we've got to take it seriously."

"I can't understand," the priest responded with a pained expression on his face. I have only tried to do God's work in Santiago. We stopped our radio program after the Government told us to. And it isn't my fault that some of our bags of corn and beans turn up in areas where the guerrillas have been. I told Captain Lucero of the army outpost in the village that we have nearly 1,000 farmers in the cooperative and we paint the stencil of the cooperative on all the bags of corn and beans we sell. We can't help it if the guerrillas buy this food. I'm sure that some of our farmers have sons who're with the guerrillas and they may take some food with them when they go into the mountains, but we don't support the guerrilla. We're just trying to help these farmers work cooperatively for the good of all."

"Well Father, I'm afraid that's not how the *Mano Blanca* sees it, and probably not how the Guatemalan government sees it, either. I've told you before. You're all being watched. I told Sister Catherine in Huehuetenango that she should not continue to allow her sisters to participate in the *Paz y Amor* prayer group, even though she says all they do is say the rosary and pray for peace. The Government of Guatemala has that group listed as a subversive organization. Anything you do to help the Indians in this country, at this time, is seen by the G-O-G as subversive activity. That's why most of the NGOs have left the country. It's impossible to work here among the Indians under these conditions. Last month there were 420 political assassinations in country, most of them conducted by the *Mano Blanca* and other extreme right groups, with the complicity of the government, but you didn't hear that from me."

"Well what should we do, Ray? We're not going back to Santiago today. We'll stay at Maryknoll House. What do you recommend?"

"I know you won't like this, Father, but what I recommend is that you leave the country for a while. Take some time off. Go home and try to raise some money, so that when you come back you can do some more good things, build that school you've talked about, put in a few new wells too, and a medical clinic, but right now isn't a good time. My own wife and kids have had to leave. President Carter put the screws to the government here, and other Central American countries that wantonly violated human rights. He cut off all military aid. And I think that Reagan will have to follow the same policy. In the meantime, you should leave the country for a while. These governments are pissed off and playing hardball.

You've seen what's happening in El Salvador—the nuns that were killed, and two of our own USAID workers."

Father Francisco put his head down and starred at his scuffed shoes for the longest while. Finally, looking up sadly at me, he said, "Maybe you're right, but I'm not leaving without Father Bocel here. We need to get a visa for him. I can't leave him here alone."

"I'm sure we can arrange that." But I had been premature in my observations at the time. The new Reagan policy on political asylum had become very restrictive. The thinking at State was that the way the U.S. could get these repressive military governments of Latin America to change was by working with them. In order to keep them as the buffer against the Cuban inspired communist movements, as Haig and the Department saw it, the U.S. had to work with them, and by granting asylum to those who charged human rights violations, it would be seen as attacking the host governments, labeling them repressive. The Reagan Administration did not adhere to Carter's Human Rights policy as closely as most human rights groups in the U.S. had hoped.

It was agreed that I would begin the process of attempting to obtain a visa for Father Bocel. While the two priests stayed at the Maryknoll house, I worked feverishly to attempt to get the visa for Bocel. Ray Baily, sitting next to me in the Blazer, had been no help, as the top guy in the Consulate. He had told me that Bocel could not get a visa because the consular rules called for an ordained minister or priest in a Third World country to have served two years in that capacity before he could apply for a U.S. visa, and Bocel had only been a priest for a year. They didn't have the same rule for European countries. It was only my knowledge of Cannon Law that allowed me to outsmart the Consul who was getting his instructions from the Department in Washington. I had spent four years in a seminary myself and had learned a little about the workings of the church.

I went to Maryknoll House to see if they had a copy of the ordination rights for priests, and they did. I remembered from my seminary days that before a priest was ordained, he was consecrated a sub-deacon two years before ordination, and as a deacon one year before. And as a deacon, he could perform many priestly duties such as giving sermons and assisting in solemn high masses where three priests or one priest and two deacons officiate. I had taken the book back to the embassy and had Baily fax a copy of the relevant pages to the Department.

After that, there was no argument. Father Francisco attested to the fact that Father Bocel had been assisting in solemn high masses as a deacon for more than a year before he was ordained and giving sermons in Quechiquel for more than two years. Case closed.

On the day of their departure, I had, with visa in hand, personally accompanied the two priests to the airport with an army of body guards and even walked the priests up the stairs of the Pan Am flight bound for Miami.

In the few months Fathers Rother and Bocel had been in Oklahoma, the war between the guerrillas and the government heated up. Human rights violations were up. Labor leaders, moderate politicians, university professors, and students were being assassinated by the right wing death squads on a daily basis in Guatemala. The guerrillas, for their part, were killing off military recruiters and some of the wealthy growers. Thus, when Father Francisco reappeared at the embassy several months later, I was shocked and angry.

"Why on earth have you come back, Father? What the devil are you doing here? Forgive me, Father, but this is crazy. Things are worse than when you left."

"I tried Ray," Father had said. "I really did. I couldn't even give a sermon in English anymore. I told the Bishop in Oklahoma City that I had to be here. This was where my work was. This was where my heart was. I wrote to the nuns at Santiago and Father Patrick, the Benedictine in Sololá, and they said things were pretty calm at the Lake. So I decided to come back. I don't sleep in my bedroom there. I move around every night, and Father Bocel stays in the city now. He will not go back to Santiago. I think it's O.K.," Father Francisco had implored.

As the Blazer arrived at the small pier at the edge of the Lake, I remembered how I told Father Francisco that things were never O.K. under this government. I walked him down to the lobby of the embassy, and having no official authority to prevent the priest from going back to Santiago, I had hugged him and told him to take care of himself. There, in the embassy lobby, in front of the Marine sentry and several people waiting on chairs, I knelt down and asked Father Francisco to bless him. That was the last time I saw Father Francisco alive.

The police launch carried the Embassy officials across the glass-still lake. The two Guatemalan policemen had only introduced themselves and shaken hands. During the half hour trip, neither of the policemen said a word. They seemed to avert making any eye contact with us. That was just as well, I thought. They should be embarrassed by what was happening in their country.

After the small craft pulled up to the pier, our group was led by the police up a narrow cobbled street in the direction of the church steeple we could see at a distance. The embassy's Guatemalan bodyguards were experienced enough to put their small Uzis in the briefcases they carried, with only the thumb holding the briefcase closed. Their side arms were kept discreetly under their coats. I noticed that there had been no Indian girls selling their wares at the pier, as on normal occasions. There was no activity in the small shops along the street, and, of course, there were never any cars in the village, as there were really no roads to this side of the lake. It was as quiet and as still as I had ever seen any Guatemalan town.

When we reached the large plaza in front of the church, I was startled to see what seemed like three thousand Indians gathered. Women were seated on the cobblestones, watching or nursing children. Men were squatted on haunches as was their custom. A few dogs walked among the thousands of Mayans. An occasional child could be heard crying. Other than this, there was no sound coming from this crowd of thousands. All of the villagers were dressed in their characteristic apparel, bright woven *huipiles* for the women, horizontal stripped pants with distinctively embroidered vests for the men. Occasionally sandaled feet, but most bare.

To me, it was among the most eerie scenes I had ever been a part of. In order to reach the church and the rectory, we had to weave our way through the mass of Indians. There was no clear path as the Indians were seated or squatting in random fashion. As we worked our way through the crowd, I sensed great anger and hostility being directed towards our group. I surmised that it was probably because we were in the company of the Guatemalan policemen, the Indians not knowing that we were not connected to them. But there was no way for me to disassociate the embassy personnel from the Guatemalan officials. Finally, we reached the stairs of the church and were greeted by the American priest from the neighboring village, Father Gregory.

"Ah, Ray, I'm glad they sent you. This is a terrible thing. How could this happen? Stan was a pious man, a godly shepherd."

"It happens Father, more than it ever should. I pleaded with Father not to come back here. I told him they were serious threats."

Father Gregory led us through the church and into the sacristy. When we entered this room where Father Francisco had donned his vestments thousands of times before going out to the altar to say mass, I was stunned to see Father Francisco laying on a table, dressed in the red vestments of a martyr. A white bandage was wrapped around his head, from under the chin to the top of the head and around the head, with a large bulge on the left side. He looked as if he were asleep, except for the bandage.

"The Indians had prepared him for burial," Father Gregory whispered. They've even made his coffin and have prepared his grave here in the church cemetery. They're in shock. They see death around them all the time, farmers getting killed in the middle of the night. School teachers left mutilated in the plaza, but they are not prepared for this. Stan was their anchor, their connection to any goodness, and salvation. They are more than distraught. They are angry too. Some of the men are talking about attacking the government offices in the town. What do you think, Ray?"

"I think, Father, that they may get even more angry. I have to call the embassy now, to see what Father's family wishes in Oklahoma. My guess is that they will want to bury him there."

"I don't know how that will go over. I think Stan would have wanted to be buried here, but I'm sure he didn't leave instructions. We always think we'll live forever."

I called the embassy on the hand-held radio and received the instructions I was dreading. The family had indeed requested that the body be flown back to Oklahoma City as soon as possible. After that bad news, I was taken into the rectory by Father Gregory, with the two Mexican missionary nuns who had found Father Francisco's body and a Guatemalan official who was in charge of the investigation. In the den where Father had slept that night, there was a pool of blood in the middle of the floor. The Guatemalan official told us that they had not touched anything or cleaned up, wanting the American officials to see everything as they had found it. I could see that Father had set up a temporary bed in the room that was otherwise his office. Bookshelves lined the walls and a large pine desk in one corner was covered with church documents and odds and ends.

"*Ya se puede limpiar aqui?*" I had inquired of the official.

"*Si, no hay problema. Ya hemos sacado fotos,*" the official responded that we could now clean up. They had taken photos. I thought that was a good idea and I instructed one of our *agenetes* to take some photos of the room as well.

After the photos had been taken, I told the nuns that they could clean up the room now, meaning Father's blood, which was beginning to congeal in the middle of the room. Baily and I then headed back to the sacristy where we were to meet with the Indian leaders of the parish, who were anxious to begin preparations for the burial. The spokesperson for the groups was a middle aged Indian who seemed a foot taller that the other five foot tall Indians. He was impressive in other ways as well, speaking slowly in Spanish, with only hints of the Quechiquel accent. While his Spanish was slow, it was clear and to the point. "*Aquí enteramos al padre. Era de los nuestros.*"

We explained to the Indian leader that it would not be possible to bury Father Francisco in Santiago, that his family in Oklahoma wanted his body returned, to be buried in the family plot. But the Indian leader was adamant, becoming irritated and expressing more agitation than I had ever seen among the Indians. "*No, no se puede llevar el cuerpo,*" the Indian said firmly. He insisted that the body could not be taken. "*Es un santo, es nuestro santo.*" He is a saint, our saint, the Indian said.

I knew that Father Francisco had been much loved by his Indian parishioners, but now they saw him as a saint, a martyr. I could not see how the embassy was going to get out of this situation. I continued to plead with the Indians, doing most of the talking as the Consul, Baily, had only limited Spanish skills. Finally, after half an hour of back and forth discussion, I told the several Indians that I had to go out to make a call to the embassy. What I really wanted was to talk things over with Baily and Father Gregory, not really wanting to call the embassy, as I was sure what the embassy's position would be.

Baily, Father Gregory, and I went to the kitchen of the nun's convent to have coffee and the Indians remained with the body of their dead priest. "This is serious," Baily said. "They may become violent if we try to remove him."

"And their violence will be misdirected, against us and Father's family," I offered. "We can't leave him here against the family's wishes. There's already going to be a major uproar back home, especially after the nuns in El Salvador. If we don't return the body there'll be even more criticism of our role here. There has to be a way to deal with this. But we're not getting anywhere with those Indian leaders."

Father Gregory repeated that he was certain that Father Francisco would have wanted to be buried in Santiago. Hadn't he come back from Oklahoma City indicating that he could not function there anymore.

"Wait!" I almost shouted. "He said something to me the day he came back and came by the embassy. He said he could not even give a sermon in English anymore, that his heart was here in Santiago."

"What do you mean?" Baily looked hard at me. "What are you saying?"

I drew a deep breath, "what if we leave his heart here? What if we leave them his heart? They can bury his heart in the casket they've made for him. Maybe that'll be enough for them."

When we three Americans returned to the sacristy, the Indians were silent and still clearly angry. Their jaws were locked and their arms crossed. I noticed *machetes* on their sides, which I wasn't sure had been there before. I began slowly, imploring them to accept the wishes of Father Francisco's mother. His mother wanted him home to be buried next to other dead family members. The family would have only this last contact with him. The Indians had had him for the last 20 years. How many children had he baptized? How many couples had he married in this church? How many Mayans had he buried here? It was only right that his family should take him now.

I noticed the Indians' expression begin to soften a bit. Finally, I said, *"les dejamos aquí su corazón. Aquí pueden enterar su corazón, el corazón se queda aquí con ustededs, sus queridos Maya."* We shall leave his heart here to be buried by you his beloved Mayans," I concluded in English so that Baily could be sure of what I had said.

The Indians left the room, following the lead of their spokesperson. Baily, looking at me with a slight smile on his face, "I think you did it. I think they will go for it." But I was not happy.

Father Gregory interjected, "Yes, I think they will accept it. They understand the importance of a mother's wishes. And the heart is a great symbol to them. The doctor that came to prepare the body lives here in town. I am sure we can get him to come and perform the surgery, or what ever it is we are doing here."

"I think it will be sacrificial, what we are doing here. It will be a sacrificial offering. Just as he was sacrificed here for doing work among the Indians." I looked away from the other men, not wanting them to see my watery eyes. Father Francisco would have liked this compromise.

When the Indian leaders returned to the sacristy, they accepted the compromise, as had been predicted. They said, they wished to bury the red vestments with the heart as Father Francisco was a martyr for them. It was agreed. I chose not to be present when the sacrifice took place. Instead, I was called back to the convent by the Mexican nuns who had cleaned up the scene of the assassination. Baily remained in the sacristy waiting for the arrival of the doctor and to serve as the embassy witness to the operation. Baily was the kind of fellow who could detach himself from any personal feelings one might have in this situation. He was a good officer. I could not do what he could.

When the nuns were convinced that I was the only one of the Americans that would join them, one of them pulled out a little plastic bag from under her tunic. *"Aquí señor, las balas que mataron al Padre Francisco."* What she handed over to me were the two slugs that had gone through Father's temple. They had flattened against the hard tile floor and had been obscured in the pool of blood, and had not been seen by the police. They also handed me two cartridges from a 45 caliber that had rolled under some National Geographic magazines that had stuck out over the bottom shelf of one of the bookcases.

"No queremos dárselos a los oficiales guatemaltecos," one of the nuns said. They had not wanted to give them to the Guatemalan officials. They handed these items over to me, rather than the police because they were certain the government was involved. Then one came up to my side and whispered into my ear. *"Vimos a los asesinos correr del rectorio. Llevaban máscaras de esquiar, hombres altos con botas militares. No nos vieron."*

They had seen the assassins run from the rectory after two shots were heard. They were tall men, the size of Father Francisco, who was a six footer. They wore ski masks and had army boots on. I had no doubt that the government was in some way responsible. If not directly, many soldiers worked as assassins for the *Mano Blanca* and other extreme right groups on their off duty hours. With these cartridges, I believed that the embassy could put some pressure on the Foreign Ministry to find the assassins. We would have to tell the G.O.G. that I had been the one who found the evidence so as not to implicate the Mexican nuns.

A pickup truck had come around the lake on the only dirt road to the village loaded with an empty casket that the Embassy had purchased in Sololá. After the coffin with Father Francisco's heartless body made the trip back around the lake, the coffin was transferred to a hearse for a more dignified return to Guatemala City. Plans were being made for a memorial service for Father Franciso at the Cathedral before the body was to be shipped back to Oklahoma. Father had many friends in country.

On the trip back to the city in the armored Blazer, I was too emotional to speak. I almost detested Baily's presence, as I felt the Consul looked upon this event as just another retrieval of a dead American. The Consular section, not political officers, did these sorts of things, most of the time retrieving Americans who died of heart attacks or auto accidents in country, without ever knowing anything about the dead bodies they were shipping home. Finally, Baily broke the silence. "I don't think we need to tell the family anything about what we did here. They might not understand."

"Yea, you're probably right. They won't open the coffin after a death in the tropics. Closed casket. We should recommend that."

No more was said for the rest of the trip back to the embassy. Halfway there, I asked the driver to stop the car. Feeling sick again, I walked behind the vehicle and threw up, vomit coming from my mouth and nose, as tears streamed down my cheeks. A year before coming to Guatemala, I had been attending posh banquets in Sacramento and giving speeches on behalf of the Jerry Brown Administration in California for whom I worked. Now, as political and human rights officer for U.S. Embassy Guatemala, I would be required to add Father Francisco's death to the monthly grim-gram I sent to the Department describing human rights violations in country, topping at 520 political killings a month. During my two years of reporting on these violations, 1980 to 1982, Guatemala was designated "the grossest violator of human rights in the Western Hemisphere," by the Department of State, but for me, it had become a very personal matter.

Renault Cartoon in Sacramento Bee, 1981
"Renault Sacbee"

Diversity Mindset
in Foreign Affairs Agencies

Speech to:The Council on Foreign Relations
New York City, May 16, 1997

W e are asked to answer the question, "Can shifts to a diversity mindset occur or must they be actively led among the foreign affairs agencies of the United States?" My response is generally that most of what has happened in the area of diversity or *affirmative action*, to use an out of date term, has happened because of court litigation, civil rights activism of a non-violent nature, and spontaneous violent eruptions in minority communities as occurred in the Watts Riots after the assassination of Dr. Martin Luther King. The majority society has been brought to the table kicking and screaming in protest and opposition to the demands for justice and equality by minorities, women's groups, and even such non-ethnic or gender-based groups as environmentalist or the physically challenged. Very little in the law has been done out of kindness, compassion or understanding, rather politicians have responded to crisis and the decisions of the courts, which, up until more recent times, have upheld these demands for an equal playing field in society.

Such is the case in respect to those who are the guardians of our foreign policy. In an April 1996 article in *The Nation*, Carl Shapiro notes that: "The State Department—long a bastion of private school patronage where change has come harder and slower than in any other Cabinet-level department—is in the midst of an internal war over racism in its ranks, particularly in the 4,000-member Foreign Service . . . a class-action discrimination suit brought a decade ago by black Foreign Service officers appears on the verge of a settlement . . . The outcome of the battle is likely to influence not only the face of the Foreign Service but the face of foreign policy for years to come."

Female Foreign Service officer filled a similar suit alleging discrimination on the part of the Foreign Service, which was filed in 1976 and only settled two years ago, which hopefully will bring about some change in the status of women in the Foreign Service. Latino and Asian Foreign Service officers, for whatever reasons, perhaps cultural or the lack of sufficient numbers, have not been aggressive in asserting fair treatment within the State Department.

That they have equal reason to demand equity is obvious by the fact that only in 1996 did the Department of State name its first Asian career Ambassador. In the case of Latinos, my views are a bit more personal. I quote from my own letter of resignation to Secretary of State James Baker in 1989:

> "I could resign in two sentences, but rather than go gently into the night, I would like to share with you some of my reasons for resigning. Having come into the Service in 1980 as one of the special mid-level officer candidates, after many successful years as a state legislator, state administrator, university professor with a Ph.D., and successful author, I assumed the Department of State's program for women and minorities was an honorable program. I am sorry to say that I have been sadly mistaken.
>
> In general, I have found the Department to be fraught with institutional racism, sexism and subtle discrimination. The proof of this statement is in the glaring statistics that are at hand. I note that of the top forty-three positions in the Department's Hierarchy, five are filled by women, 2 by blacks, and none by Hispanics or Asians. (The 2 blacks are in EEO-type positions and 3 of the 5 women are in decorative protocol or information positions.) Currently there are no Hispanic Ambassadors nor Deputy Chiefs of Mission at the more than 300 possible positions at overseas posts."

After my return to Washington as Director of Minority Recruitment for the Peace Corps in 1994, there were many occasions when I had to visit the State Department building. In my last visit in December of 1996, I noticed that in the Department's public exhibit area where the photographs of the Department's highest ranking officers are proudly displayed, little had changed. There still was no Hispanic among the 48 top officers, no Asian and an increase of two black, two still holding the EEO positions and a slight increase in the number of women.

Though my observations are somewhat personal, and reflect my reaction at having come up against the "tortilla ceiling," other entities have commented on the Department of State's personnel policies. In 1989 (the year of my resignation) the House Subcommittee on the Civil Service found that minorities in the Foreign

Service were denied tenure at a radically higher rate than whites, with black men selected out at roughly six times the rate of whites.

In September of last year, the General Accounting Office issued a report noting that, "the percentage of African-Americans in the Foreign Service's crucial middle ranks—tenured officials poised for promotion to senior positions—declined between 1984 and 1992. Further it concluded that, "the Department of State had one of the poorest records on minority and female employment and showed the least improvement over the decade." This moved Ambassador Terence Todman, one of the highest ranking Black Foreign Service officer ever, to comment, that Department of State officials have managed to evade affirmative action over the years by covering up the depth of the problem. "We are talking here about people who have a long track record of cooking the books to avoid the necessity of change."

Historical Problem in Foreign Policy Agencies.

At the professional level, I recall being the first and only Mexican American on the faculty of the community college I began teaching at in the 1960's. There have been a lot of firsts in my own life, not because I was extra ordinary, but because there were so few of us around at the time. (In 1968, only 12 Mexican Americans graduated from UCLA). I was the first Ph.D. from my community and the first state assemblyman elected to the state legislature from the San Joaquin Valley of California. But this is not about me.

Consider the changing demographics and the impact of immigration on our country. Let me just highlight a few items that I am sure most of you are already aware of. Demographers note the impact of recent immigration on the changing face of America. In New York, Los Angeles, Chicago and Fairfax County Virginia, a bedroom community for Washington, D.C., over 100 languages are spoken in the public schools. By the year 2005 in California, minorities which are now 45% of the population will become 52% of the population. That is just 8 years from now, and by the year 2040 minorities in California will be 68% of the population, with Latinos becoming the plurality of the population by 2020. Even today, minorities constitute a large majority on the campus of the University of California at Berkeley, nearly 60%.

And what is the effect of these statistics on the work force of the country? More than half the U.S. work force now consists of minorities, immigrants, and women; so white, native-born males, though undoubtedly still dominant, are themselves a statistical minority. However they are not in immediate danger as a recently released Government study shows that they still retain 97% of the top positions in the workplace.

The Hudson Institute's study, *Workforce 2000,* points out that in five years, 85% of the new job entrants into the workforce will be made up of women, minorities and immigrants. To many, this is a frightening fact, which causes extreme reaction in some sectors. Just what is the reaction among the so-called majority to these changing demographics?

In California it was SOS, Save Our State, otherwise know as Proposition 187 in statewide elections of 1994, an initiative based on fear, fear that often erupts during periods of tough economic conditions. In California the economic scene had perhaps been the toughest in the Nation at the time because of the cut-backs in the defense industry and the many military bases that had been closed in the state.

There are those in Congress today who would like to pass some sort of Proposition 187 legislation aimed at these new immigrants. Last year's bill did go so far as to deny certain benefits to even legal immigrant. And now the xenophobia and isolationism that causes some of our countrymen to fear immigration has led to another fear, the fear of affirmative action.

So what do we do about minority recruitment and affirmative action under the present circumstances? How do we recruit in government and foreign affairs agencies in light of the new attack on affirmative action?

Borrowing from the words of Mr. Roosevelt Thomas in his article, "From Affirmative Action to Affirming Diversity" published in the Harvard Business Review several years ago; he writes "Sooner or later affirmative action will die a natural death. Started more than 30 years ago to correct injustices in our society, legal and social coercion were necessary to bring about the change."

The truth is, as Mr. Thomas notes, "Affirmative action is an artificial, transitional intervention intended to give managers a chance to correct an imbalance, an injustice, a mistake," and the government has imposed it by law because of real, not perceived injustices of the past.

As many political pundits predicted, "Affirmative Action became the Prop. 187 issue of the 1996 elections. Such well know liberal columnist as the Washington Posts', Richard Cohen, even admitted that, "Ultimately, affirmative action is doomed. The electorate loathes it and the courts are giving it another look, probably a critical one . . . Whatever good it has done, it violates the American creed that we must be judged as individuals, not on the basis of race or sex—a group membership over which we have no choice. The civil rights era is over. The civil liberties era must begin."

Today, in government circles we don't call it affirmative action much anymore. The new buzz word is DIVERSITY, a word in the title of this conference too.

Let us examine the difference. In the U.S. we have had two versions of diversity. In the past our DIVERSITY was ASSIMILATION.

The ethnics of the past became part of that melting pot theory. Less than a stew, they were supposed to become a puree. Thus: "those long-haired, wild-eyed, bad-smelling . . . reckless foreign wretches" . . . were expected to blend in. And they did.

But today there are just too many of them to blend in. Just as women went from 4% of law school students in 1965 to 45% in 1995, truly a critical mass, minorities are 33% of the national population and growing at a rate five times as high as the white population.

Remember that today white males alone constitute 40% of job entrants, but in just five years they will constitute only 15%. Remember also that minorities and immigrants will represent the largest share of the increase in the population and new entrants to the labor force.

Almost two-thirds of the new entrants into the workforce will be women (both minority and white), and immigrants will represent the largest share of the increase in the population and the workforce since the First World War.

Dr. Troy Duster, sociologist from U.S. Berkeley and author of many works on the impact of changing demographics in the country speaks of the various stages of affirmative action/diversity.

He outlines it this way in discussing the position of women in our society: **Stage One** was that of Assimilation: females had a choice of assimilating or being marginalized. In 1965 women constituted 4% of all law school students around the country.

Stage Two goes like this: now in 1995 women are 45% of all law school students, truly a critical mass. Males feel threatened not just by the female presence but also by the female orientation. Females threaten the institution. Because they have reached a critical mass in the law schools, they are no longer willing to just be marginalized, strength in numbers as the saying goes.

What they now want is a change in the "white male-controlled institutions." And the changes they want are not just personal. They are not talking just about a "glass ceiling." Females are demanding more family law courses, social law, environmental law, rather than the standard corporate law, and business law, or criminal law that the majority of white male law students felt they had to have and what white male law professors felt was their obligation to teach. Females are demanding a change in the curriculum.

Today at the University of California Berkeley, 54% of the students are female. This is true in law schools, medical schools, graduate programs in general. It is true in the Department of State, the CIA, and many other entities at the federal, state and local levels. Minorities are in the same transition and critical mass levels as females. Especially in states like California, New York, Texas, Florida, New Jersey. U.C. Berkeley is 58% minority today, with Asians a plurality. UCLA is at 55%.

The problem with those who have been running the institutions of higher learning and government agencies over the years is that they have been trained only in Stage One. "Come in, sit down, and enjoy the show. Don't upset the program, and above all, don't make demands."

The dogma of the law school elites was, "We are the keepers of the cannons. We know the law. We will tell you what you need to know."

This same attitude prevailed among academicians in the Sixties. But then minorities began to come onto campuses in greater numbers and the civil rights movement led to their demands for ethnic studies and what they called, a more relevant curriculum. The white faculty, which I might add, controlled the institutions, responded by saying, "You are being political. We are the neutral carriers of the curriculum. History cannot be Black or Brown. It is neutral." Because the white administrators, deans and faculty controlled the show, they were the ones who established the "defining categories."

But because the students of the 60s didn't just come in, sit down, and enjoy the show, great upheaval occurred at our institution, and it continues to occur. The demand for ethnic studies has had a profound effect on our institutions. This has even liberated many white professors and students. It has changed the manner in which we teach U.S. history, political science, sociology, medicine, and the law. It is no longer sufficient to devote two pages to the institution of slavery in American history, or a page to the 1848 War between the United States and Mexico in which the former, motivated by "the White Man's Burden" and its supposed Manifest Destiny, doubled its territorial size and the latter lost one half of its territory, in a dubious victory, an unjust war which caused consternation among our population, not unlike the Vietnam War.

I challenge anyone to go back and thumb through a U.S. history text of the 1950s or earlier and compare it to any U.S. history text used in schools today, and I'm not talking just about the addition of current events. Look at how Manifest Destiny is treated, how the Spanish Mission system of the Southwest is dealt with, or the American Indian's Trail of Tears is related.

Absent in my studies of American history as a high school student and even in my early days as a collage student was an accurate discussion of such events as the War with Mexico or the Spanish-American war of 1898. I heard little to nothing of the U.S. Anti-Imperialist League, or the fact that one of our greatest American writers, Mark Twain, devoted the last ten years of his life in support of the Anti-Imperialist League. In fact, not until 1992 did scholars compile many of Twains unpublished works in this effort. In one address, Twain noted, "From Biblical days, there has rarely been a welcome mat for the bearers of unwanted messages . . . . The abolitionists are honored mostly in retrospect. They were despised and ostracized, and insulted by the patriots." Again in a speech on True Citizenship at the Children's Theater in 1907, he noted, "I remember when I was a boy and I heard repeated time and time again the phrase, 'My country, right or wrong, my country.' How absolutely absurd is such an idea. How absolutely absurd to teach this idea to the youth of the country," Twain noted.

Herbert Eugene Bolton who established a school of Inter-American studies at the University of California at Berkeley in 1911 and is credited with the definitive challenge to the Teutonic School of American History coming out of John

Hopkins University at that time, stated in an address to The American Historical Association in 1932, "There is a need for a broader treatment of American history to supplement the purely nationalistic presentation to which we are accustomed." In an earlier address he had noted:

> My early environment and outlook were typically Yankee American, that is to say, provincial, nationalistic. My unquestioned historical beliefs included the following, "Democrats were born to be damned; Catholics, Mormons and Jews were to be looked upon askance. The Americans licked England; they licked the Indians; all good Indians were dead; The English came to America to build homes, the Spaniards merely explored and hunted gold; Spain failed in the New World; the English always succeeded; their successors, the Americans, were God's elect . . . the Americans virtuously drove the Mexicans out of New Mexico, Colorado, Texas, Arizona, and the rest, and thereby built a great empire. Everyone of these concepts is false in whole or in part, but it took me half a lifetime to discover it.

So the conflict that exists in Stage Two is what Duster calls the "Schlesinger Nightmare." In his recent book, "The Disconnecting of America," Arthur Schlesinger celebrates Stage One, morns the death of order and control. It is a nightmare for those who have lived in Stage One, for now they have to contend for the scarce resources with competing groups like women and minorities. Funding, positions, careers are at stake as well as their self-aggrandizing notion that they are the "keepers of the cannons." That is why a Tex Harris, President of the Foreign Service Association, and a friend of mine with whom I served in the Refugee Bureau during my days at State, could write to the Secretary of State in a letter attacking Affirmative Action: "A continuation of diversity efforts can only engender further resistance by officers who feel disadvantaged by them . . . We are not talking about racism here. We are talking about contradictory standards that are quite destructive of morale . . ."

Whose morale is being harmed, certainly not the litigants involved in Thomas v. Christopher. Certainly not mine. My morale was harmed for the opposite reasons, and I chose to resign from the Foreign Service rather than to wake up and angry man every day I served at American Embassies overseas. Life is too short. It is too precious. There are more important things to do than to singularly wage war against the Department of State's personnel policies.

Ideally, we should be in a Stage Three. This is a stage that should enrich our sphere, our society because of the diversity found in our country, and perhaps not found in such degree in any other country of the world.

Analogies are used; Stage One was to be the melting pot, the porridge as it were. Assimilation, the blending of flavors, but the white meat and potatoes was the prominent base. But Stage Two intervened. A lot of garlic, and cilantro, and greens, were thrown in.

Borrowing again from Dr. Roosevelt Thomas, "Today the melting pot is the wrong metaphor even in business (and government). If it ever was possible to melt down Scotsmen and Dutchmen and Italians into an indistinguishable broth, you can't do the same with Blacks, Asians, (Latinos) and women. Most people are no longer willing to be melted down, not even for eight hours a day . . . ."

Stage Three should celebrate diversity, because it enriches our society. Because as the President has stated, our government should look like the face of America and that face is no longer just a white face. And the question we are asked at this conference here today, "does this change in the complexion of our country make a difference in the direction of our Foreign Policy?"

This, after all, is the theme of this Symposium. **"In the National Interest: Dose Diversity Make a Difference?"**

It does in the following ways: Diversity begets creativity. Diversity leads to solutions that are not based on ideology or dogma, but based on survival and peaceful coexistence, to use an old phrase. The need to survive causes conflict, conflict causes tension, and tension is met by creativity, which should lead to elegant solutions. Joel Barker, a futurist writer who has much to say about changing traditional paradigms notes: "When we gather in groups of people, whether they are businesses, (government), cultures, we aggregate the problem solving power that each of us has with our specific paradigms to deal with the larger world . . . It is our diversity as a group that lets us deal with the complexity of the world through the application of many paradigms . . . For that reason, whenever I hear people speak against immigrants of different cultures as "weakening" the United States, I object. Because I know that their differences have increased the potential problem-solving capacity of the nation."

Affirmative action in the past recognized a mutuality of rights and was moved by an accumulation of power and the use of this power against one another, thus the hundreds of court cases where the mutuality of rights was to be determined by the courts. But this is the old win-lose paradigm, the win-lose treadmill. If you look today at successful work places you will find that they are the ones where what works is what is used: Interest based decision-making. Arafat and Rubin, Mandela and DeClerk agreed because it was in the best interest of their constituents that they should agree. Unfortunately there are still many who would use the old accumulation of power to resolve differences.

Consequently, the Office of Minority Recruitment at Peace Corps has laid out a recruitment plan which seeks to increase recruitment efforts by seeking the real diversity in our country. We are recruiting at the 144 Historically Black Colleges and Universities (HBCU's), the 113 member institutions of the Hispanic Association of Colleges and Universities (HACU), the 22 Tribal Colleges, and the hundreds of community colleges where we know that 54% of all minorities in higher education start their college years. We are also focusing on hundreds of community-based organization in the barrios, the ghettos, the Asian neighborhoods and reservations.

While we know that up to now, the majority of minority Volunteers are presently recruited at majority campuses, we also know that many of the HBCU's and HACU institutions are producing the kind of trained specialists we need in today's Peace Corps. We plan to focus as much attention on these minority rich institutions as Peace Corps has focused on the Ivy League campuses and the Big Ten schools in the past. We know that one of the image problems Peace Corps has had in the past was that it was a white-middle-class-kids organization.

Many potential minority Volunteers are now thinking globally as they plan a career and Peace Corps is quick to point out that the Peace Corps experience gives the Volunteer very useful skills in international, cross-cultural experience, and usually an added language or two. This is the type of experience that international employers and the U.S. Government are interested in. Thirteen percent of new Foreign Service officers are former Peace Corps Volunteers.

One of the selling points the Office of Minority Recruitment focuses on in its approach to potential minority Volunteers is to stress the value of international experience in the rapidly changing world. The global village concepts appears to have great appeal to many minority students who are now looking far beyond their own neighborhoods for exciting career choices. The Peace Corps of the 90s is at the leading edge of U.S. programs which are reaching out to the Pacific Rim and the new democracies of the Former Soviet Union in Eastern Europe. Such developments as NAFTA, GATT, the Summit of the Americas and the invitation of Nelson Mandela for a Peace Corps program in South Africa have opened up exciting possibilities for all potential Volunteers and especially for minorities who heretofore have not always recognized the value of international experience for career opportunities, or whose parents have been somewhat resistant to international job opportunities.

With the goal of 7,000 Volunteers in 1995 and challenges to affirmative action programs now working their way onto court dockets and in the Congress, the Office of Minority Recruitment at Peace Corps believes that a sufficient number of very qualified, potential minority Volunteers can be successfully recruited off colleges campuses, especially the HBCU's, HACU institutions, Tribal Colleges as well as heavy-minority-enrollment majority campuses, without any special admit concessions. Peace Corps has thousands of opportunities available to individuals interested in expanding their world view, refining their leadership skill, and gaining personal satisfaction by working in humanitarian endeavors at levels of responsibility far above those of their stateside counterparts.

Finally, let me return to the question posed for this conference about the value of diversity in the foreign affairs agencies and relate it to my own personal experience. My reasons for resigning from the Foreign Service of the Department of State are as much over the institutional discrimination which I have noted with respect to Hispanics as they are over my own personal discouragement. As a Hispanic, one cannot be very encouraged by seeing the lack of diversity within the Department. Clearly there are no Hispanic role models to be found in positions of influence and authority within the Department's structure, not a single ambassador nor DCM at this time out of 300 possible assignments worldwide. Instead, Hispanics seem to have been so beaten down within the Department that they do not even raise their voices in protest of this shabby treatment. Women have at lest filed successful class action lawsuits and blacks have organized an effective lobby group also considering litigation. And in other agencies such as the FBI and INS blacks and Hispanics have demonstrated effective action, but at State, submission seems to be the preferred "dignified" behavior.

I have grave concerns about the efficacy of the Department's entry program for women and minorities. Over the last few years I have repeatedly asked the Department for statistics demonstrating the promotional rate of mid-level entrants to the Department. Nothing has been forthcoming. In private discussions with other mid-level entrants, I find that their experience is similar to mine. While I find that the Foreign Service personnel system tends to demoralize most officers in the Service, it is especially vicious as regards minorities and women, and is the most significant reason for resignations among this group.

A large number of the mid-level entrants like myself have resigned for the same reasons as I did, they simply could not buck the system. Many of my comments upon resignation could be repeated by Hispanic State Department employees resigning in 1994. There is still not one Hispanic among the 34 appointees at the 8 top levels of the State Department. Among the 16,534 civil service employees at State only 704 (4.2%) are Hispanic and mostly below the GS-8 level. Among the 4,000 Foreign Service Officers the figures are even lower. With 14,000 individuals a year taking the Foreign Service Exam, and only 140 being accepted annually as Foreign Service Officers, the odds for Hispanics or Blacks making the cut are pretty grim. Thus, the good 'ol boy network perpetuates itself as it controls the entry level process. It seems only to change when lawsuits are filed.

If President Clinton and Secretary Christopher truly wanted to change things at the Department of State, even though they have already had two years in which to do it, they could do so almost instantly at the top, since they have 34 exempt positions and over 100 other appointable positions not requiring Senate confirmation for which they have the power to hire and fire at will. It seems clear that they are not willing to rock the State Department boat and turn the page on the American diversity, which is a reality and which President Clinton has stated should be reflected in the make up of government. I know there is at least one highly qualified Hispanic available to serve immediately as my resume has been with the White House Personnel Office for nearly two years.

The Two Big U.S.-Mexico Problems Continue: Oil And Immigration

The Sacramento Bee, **May 20, 1979**

The recent great oil discoveries in Mexico, accompanied by the decline of United States diplomatic fortunes in the Middle East, have placed the two countries on a path from which there is no return. Mexico and the United States are either on the verge of a new and egalitarian diplomatic and economic relationship or headed toward a disastrous collision. Both countries would do well to ruminate on past history. The new-found oil fields south of the border are not too unlike the discovery of gold in California during the 19th Century that precipitated perhaps the most bitter period between the United States and Mexico.

Fear of exploitation by the "colossus of the north" extends far back in Mexican history. President Benito Juárez, 1857-72, declared on one occasion that, "between the center of Mexico and the country to the north, there should always exist a great desert (the Sonoran Desert)." Juarez was so fearful of the U.S.'s desire for exploitation of Mexico's natural resources that he resisted, during his presidency, the urging of many of his advisers and the U.S. business interests to build a railroad from central Mexico to the U.S. border.

It was not until after his death, and during the dictatorship of Porfirio Díaz, who had been one of Juárez' top generals in the war against the French, that the railroad was ultimately built. For the 31 years of the Díaz dictatorship, Mexico was virtually sold out to U.S., British, and French interests. So severe was the rape of the country that the culmination of the "Porfirian era" was the Mexican Revolution of 1910, the first revolt of the proletariat in the 20th Century. The heroic figures such as Pancho Villa, Emiliano Zapata, Alvaro

Obregón, stand out as symbols of "los de abajo" (the underdogs) against both local and foreign oppression.

There should be little doubt that Mexican President José López Portillo's recent toast to visiting President Jimmy Carter of the U.S. is a strong indication that the Mexican revolution is alive and well. In what has been referred to as the "battle of toasts," President López Portillo made it clear that he was more aligned with Juárez and former President Lázaro Cárdenas, who nationalized the Mexican oil industry in the 1930s, than he was with dictator Porfirio Díaz, who made it his policy to sell Mexican resources to the highest bidder.

López Portillo, in referring to U.S. Energy Secretary James Schlesinger's scuttling of last year's proposed natural gas deal between the two countries, welcomed Carter with very strong rhetoric: "Among permanent, not casual neighbors, surprise moves and sudden deceit or abuse are poisonous fruits that sooner or later have a reverse effect. No injustice can prevail without affronting decency and dignity."

Even before Carter's arrival in Mexico, there was an indication that the Mexican President, highly regarded as both an intellectual and a pragmatist, was prepared to show the U.S. President that "Montezuma's revenge" did not consist of merely a lower digestive tract malady. In a press conference just prior to the U.S. President's arrival, López Portillo declared that "I hope Mr. Carter doesn't intend to come here and negotiate with beads and trinkets with a man still wearing feathers."

Perhaps the most serious problem for both countries is how to deal with the development of Mexico's vast newfound oil reserves. The issue is important to the U.S. because of its declining influence in the Middle East and the Arab world's obvious intention of bringing the U.S. and other western powers to their knees.

For Mexico, the oil issue is equally important even though for other reasons. There is no doubt that the high unemployment rate of the country, estimated at higher than 30 percent, would be relieved by the development of the oil and related industries. But President López Portillo, as a pragmatic and knowledgeable student of economics and world events, recognizes that there may be a great danger in developing Mexico's oil fields primarily to fulfill the needs of the gas-guzzling western world. Reflecting on the cultural shock following Iran's ill-prepared effort to make the adjustments required by new-found wealth, López Portillo declared: "We shall develop our oil industry at a rate to meet our own domestic needs not because others need our natural resources."

What the Mexican president fears most is adding to the high rate of inflation that would result from an infusion of foreign money. He fears that Mexican citizens would indulge themselves in the purchase of luxury items manufactured abroad rather than to develop their own industries. The lack of entrepreneurial efficiency in Mexico and most of Latin America has resulted in the slow industrialization of that part of the world. There has always been a penchant among the business community of Mexico to invest its money abroad rather than to convert it into the development of its own industries. Even at a time when Mexican banks were offering a 12 percent interest rate on savings, Mexican middle-class and upper-class citizens preferred to save their money in savings and loan institutions in the United Sates that were offering a mere five percent interest. This has resulted in the past in the unavailability of capital in Mexico for the development of its own industries.

Additionally, López Portillo is interested in an expansion of the Mexican oil industry that would be controlled by PEMEX, the government operated oil company, rather than by foreign oil company technology, and which would be directly tied to other sectors of the Mexican economy. Thus, López Portillo continues to insist that "Mexico will develop its fields according to its capacity to digest income from oil exports."

Obviously, the U.S., as the world's largest oil consumer, more than 8 million barrels a day, should not expect Mexico to be willing, or even able, to quench the U.S.'s insatiable demand for oil. Mexico is currently producing one million barrels a day with plans of reaching 4 million a day by 1985, making it second only to Saudi Arabia in potential oil exportation. In spite of this extraordinary potential, however, there is nothing to guarantee that the U.S. will be Mexico's only customer. López Portillo, just a week prior to Carter's arrival in Mexico, announced in an interview with TIEMPO, Mexico's leading new magazine, that "Mexico's oil will be for sale to whomever wants to buy under the conditions that are the most favorable to Mexico."

THE TORTILLA CURTAIN—Of equal significance, in current relations between the U.S. and Mexico is illegal immigration. Obviously, to Mexican President López Portillo, the situation is both one of human dignity as well as economics. He feels so strongly about it that he did not fail to make it part of his somewhat chilling toast to President Carter upon the latter's visit to Mexico. López Portillo admonished: "The most serious issue of our times is the fact that there are men who can buy men and that there are men who have to sell themselves, and this happens very frequently with our poor people who go to the United States."

Of course, López Portillo tells only the philosophical side of the story. Mexico's chronic unemployment situation and its need to develop between 800,000 and one million jobs a year for its youthful population cannot be satisfied even by the development of its oil industry. Currently, private enterprise in Mexico is developing as little as two percent of the jobs needed annually while Mexican workers in the U.S. return to Mexico with $2 billion annually that are pumped into the Mexican economy.

Consequently, the U.S. serves now, and historically has always served, as a safety valve for Mexico's labor problem. However, the issue has never been entirely one-sided. U.S. farming and labor-intensive industries like the railroads have traditionally relied on this cheap labor force from Mexico.

Indeed, though the current U.S. administration views the illegal immigration a crisis situation, the reality is that former U.S. policy is greatly responsible for the three million "illegal" border crossings that occur each year. At one time, the migration north from Mexico was legalized under the name of the "*bracero* program" which was begun in 1942 primarily for the purpose of providing cheap labor in agriculture and railroad work during the war years when the U.S. was experiencing a labor shortage.

The program proved so popular with U.S. agricultural interests that it was extended by Congress until 1964 when the pressure of the civil rights movement and the organization efforts of the CSO and United Farm Workers Union caused Congress to end it. It is difficult now for the Mexican government and the so called "wetback" to understand the supposed change in U.S. policy when in reality it is clear that U.S. business interests continue to provide work for the estimated 8 million to 12 million "illegals" who are currently employed in this country. Nearly 80 percent of these illegals are employed in metropolitan areas where they compete for low-paying jobs with Blacks and other Latinos as busboys, dishwashers, janitors, maids, cooks, hod-carriers and the like.

It is this competition for employment, especially among their American cousins, the Chicanos, that has produced the greatest dilemma for the U.S. Last year President Carter failed to get a law passed by Congress that would impose strict monetary penalties on any employer knowingly employing illegals. Also included as part of the plan was a form of modified amnesty for illegals who could prove that they had been in the country for a certain number of years. The plan was immediately criticized by all sides. U.S. Chicanos felt that it would be a discriminatory law subjecting brown-skinned U.S. citizens to harassment by government officials. The business community as well was opposed to the plan feeling that it would be subjected to raids and harassment by Federal officials.

It is evident that the U.S. and Mexico must resolve some very sticky problems in the coming months. Carter's handling of the issues of oil and immigration will become even more important as he nears the primary election period. The Latino community is rapidly emerging as the largest minority group in the country and it is clear that both Ted Kennedy and Jerry Brown have an inside track with this group in their presidential bids.

Despite the fact that certain animosities do exist, especially over the oil and immigration issues, the U.S. and Mexico have intertwined destinies. Besides sharing more than a thousand miles of common border, their history has always been linked; whether it was General Winfield Scott marching into Mexico City or Pancho Villa raiding the border town of Columbus, New Mexico, in both war and peace the two countries have shared history and geography.

While the U.S. is in desperate need of Mexican oil, it also reaps a great deal of profit from its trade with its southern neighbor. Over 63 percent of all goods imported into Mexico come from the United States. Mexico, for its part, depends heavily on the U.S. dollars that currently flow into Mexico, through tourism, the purchase of winter farm crops, and the $2 billion that enter annually with returning workers.

These three economic elements alone constitute over 50 percent of Mexico's gross national product. Even a cooling of the tourist trade from the U.S., such as occurred during the presidency of Luis Echeverría as a result of Mexico's 1975 anti-Israeli vote in the United Nations, could prove disastrous for the country. The impact was so severe on that occasion, since tourism is one of the country's leading industries (second to agriculture), that Mexico had to devalue the peso for the first time in 22 years, partly as an inducement to potential U.S. visitors.

There is no doubt that oil, immigration, tourism, and trade constitute the huge ball that Presidents Carter and López Portillo must attempt to roll in the same direction if the U.S. is to maintain cordial relationship with its nearest neighbor.

Fortress Europe?
Or a Challenge to America?

Speech to Kiwanis of Kern County, **May 1990**

News Item;

"Four decades ago, the United States accounted for some 40 percent of World Trade Production. Today, for only 23 percent . . . US share of monetary reserves dropped even more dramatically, from 50 percent to 9 percent during this period.

News Item;

"Foreign investors accounted for half of American patents last year, compared with one-third a decade earlier."

News Item;

"American science students ranked 14th out of 17 countries surveyed in 1988. One-fifth of America's engineers are foreign born. A quarter of high school students drop out."

News Item;

"Research and development in the US has been at 1.8 of GNP for two decades, while it has increased to 2.8 and 2.6 percent in Germany and Japan respectively . . ."

If these figures and comments were not enough to make us choke on our imported truffles, we should also consider the recent trade skirmishes the US has been engaged in with our European Trading partners.

First, there was the Pasta war, then the Fats and Oils war. Most recently, during the last year, it has been the Hormones war. The US Government and the US Business sector are engaged in a growing, though undeclared, Trade-War with the twelve member nations of the European community, or EC for short. This European Super Common Market, headquartered in Brussels, Belgium, has been in existence for over three decades, and while many skeptics thought that countries as diverse as England and Greece could have little in common, the need to coalesce has become essential, as Europe, too, faces increased trading competition from Japan, China and the other Pacific rim countries, as well as from continued competition with the US.

A Little Background

Back in 1957, the Treaty of Rome envisaged the creation of a single, integrated market, free from restrictions on the movements of goods, services, capital and people, the removal of distortions to competition; a common policy on transportation; agreement on laws affecting industrial activity; and the harmonization of indirect taxes.

All of this was to be accomplished in 12 years—i.e. by 1969. In fact, after rapid progress in establishing a customs union, and some progress on indirect taxes, the effort lost momentum somewhere in the mid-1970s without even beginning to address most of the requirements. The slowness of progress during this period could perhaps be attributed to the poor economic environment during the last decade.

The Process finally got back on track at the Copenhagen Summit in 1982, when the EC leaders pledged themselves to completion of the internal market as a high priority.

This led to the 1985 publication of the Commission "White paper on completing the internal market," a truly remarkable document laying out a time table for the adoption of some 300 directives by 1992, with individual target dates for approval by the Commission.

The program received a further boost in July of 1987 with the enactment of the "Single Europe Act" which allowed for a simple majority vote among the 12 members—rather than requiring unanimity. The Act also enhanced the role of the European Parliament, leading to further European unity.

As these twelve member nations of Germany, France, Italy, the UK, Spain, Belgium, Greece, the Netherlands, Portugal, Denmark, Ireland, and Luxembourg ride toward a true common market of some 350 million people by 1992, the rest of the trading world is watching with bated breath and some degree of anxiety.

Just what will this common Market mean? To some degree it will result in the dropping of barriers, which will, in some instances, make trade among the twelve less cumbersome than our own inter-state commerce.

Three Broad Categories are:

1). Removal of physical barriers, i.e. all those that give rise to border controls (vehicle safety checks, veterinary and photo sanitary controls, police checks, etc.);

2). Removal of technical barriers, i.e. industrial product standards, public procurement—practices, restrictions of capital movements, and the absence of a common legal framework for industrial activity which have made it difficult for companies to work together across national frontiers; and . . .

3). The removal of fiscal barriers, i.e. differences in value added taxes and excise taxes which tend to distort trade along frontiers.

These three areas, especially the directives removing the technical barriers encompass many of the issues of interest to American exporters and investors.

The issues now are just how far will the EC go in becoming a stronger competitor in World Trade in the next decade and the 21st century?

Clearly the EC is not just aimed at dropping internal trade barriers on traditional industrial sectors, but more importantly on new areas such as science and technology, telecommunications, banking and financing, insurance, transportation and informatics.

What does all of this mean to non-European countries? The answers will not really be available until well after 1992, but in the meantime, there is a growing concern over the development of 'Fortress Europe'.

And how does this affect the state of California, which is the 7th largest trading country in the world, producing 25% of this nation's agricultural export and leading the nation in Hi-Tech production and export?

Example

The Beef Hormone War and the Air Bus War are really just skirmishes in a long war that will eventually result in a new world trade order. Over the years the idea of free trade economies were accepted as good for everyone, but in fact only benefited primarily the stronger economic powers. In the 19th century that was Great Britain. After WWII it became the United States. London based economist Bernard Nossiter writes, "The United States deliberately built up the economies of defeated enemies and prostrate allies (so as to make them purchasers of American goods). By 1971, it had lost dominance, so along with the industrial nations, it has abandoned free trade for a mixed economy, substantially protectionist."

Nissiter goes on to point out that U.S. military interests are a crucial component of this newly developing economic order.

While in the past, Washington accepted EC trade discrimination for the sake of unity to the NATO Alliance, this has ended. "The West Germans and Japanese used to hold onto declining unwanted US dollars as a disguised payment for American defense, but no more."

As the face and physiology of Europe are changing, as Gorbachev's Glastnost and Perestroika begin having more and more appeal in Europe, and West German political and military figures begin to call for the removal of foreign—mainly US troops—from their soil, all of Europe, except Margaret Thatcher, calls for immediate nuclear arms reduction. There does not appear to be among the Europeans a great sense of sacrifice of jobs and profits for the sake of perpetuating the common defense that has existed since WWII.

The US will have to face the 1990s and the next century essentially on it's own. Whether there is really a Fortress Europe and a bamboo fortress, one thing is certain; the US has lost it's competitive edge. No other country has done so much for so many in so short a time—with the Marshall Plan, we essentially rebuilt the world after the last World War. Now we are suffering because of our own goodness. I would not undo the unselfishness of our effort, nor the inherent kindness of the American people, but I believe it is time for Americans to exhibit that pioneering spirit which has made this country great.

I could talk about the fact that we have allowed ourselves to be outsold in World Markets . . . That the quality of many of our goods has been mediocre . . . That we have failed to build a greater capacity for expanding export markets . . . That we have made it easy for our internal market to be penetrated from abroad . . . That we have been too slow with the research and development . . . But you know all of this.

What we need is a change in attitude, our attitude. Certainly we don't need Teddy Roosevelt's big stick, but we do need some kind of leverage.

We are still the richest market in the World. There are more of us, buying more of everything, every day, than there are in all of Europe and the Far East. We must understand that they need us more than we need them, but we must not forget that we need each other. We must be tough negotiators, tough traders, tough speculators. And above all, we must be firm in our conviction that we are still the greatest nation in the world and we must recapture those qualities which created this greatness . . . "Resourcefulness . . . Commitment . . . Industry . . . and Fair Play."

The Bureaucratic System Gets Pat On Its Red Tape

The Sacramento Bee, **March 6, 1977**

T his year, more than ever before, we saw presidential candidates running against it; we saw legislative candidates running against it; we saw local government candidates running against it. This tyrant of the political scene and the object of much campaign rhetoric can be summed up in one word—*bureaucracy*. While one candidate assailed the "uncontrollable growth of bureaucracy," another complained we have "too much government" or that we can't afford "all the freeloaders on the government payroll."

Now that the fury and fire of campaign rhetoric has cooled, it might be appropriate to come to the defense of the "American bureaucratic system." We might begin by pointing out some of the characteristics bureaucrats can honestly proclaim have saved this country from political instability, military coups, and revolutions, and allowed the country to set an example to the world of a somewhat stable polity. We have survived 200 years as a country, at times a bit tarnished, at times a bit embarrassed, but nonetheless still a standard of the democratic process for the world.

Why was this country able to move forward in the midst of a world war upon the death of President Franklin Roosevelt? Why was the country able to move forward in an orderly fashion immediately after the assassination of President Kennedy? Why did government continue to function after the fall in disgrace of both President Nixon and Vice President Agnew?

The answer to these questions may surprise many: This country, more than any other in the world, has established a very competent, albeit at times slow, bureaucratic system which has resulted in our two centuries of political stability.

Martin C. Needler in his book, *Instability, Violence and Evolutionary Change,* has suggested that a system of government is stable when it reflects the informal distribution of power, when it gratifies the needs of those subject to it, and when its ideological and political bases are accepted by those governed. In simple terms, stability exists when those governed have a part in running government, when their social and economic needs are met, and when they accept the method by which those in the leadership roles have come to power.

In contrast to most of the developing nations of the world, these three elements exist in the United States. Power is distributed among the various branches of government. The government attempts to meet the needs of the citizenry and, finally, leaders are generally elected or appointed in an established and accepted orderly process. In each of these instances the bureaucracy plays a critical role.

Why is there so much political instability in Latin America or the Middle East or Africa? Perhaps the most obvious, yet often neglected, answer is that there is no established bureaucratic class in these regions of the world.

John J. Johnson states that political instability, military coups, and revolutions occur frequently in Latin America because of the "low bureaucratic professionalization." Johnson points out that basically there is no permanent class of bureaucrats to keep a country functioning after a military coup has occurred, or a president has been ousted, or the leader of the country suddenly assumes a dictatorial role.

In developing nations in Latin America and other parts of the world, after the political shock of change has occurred, whether militarily or peacefully, the existing bureaucratic class is effectively eliminated. From cabinet minister to local police chief, the friends, relatives and associates of the new regime assume the roles in the bureaucracy. This patronage system flows to the lowest levels and in the case of military *juntas,* which assume power, the bureaucratic class often is made up of officers and sergeants now entrusted with keeping the railroads running and the sewage plants functioning.

Because of this often-occurring factor of substitution of bureaucratic class, government cannot possibly provide the three elements Needler points out are essential to political stability. In the absence of a well-defined and long-established bureaucracy, a "patronage bureaucratic system" cannot reflect an even distribution of power, it cannot see to it that the social and economic needs of its citizens are met, nor is it likely to be an acceptable governmental structure to the citizens. Consequently, the developing nations of the world, many of which have been in the developmental stage for several hundred years, are constantly plagued with military coups, civil wars, and illegal assumptions of power.

The United States has had only one constitution in its 200-year history while some countries have had as many as 35 in the same period. Additionally, the United

States, despite a civil war and any number of political scandals, has continued to function with relatively few major changes to its political structure.

All this does not mean that the creation of a large bureaucratic class with a formalized merit civil-service structure is without fault. In a classic article on *Bureaucracy and Social Change*, Stanford University professor Seymour Martin Lipset points out "there is no simple solution to the dilemma of keeping government administration efficient as well as responsive to the will of the electorate." He reflects the same basic theme as recent political candidates when he comments, "The increase in the power, functions, and sheer size of modern government necessitates the search for some means of controlling the bureaucracy."

The real political and social dilemma the State of California faces, as does the entire nation, is to control bureaucracy at the same time the citizenry is demanding more . . . . social services. In terms of political scientist Needler, this constitutes "government's attempt to gratify the needs of those subject to it."

Public opinion polls and various surveys indicate a majority demand for national health insurance, more governmental support to local schools, increased child-care services, and aide to the aged. Yet those same surveys indicate a criticism of bureaucracy—too much red tape, too slow to act, too wasteful. The citizenry itself is in a quandary. It desires the benevolence of a great provider and the simplicity of a TV dinner.

The answer, perhaps, may be in the approach by California's Gov. Jerry Brown and promised by President Carter, a combination of social liberalism and fiscal conservatism. It seeks to eliminate the waste of the "great society" social programs. The concept would retain the humanistic commitment at the same time it seeks to employ the fiscal frugality of the old-standard Protestant ethic. It attempts to infuse the humanistic qualities exemplified during the few years of the Kennedy administration while also recognizing revenue limits. The State of California now employs approximately 201,000 civil servants; the federal government, including the military, employs, 2,750,000. For California, civil servants constitute only 8.7 per cent of the total population. Consequently, the burden of providing services such as health care, highway construction, employment services and the like to the other 91 per cent falls upon a relatively small minority.

The real challenge facing both politicians and bureaucrat alike, is to eliminate bureaucratic resistance to those humanistic social changes that are both promised by candidates and desired by the people. As Lipset has pointed out, the bureaucracy itself *does* play a significant role in determining policy. The goals of civil service are often seen as self preservation rather than maximum efficiency or concern. Social reform, which may be generally desired by the population but that disrupts the established practice of a given agency at the same time, may be resisted by the management-level civil servant. The task of any new leadership is to institute progressive changes without ruffling too many bureaucratic feathers.

To expand and streamline the needed services desired by the population without grossly expanding the size and cost of government is the test of the future. The job, perhaps, may indeed require a governor like Brown who meditates and a president like Carter who prays a lot.

The often-maligned "bureaucratic system," in spite of its cumbersomeness and complexity, generally serves us well. Additionally, it employs several million basically honest, hardworking American citizens who contribute daily to the well being of the entire population, in spite of the negative things we may say or write about them.

IV

Education Issues

Summary of Articles

T he final section of *Dissent* deals with several controversial issues in education such as affirmative action, English Only, and bilingual education. It is ironic that the piece on "Official English" that was carried by the Hispanic Link News Service in 1998 has become one of the contentious issues being debated by the Congress as they struggle to pass immigration legislation this year. Clearly, the article "Education Number One . . ." demonstrates to the Congress and the general public alike that Latino immigrants are just as anxious to become full participants in the American Way of Life as were those immigrants from Europe who came to our shores in other centuries. The fact that in California today a majority of children under the age of 18 are Latinos is clear evidence that the Latino community must assume a leadership role in promoting relevant and practical global education for its children and the other children of the state and nation.

The Growing Latino Community: Education Number One

Latino Vote, **July 1998**

Dramatic Demographic Change

P undits have referred to the Latinos over the years as "the sleeping giant" and "the invisible minority;" or by harsher critics as, "cholos, spicks and wetbacks," but today these terms have given way to references of a different nature, which connote the obvious change that is taking place in the Latino community. Obviously, one of the most dramatic changes has been the Latino impact on the demographics of the state as a result of increased immigration and a significantly higher birthrate. *The Sacramento Bee* recently noted that, "since the early 1980s, California has been on the receiving end of an immigrant wave that demographers have compared with two other historic spurts of migration to the United States: the great surge of famine-induced Irish migration in the late 19th century, and the subsequent arrival of southern and eastern Europeans—a diverse population of Jews, Italians, Lithuanians and more—from the turn of the century until the 1920s."

This third and present immigrant wave is coming, not from Europe like the other two, but from Pacific Rim countries, the Philippines, Southeast Asia, Central and South America, and especially Mexico. This wave began after the 1965 immigration law removed national quota restrictions, and opened the door to millions of immigrants of color from the Third World. Mexicans alone constituted 43 percent of the new immigrants to California with Central and South Americans becoming an ever-increasing percentage. More recently, during the 1980s, as a result of the 1986 Immigration Reform and Control Act, over 8.6 million immigrants arrived in the U.S. according to the U.S. Census Bureau. In California alone, as a result of the amnesty granted under the act, over 1.6 million illegal immigrants became eligible for permanent residency, in addition to several million legal arrivals.

Beyond just the sheer numbers of recent Latino immigrants, the nature of these immigrants to California is a significant factor. Many of these immigrants, in large numbers fled Central America during the 1980s, a time of great turmoil in that region. Guatemalans, Salvadorans, and Nicaraguans especially, fled countries where human rights and political rights violations were the governmental policy of the day. Today, these new immigrants tend to have a very healthy respect for the democratic process that was denied them in their countries of origin. They are hardworking, aggressive and more politicized than the millions of farm laborers that came before them during the 50s, 60s. and 70s. Many of these new immigrants choose to work in service areas rather than farm labor, and have joined unions such as SEIU (Service Employees International Union) and others that put a premium on political participation. With the possible exception of César Chávez' efforts with the United Farm Workers Union, most Latino immigrants, involved in farm labor in the past, tended to live on the margins of the political life of the country, not so with more recent arrivals.

Clearly the sheer growth in the Latino population of California since the early 80s has been dramatic. Today the Latino population in the state is approaching 12 million, a 48.8% increase in this last decade. In the next forty years in California this same population will experience a phenomenal growth rate, reaching 31.5 million. At the same time, the present white majority population will grow by only 19%, from 17.1 million to 20.5 million, and cease to be the majority by the year 2005, when minorities become the majority. Latinos will become the plurality in the state by the year 2020 and the majority by 2040. But sheer numbers are not the only changes taking place. Latinos are becoming active participants in the political life of the state. In California, the results have been particularly dramatic. From the general elections of 1994 to the general elections of 1996 the California Latino vote had increased from 9.6% to 13% of the electorate. At the end of the 80s Latinos had been less than 8% of the state's voters. The most recent 13% turn-out in the last statewide election of 1998 indicates that the Latino vote has increased by nearly 50% in less than a decade. These new voters tend to be those more politicized and active voters mentioned above, 26 percent of whom are new citizen, first-time voters.

In the April 1997 local elections in Los Angeles county, Latinos also demonstrated a high sense of civic-minded self-protection. Proposition BB, a school bond measure that sought to make available 2.5 billion dollars for repairs, construction and improvements in the L.A. Unified School District received its strongest support from Latinos. According to a Thomas Rivera Center exit poll, Latinos voted an amazing 91% in support of the school bond measure. Officials credit the Latino vote in providing the margin necessary for the success of the bond measure which was required constitutionally to pass by a difficult two-thirds vote margin. Latinos angry already about Propositions 187 and 209 appeared to be motivated by the fact that their children made up 68% of all students in LA Unified, the second largest school district in the nation. White children constitute only 11% in the school district, and the white vote in the county over the years had voted down school bonds on a regular basis. Latino leaders in the community noted after the April election that, "the strong turnout and the success in helping win passage of Proposition BB would have a dual effect, simultaneously demonstrating the growing clout of Latinos and expanding that clout as victory reinforces the idea that participation is meaningful." Particularly significant is that Latinos appear to be acutely aware of the importance of education for themselves and for their children.

The Significance of Education for Latinos

Most significant, however, is the youthfulness of the state's Latino population, which is twelve years younger on average than the white, non-Latino population. The projected school enrollment figures give an idea of just how large this youthful Latino population already is. In the potentially vote-rich San Joaquin Valley, Latinos have been the majority of the 18-years-and-under population since 1990. While statewide, Latinos became the majority of the 18-years-and-under population this year. The impact of these figures on education is tremendous. By the year 2005 Latinos will constitute 50% of all children enrolled in school K through 12 in the state, while the white population will be only 28%. High school graduation for Latinos is also expected to increase by 60% in these years.

It is in the education future of these children where the dreams, hopes and aspirations of Latinos for a more significant role in the political and civic life of their communities rests. But one cannot assume that the Latino vote will be a monolithic vote. As a group they have proven to be less liberal than the Black or Jewish voter, yet not as conservative as the white voter on a variety of issue. Overall, as a group, Latinos appear to have a moderate agenda with wavering Democratic Party loyalty. Assembly Speaker Antonio Villaraigosa suggests that, "the older Latinos will probably stay with the Democratic Party the rest of their lives, but with their children there is no guarantee. I would never argue that this Democratic vote will be for time immemorial."

Towards a Cause for Rebels in Education

Under Fire: Voices of Minority Males, Vol. II,
An Anthology, editors Jess G. Nieto & Patricia Rainey.,
Published by: Heritage of America Educational
& Cultural Foundation, 1993

Introduction:

> It is funny how things aren't like they used to be. It used to be that
> *LA LLORONA* was a ghost, a shadow, a cry one heard in the brush of
> the river . . . Now it's becoming more and more real, now it's a cop's
> siren. Now we can see it. We actually see it eating up the men of the
> barrio . . .
>
> **Rudolfo Anaya. HEART OF AZTLAN**

Income is tied to employment opportunity, which in turn is tied to educational opportunity. And if we accept the conclusions reached by most leading sociologists, anthropologists and even some criminologists, lack of adequate income and the loss of self esteem that often accompanies it, leads to criminal behavior among many. And even more significant conclusions can be reached as to who the perpetrators of this criminal behavior are.

Afro-Americans currently account for half of all arrests for assault and murder, and two-thirds of all arrests for robbery in the United States. They are responsible for half of all reported rapes. Twenty-five percent of black males have been incarcerated at one time or another. One in twenty-one black males will be killed this year, most likely by other black males. (1)

If we look at statistical data for Latino males in the Southwest, where most are located, the conclusions are similar. In California, Blacks and Latinos constitute 70 percent of the inmate population in the state's prisons, a population that is at 140,000 now and growing by 10,000 every year. Seventy percent of these minority inmates will return to prison for a second, third, or fourth stay. (2)

Some authorities have concluded that the Los Angeles Riots of 1992, the largest civil disturbance in the nation's history, was the result of thousands of "criminal types," primarily African Americans and Latinos, exploding in a frenzy of violence. This explosion, some say, was the result of poverty and joblessness created by the failure of an education system that no longer educates and an economic system that no longer produces jobs at a level to sustain the population.

The educational establishment of teachers, administrators, and school boards responds that it is being asked to solve societal problems caused by 200 years of racial polarization, unequal educational opportunities, and the deluge of new immigrants into this country. This old educational establishment, run primarily by white males, based on a long-gone agrarian society and blind to the predictions of the research found in the report by the Hudson Institute, "Workforce 2000" (3) is clearly failing. But the educational system is not alone in its failure; governmental agencies and the once infallible American business sector are also in disarray.

To avoid chaos in our society—in education, in government and in the business sector—radical change is needed. This change must begin at the earliest levels of education and reach to graduate schools and corporate headquarters. This change can be led by a growing cadre of minority educators who must shed the "wimp" image that many have assumed over the years, as they have settled into comfortable positions of authority, seduced by promotions, large salaries, and suburban assignments.

Hispanic, Afro-American and Asian educators, themselves, must take bold steps in challenging the old guard of education—teacher unions, administrative organizations and school boards. Some of the "sacred cows" of education must also be led to the slaughter. The new educational establishment must propose that the old school calendar, based on the agrarian society of the 1800s be thrown out. They must question whether "local control" really means local surrender. They must challenge some of those "terms and conditions of employment" that unions hold sacred, but which may work against the real educational needs of children. They should challenge the concepts of tenure, sabbatical leaves, and 10-hour work-weeks for university professors. They should question whether research at public universities, which is not population-centered, is really a proper expenditure of tax-payers' money or might just be a subsidy to big business. The new educators must challenge the hundred thousand dollar salaries of school administrators and the under-the-table deals made by trustees and chancellors to benefit favored administrators.

The fact is that, for the most part, education in many of our inner cities is a failure. Our inner city schools are the "killing fields" in our own country, not some third world country across the sea. There were 75,609 assaults on school grounds in California last year. Over 10,000 weapons were confiscated in the state. Thirty individuals were killed on school grounds in the U.S. in 1992. (4) It is easier to buy drugs on our public school grounds than in Bogotá, Columbia. We cannot simply change the present system of public school education; we must eliminate it. And in its place, build a new system equipped to deal with the realities of the 21st Century. Those advocates of the voucher system have already concluded that they do not even want to try to fix the public school system. What they advocate is another extreme that is not based on a concept of public education, but on the privatization of the educational process. This would create even more disparity in the education of our children.

THE SETTING—OUR CHILDREN'S KILLING FIELDS

The inadequacy of the present education system with respect to certain Afro-American and Latino males is not limited to inner city schools alone, nor is it only an issue of violence on the school grounds. Rural areas, which must deal with the constant stream of migrant children, are faced with a different set of problems, but the results are often the same. The Delano Joint Union High School District, located in California's Central Valley, had a dropout rate of 42.5 percent in 1990. The District is well over 60 percent Latino. Likewise, the urban Los Angeles School District, which is more than 86 percent students of color, had a dropout rate of 52 percent for Blacks and 43.6 percent of Latinos in 1990. (5)

But statistics alone do not tell the real story of what is happening or not happening in those schools attended by a majority of minority children. Educator Kenneth Clark has noted that "ghetto/barrio schools regularly succeed in lowering the IQ's and intellectual curiosity of their pupils." (6) They do so because many of the children who pass through their doors enter already intellectually handicapped as a result of poverty, violence and neglect in the home and in the neighborhood environment.

A kind of reverse Darwinism is at work in our inner cities. It is no longer a question of "white flight" from the inner cities. Those minority members who can escape the inner city do as well. They cannot remain there. They will not survive. Instead, the survivors in the inner cities tend to be the lowest of the low, the sickest, the most needy. Some of these inhabitants of the inner cities also become the most violent. The "fittest" do not survive in the ghetto/barrio. The fittest generally survive only by escaping, by fleeing to suburbia, following behind the whites European ethnics who fled a generation ago.

Now those "colored ethnics" who have moved to suburbia have many of the same middle class values as their white neighbors do . . . home mortgagees, kids in college, retirement plans and RVs. Their flight is a flight for survival, like the unsuspecting bird that walks along a tropical riverbank, suddenly takes flight as a crocodile lunges towards it. The new class of minorities in the suburbs have less in common with the inner city minorities than they do with their White neighbors. They are, at times, even embarrassed by the behavior of the urban poor who seem to speak another language (Ebonics) and possess very different behavior patterns.

What is often left in the inner cities is a mass of sick ones, the socially disabled. A few old-timers cling to the neighborhood, mostly because there is no place else they can afford to move to. But the reality is that the inner cities are now dominated by the most incapable, the least likely to succeed. Certainly there are exceptions, especially among arriving immigrants who have not yet been totally damaged by the despair of welfareism and poverty. The emerging gang warfare does suggest, however, that they are well on their way. The politicians who represent the inner city dwellers do no really live among them. The human ecosystem of the ghetto/barrio is dominated, not by the fittest, but by the most incapable in the broadest sense. This reverse Darwinism allows this species to use its survival skills on the mean streets and killer byways of the cities, but not in the greater, outside world. They become predators upon their own.

"The enormous concentration of poor children at the bottom of society's ladder is a depressing dynamic fact." (7) In 1992, twenty-five percent, one in four children in California, lived in poverty. (8) It is made all the worse by the incredible inferiority of public education in the slums, where so many children are unfit for anything but marginal working lives at best as demonstrated by the high drop out rate and low test scores.

Today, poverty is vicious. In its viciousness it leads to violence and a myriad of other social problems. The poverty of the Great Depression was benign, even hopeful by comparison. The farm boys came out to the city seeking their fortunes. The European immigrants arrived in staggering numbers. The New Deal was really new and it was really a deal. There was an "insatiable need for unskilled and semi-skilled workers." There were even jobs for grade-school dropouts, those who were illiterate, and foreign-language-speaking immigrants from the old countries. In the West, Mexicans and Filipinos arrived to replace the Okies who left the farm fields for the oil fields and defense plants with the arrival of WWII. (9)

In the Thirties militant poverty played a role in a climactic moment in American social history. Millions of poor participated in the organization of unions, particularly those of the CIO, and the political struggle for the New Deal. They and their ethnic drive and community hopes, became an important constituent of a new political coalition which translated the dreams of the liberal reformers and socialists into law—the Wagner Act, Social Security, minimum wage and the like.(10)

In those exciting days it was a question of "militant poverty" which made an impact on our American way of life. The millions of poor organized, worked together, had mutual causes. Their diverse ethnic backgrounds had one common interest, a desire for a better tomorrow for themselves and for their children. Their "robust" enthusiasm took the form of constructive political activism. There was a sense of neighborhood, of belonging and looking out for one another. Doors were left open so the milkman could put the milk in the icebox if you were not home. Above all, there was a sense of great optimism.

Today's poor have no such optimism. Some might argue that this is because today's poor, in the inner cities, tend to be people of color, but that begs the question. They have moved into the same neighborhoods that were previously inhabited by Poles, Jews, Italians and Irish. The difference is not simply a matter of color, the difference is that we are another country today. Our economic system is bankrupt. Technology is replacing manufacturing. Those same jobs that were in industry before, in the steel plants and assembly lines that could be occupied by non-English speaking Italians and Poles are no longer available for today's immigrants in the same numbers. Today, the semi-skilled or non-skilled may find work at a car wash or a melon field, but certainly not at a high-teck firm or at an aerospace company.

Instead of the "dynamic poverty" of the Depression years, we have the modern term—the culture of poverty. This theory of poverty holds that joblessness creates slum conditions, which cause despair. This in turn leads to "high rates of disorder, indulgence, family instability, dependence on public assistance and abuse of drugs and alcohol." The Black and Latino males in the cities complete the circle of poverty as "rootless men seeking short term gains in crime and often marginal activities," often leaving behind fatherless families, unable to socialize the next generation. This further impoverishes the slums and makes them ready to burst into flames with the slightest provocation, reaffirming a destructive impulsiveness, thus, the L.A. Riots of 1992. (11)

These inner city poor males are characterized by "economic underachievement," so dramatic that it is a source of great depression and anger among these males. It is often a mirror of their lives. This was seen during the riots when Black and Latino males took out their frustration on the Korean, Arab, and Pakistani merchants who had moved in to replace the culturally familiar "mom and pop" proprietors in the old neighborhood businesses. This alien entrepreneurship in the old neighborhood was another manifestation of Black/Latino male feelings of inadequacy, even if they were not aware of it.

Thus, Jack Newfield and Jeff Greenfield in their *POPULIST MANIFESTO* that signaled the full-fledged arrival of our new poverty in the 60s could write:

> We share the belief that the fundamental sources of crime are rooted in the pathology of poverty: jobless, purposeless men and women, broken families, a school system that does not educate, and the consequent epidemic of alcoholism and drug addiction. "The slums of the great cities are the breeding grounds of crime." Anatole France said, and that view is still sound . . . (12)

The outside world's response to these inner city problems were the government's Great Society, the War on Poverty, Vista, the Job Corps. But except for the professionalizing of a handful of Sixties militants, these programs were a colossal failure, if measured by existing conditions. The slums are bleaker, the crime rate is higher, families are in greater crisis, and children are in graver danger of suffering spiritually what the children of Somalia suffer physically.

At this point, everyone, even those outside of the ghetto/barrio, seems to have given up. The business sector has pulled out. Supermarkets, chain stores, and banks have long since fled the neighborhoods. Government agencies do not speak of gains or progress, only of containment. The Los Angeles Police Department admits that it has lost the war on drugs and gangs. The best that can be done is to contain them, paint over their graffiti, keep them inside of the ghetto/barrio, and even this may not be possible for much longer. And amidst all of this, schools are supposed to teach. Society is expected to provide a meaningful educational foundation for the children of the socially undernourished and disabled so that these children can become worthwhile members of society. Instead they become the reflections of many of their parents.

EDUCATING THE UNDERNOURISHED

Because the problem is so grave and our failure so complete, the education system in the inner city cannot be fixed. No simple Band-Aid solutions will do. The large Los Angeles school district is contemplating breaking itself up into seven smaller districts to attempt to solve its tremendous problem. The school voucher gang runs around the state of California dangling a promise of $2,600 for every child so that parents can select the schools of their choice, including sectarian schools.

While the deplorable condition of cities is one major factor in the failure of our schools, it is by no means the only cause. The education establishment is also responsible to a large degree. The unionization of the teaching profession has resulted in making the occupation more a trade than a profession. The fight for "wages and terms and conditions of employment" has led the teacher organizations down a path that is fraught with danger and may be one reason the voucher advocates have arisen. The unionization of teachers is in contrast to the national trends where union membership in the labor force has dropped to an all-time low of 17%.

The taxpaying public is uncomfortable with some of the new trends of education. The issue of teacher strikes, for example, does not have the interests of students and parents at heart, despite what teacher unions might say.

A strike in the private sector is an economic weapon against the employer: the strike causes economic losses as the employer's production sales drop. In the public sector, however, a strike does not have a financially detrimental effect on the government employer. In the public sector, therefore, a strike is not an economic weapon. It is aimed not at the employer but at the public . . . the public employee strike must necessarily harm the public in some way in order to reach its goal of influencing the government employer. In public school strikes, this harm comes from withholding education from students. Such strikes result in depriving children, most of whom do not have the economic means to seek an education elsewhere, of their fundamental interest in receiving education and should not be recognized as a legitimate bargaining tactic. (13)

Some activities of teacher unions, as well, do not seem to support the interest of many minority or inner-city students. Faced with declining enrollments among Anglo students (just the opposite of what is happening with Latinos and Asians), teacher unions and school administrators have sought to retain teacher positions for less needed monolingual teachers when the need for bilingual teachers is critical in many areas. The result is that policies of a labor relations nature has been more of a factor in the controversy over bilingual and migrant education than teacher unions wish to admit. Questions of tenure and retention may have become more important to unions than are the basic educational needs of children, at least to the organization, if not to the individual teacher. The unions are faced with the same problems industrial unions had to face when technology and specialization began to impact on older, obsolete union members such as boilermakers and firemen on the railroad trains.

Many other issues at the school site, the hours of operation, the length of the school year, the credentialing requirements, textbook selection, all of these matters have developed over a century of time. Perhaps they must all be re-examined. Is the concept of tenure, (job security regardless of performance), perhaps something that our society can no longer afford? We have chosen term limits for our politicians, should our teachers be next? Are sabbatical leaves something that our society can still afford to pay for? Why do children attend school for only 175 days of the year? Why are they let off for three months in the summer and three weeks for Christmas and Easter? Japanese children go to school for 240 days a year. Is this agrarian calendar something that our society can still support at a time when only two percent of the population is employed in farm work? Why are students sent home as early as 2:30 in the afternoon? Would it not make more sense to keep them in school for some type of creative play rather than to send them out to the mean streets of the inner cities before their parents have returned home? Many of these questions will not likely receive a favorable response from teacher groups, school administrators and some parents, but an alternative to the voucher system can only be devised if we take drastic action now to improve the public school system. Educators should accept the fact that there is a growing perception among tax payers that they are not getting their money's worth in public education from kindergarten to university.

At our universities, college professors teach two classes a quarter. That amounts to less than 12 hours a week in the classroom. The rest of us have gotten used to a forty-hour work-week. We spend millions of dollars at these universities funding teacher-credentialing programs without any assurances that teaching credentials have any real meaning in the classroom. Catholic high schools, for example, do not require credentials for their teachers, yet they consistently produce a much higher percentage of college eligible students, well over ninety-percent in most instances, (14) even if these schools can be more selective in the students they enroll, there is no proof that the lack of a credential hinders their teaching.

As previously mentioned, the needs and interest of minority children in the inner cities and rural migrant population schools may be at odds with the professional education establishment and other government entities. Dan Lungren, the Attorney General of California, for example, proposes to solve the problem in our schools by taking a law and order approach. He put forth a program of "information, prevention, deterrence and punishment." He believes that, "a policy maker at the state and local level needs accurate and timely information about the scope of the problem . . . . We can prevent school violence, in part by instructing our teachers in true principles of school safety . . . Weapons, such as guns and knives, have no place in our schools . . . Tough new laws to implement drug-free, gang-free, and gun-free zones was going to deter homicides, which have gone up every year since the death penalty was enacted, around our schools will underscore our zero tolerance message, to those who would use school areas for criminal activity."(15) The Attorney General's plan is as naive as the notion that the death penalty was going to deter homicides.

The fact is that the loudest advocates of "law and order" often promote the very policies that increase crime rates. They pass laws that affect the dispossessed, the very class of people that bears the brunt of muggings, rapes, purse snatchings, burglaries, and murders. (16) Politicians raise the hysteria level by taking political cheap shots and grandstanding on the issue of proposing punishment rather than diagnosis and cure. One law enforcement official responding to the Attorney General's approach noted, "It's a war zone in those neighborhoods. You can't send our kids anywhere in there. Gangs hold the community hostage. There are no laws that will fix those kinds of social problems." (17)

REAL SOLUTIONS—HARD CHOICES

The needs in education are astronomical. There is not merely a need to radically change the delivery system in the ghetto/barrio schools. The entire system needs a radical change. If we are to heed the warning of the *Workforce 2000* report, we must improve the educational preparation of all workers. "As the economy grows more complex and more dependent on human capital, the standard set by the American education systems must be raised." (18) Speaking specifically to the needs of Blacks and Hispanics, the report states:

> The shrinking numbers of young people, the rapid pace of industrial change, and the ever-rising skill requirements of the emerging economy make the task of fully utilizing minority workers particularly urgent between now and 2000. Both cultural changes and education training investments will be needed to create real equal employment opportunity . . . . Education and training are the primary system by which the human capital of a nation is preserved and increased . . . . Without substantial adjustments, Blacks and Hispanics will have a smaller fraction of the jobs in the year 2000 than they have today, while their share of those seeking work will have risen. (19)

Given the tremendous task ahead, of noting the continuing growth requirements in California, where the state must build thirteen new classrooms everyday to keep up with the growing population, and noting that half of those classrooms will have to be for bilingual instruction, the task seems almost overwhelming. The following are some approaches that should be considered if we are to put an end to the decline and hopelessness encountered in the ghettos/barrios of our country and exported to the rest of America. Many of these suggestions might have some value for the population at large as well:

    *   An especially trained teacher corps must be nationalized for duty in the inner cities where ordinary teachers, despite their good intentions, have neither the skills, nor the temperament to deal with many extreme educational and social problems.
    *   The old concepts of teacher tenure must be reviewed. In almost no other profession is an individual guaranteed employment for life. The notion of keeping

one's job in perpetuity except for criminal violations, often results in teachers becoming complacent and lacking in new ideas and needed energy.

* The present nine-month school calendar should be reconsidered. A forty-hour work week is reasonable in most occupations, especially where manual labor is not required. Modern technology, computer based testing, educational video programs, and the like, greatly reduce the need for teachers to "be on" at all times. The notion that teachers need the summer off is as outdated as the notion that children also need the summer off. Farm crops are now harvested by machines, more than they are harvested by school children as they were in the last century when the nine-month school calendar was initiated. While teachers may have to keep abreast of developments in their disciplines, their need is no greater than a physician or an engineer who is required to brush up on their own time, not on taxpayer supported three month vacations.

* The present generation of junior high and high school students in the ghetto/barrio may already be lost to some degree. Some children should be voluntarily placed in "educational protective custody," and with consent of parents, be placed in high-powered environmentally rich boarding schools.

* Teacher credentialing may be more of a hindrance than a help. Teacher training institutions may not be preparing teachers for realistic teaching. The university education bureaucracy appears to have created the teacher training industry with little proof that children benefit. By tying salary schedules to the number of post degree units taken, the education credentialing institutions perpetuate themselves and may have little effect on the quality of learning.

* State college and university systems are insulated systems, steadily loosing touch with the real world. Academic senates and employee organizations have lost sight of their mission. The notion of "publish of perish" is detrimental to real teaching in the long run. In the short run, it is costly. Research of a non-educational nature should be left to the private sector. Sabbatical leaves with pay, released time for campus politics and research, excessively light loads and tenure are great benefits for university teachers, but have little educational value to the students who attend the institutions. Instead, these sacred cows of academia end up prolonging the time that it will take a student to graduate.

* *Workforce 2000* recommendations should be like a biblical manual for public institutions for the rest of this century: "Education and training are the primary systems by which the human capital of a nation is preserved and increased. The speed and efficiency with which these education systems transmit knowledge governs the rate at which human capital can be developed . . . ."

* If we are to avoid a voucher system that is aimed at the throat of public education, we, as educators, must heal ourselves. We must completely sever that which is dead and useless and replace it with new life in the form of innovative, bold, iconoclastic programs.

Again, "these are the times that try men's souls." As we prepare for the next century, we must leave behind a system of education that served us for the last two hundred years, but has now outlived its viability. Just as Horace Mann blazed the educational trail that we have been following for so many years, we must now set a new course, one that is driven by the needs of the technological world we are now exploring. The old tree of learning is dead, but from its roots a new tree of Knowledge that will shelter future generations must grow.

ENDNOTES

1. Several of its major findings included: The U.S. workforce will grow slowly1. Levin, Michael. "Implications of Race and Sex Differences of Compensatory Affirmative Action and the Concept of Discrimination." JOURNAL OF SOCIAL, POLITICAL, AND ECONOMIC STUDIES. Vol. 15, No. 2. Summer 1990, p.207

2. Huber, Walt. STATE AND LOCAL GOVERNMENT IN CRISIS, COVINA CA. Education Text Book Co. 1992, p.218

3. Johnston, William B. Project Director, WORKFORCE 2000. Hudson Institute, Indianapolis, Indiana. 1987. The Hudson Institute, a private non-profit research center, published in 1987 one of the most convincing studies of what the United States must do in order to remain competitive in the world in the 21st Century., becoming older, more female, and more disadvantaged and; the new jobs in the Service industries will demand higher skill levels than the jobs of today. Both of these items will have serious implications for how our educational institutions educate the previously undereducated minority groups.

4. Merl. Jean. "Progress Seen in Dropout Rate." LOS ANGELES TIMES. (May 29, 1991). p. 3 Metro Section.

5. Martinez, Lionel. "Cultural Differences Affect Latinos in the Classroom." (THE BAKERSFIELD CALIFORNIAN)

6. Harrington, Michael. TOWARDS A DEMOCRATIC LEFT. Baltimore: Penguin Books, 1969. p. 58

7. Ibid

8. Huber, op. cit. p. 4

9. Harrington, op. cit. p. 60

10. Ibid

11. Levin, op. cit. p. 208

12. Newfeld, Jack and Greenfield, Jeff. A POPULIST MANIFESTO. New York: Warner Publications. 1972, p. 142

13. Gonzales, Raymond J. "Sand Diego Teacher's Association v. The Superior Court for the County of San Diego." Before the California Supreme Court L>S. No. 30977. Nov.1, 1977. Gonzales as a member of the Public Employment Relations Board for the mentioned case. The cite is taken from page 9.

14. Celis, William. "Colleges Battle Culture and Poverty to Swell Hispanic Enrollments." NEW YORK TIMES (February 24, 1993), p.17

15. Lungren, Dan. News release from the Attorney General's Office relative to his plan to combat the increase of violence in California schools. April 26, 1993. Sacramento, California. Reports were carried in major newspapers such as the Los Angeles Times, Sacramento Bee, and the Bakersfield Californian.

16. Newfeld and Greenfield. op. cit. p. 139

17. Henry, Lois "Violence on the School Ground." THE BAKERSFIELD CALIFORNIAN. (April 26, 1993) p.1 local section.

18. Workforce 2000, p. XIV

19. Ibid., 114-115.

Pouring $6 Billion Down the Drain?

The Sacramento Bee, **March 7, 1975**

The average reading level in Los Angeles County is the eighth grade; 51 percent of all students entering the University of California are required to take "bonehead" English; more than 480 teachers in one school district were assaulted by students last year; more than 50 percent of all Chicano students in California never graduate from high school; over 31 school districts in California had teacher strikes in the last two years.

What does all this mean? Are these significant statements? Do they reflect the perilous situation of public-school education in the state or have these conditions always existed? Better yet, should we expect these conditions to always exist?

There is perhaps no better barometer than society itself to gauge the effectiveness or ineffectiveness of our school system. If the juvenile crime rate is up, if drugs among youth run rampant, if the job market is flooded with unskilled semiliterate high-school graduates, if test scores continue to plummet, we might assume that the $6-billion a year that we California taxpayers are paying for education is money down the drain.

There are some very vital questions that education professionals, politicians and parents must begin to face if we are to avoid the total collapse of public-school education in California in the last quarter of this century. The courts have already told us that we must restructure our funding system (Serrano vs. Priest) and that we must integrate our school systems (Gitelson Decision), and that we must offer equal educational opportunities. More significantly, test scores tell us that in the basic skills such as reading, math and language arts, our children seem to be going backward. As an example, college entrance exam scores for California high-school graduates declined another three points this year.

In spite of Sesame Street and Mattel Toys, the average child in California is receiving less than an average education. Many parents are beginning to shout for a return to the three R's, and to hell with the new math. The school dollar is getting thinner and thinner. And Johnny not only cannot read, he has just popped two bennies and stolen a car. Wilson Riles' request for more funds to invest in his "highly innovational" early childhood education program is met with skepticism by those who say he's asking for more money to do what he's supposed to have been doing all along.

Perhaps the most obvious yet forgotten criticism of our schools is that they are vestiges of another era. We have filled the classrooms with 20th century gadgetry—overhead projectors, reading machines, and more—yet we have failed to bring our system out of the agrarian past in which it was conceived.

Consider, for example, our school calendar. In California, schools are required to be open 175 days a year, which means they are closed for 190 days. At one time in our agrarian past, schools were closed during the late spring and summer months so that children could assist their agrarian parents in the planting and harvesting of crops. As late as the 1950s, rural school districts in California were allowed to close their schools several weeks early, in mid-May, and reopen in early October so that farmers could get their crops harvested and migrant families could make their annual treks along the verdant valleys of California.

Still, today, in 1975, we continue to artificially close our schools in June to accommodate the family farmer who doesn't hardly exist, and reopen in September as if all our children had participated in the harvest.

Economically, the closing of our schools for three months in the summer is one of the biggest wastes of tax dollars continuing into the last quarter of this century. Not only do entire school plants sit empty and idle for the summer, a massive labor force of 600,000 teachers, administrators and support staff in California continue to receive their paychecks for an obviously reduced workload, or no workload at all. In addition, parents, who in another era welcomed the return of their children to the routine of farm life, must now scurry about locating babysitters or summer camps to help them out of their situation, as both parents in a many families now work to make ends meet. With more than 51 percent of the female population now actively employed, one wonders who stays at home from June to September to supervise the children.

Today, even many professional educators are questioning the necessity for such a long vacation. Psychologists insist children do not need that kind of time for pure recreation. Learning or the desire to learn does not simply disappear towards the end of May. If students' attention begins to stray, it is perhaps only because both they and the teachers have grown to expect the long vacation. Given the fact that students will someday find themselves in jobs where they will work from 240 to 250 days a year rather than 175, it might be wise for our educational institutions to ease them into that type of work schedule.

Related to this antiquated school calendar is the entire issue of school finance. The California courts have told us in the Serrano v. Priest decision that our present method of financing public schools is unconstitutional. They are suggesting, perhaps, that the local property tax is neither a fair nor an adequate way to fund education. And since teacher and staff salaries constitute more than 80 percent of school costs, it is impossible to separate the salary issue from the overall question of school finance.

Just as in the case of the 19th century school calendar, teachers' salaries are based on a 19th century premise that somehow educators were to be set apart from the rest of the working class. We have come from a time when most teachers were women, and often second-income earners in a family, to a period when teacher groups are militantly taking to the streets to demand a fair wage and better working conditions.

What in fact do teachers earn in California? Salaries can begin as low as $7,200 a year and reach a statewide average of $12,000. This isn't too bad for 175 work days. The real issue and the reason for the strikes, however, is the fact that after a minimum of five years of college a teacher in California earns less than most truck drivers, firefighters, correctional officers, and craft workers. Teachers are faced with the dilemma of choosing between days off or a decent wage.

Among the general public, there appears to be little sympathy for teachers. Inevitably the antiquated school calendar emerges. The teacher's three months of summer vacation, two weeks for Christmas, a week for Easter, explode in the face of the so-called "working stiff" who has to be satisfied with a couple of weeks off every year. He finds it difficult to sympathize with the teacher. To the taxpayer, teachers are overpaid and under-worked.

The reality is that teachers are actually overworked because their work is crammed into 175 days a year, their classrooms are overcrowded, and their salaries are spread over a 12-month period.

The requirement that teachers attend classes on college campuses during the summer months only adds insult to injury because at their own expense they must fulfill unit requirements by taking watered-down courses invented by schools of education to entertain teachers during the summer.

Not every ill in our school system can be solved by taking a more updated approach to the school calendar but it certainly would be a beginning. We could make much better use of our school facilities by extending the 175-day school year. And, to bring some relief to the state at the same time we are extending the school year, it might be possible to cut a year or two off secondary schools. The State of California must deal with these issues, or our declining ranking among the states of this nation with respect to amount of our educational investment, will have no end.

New Decision Makers In Education

The Sacramento Bee, **June 9, 1978**

T he collective bargaining law for public school employees in California
is less than two years old, yet several significant trends appear to be
emerging. These trends may lead opponents to call for termination of the law
while supporters seek expansion.

The Educational Employment Relations Act (EERA) of January 1976 gives
public school employees the right to seek to bargain collectively with their
employers (local school district governing boards) on matters related to "wages
and other terms and conditions of employment."

As stated in the preamble of the law by the author of the bill, Sen. Albert
S. Rodda of Sacramento: "The legislature intends that it is the purpose of
this chapter to promote the improvement of personnel management and
employee-employer relations within the public-school systems in the State of
California . . ."

What has emerged during the last two years, however, falls somewhat short
of this noble intention. There are four factors which may determine whether, in
the eyes of the taxpayers, the law succeeds or fails within the next few years:

- It would appear that a third entity, separate and distinct from the employer
  and employees in any given school district, is acquiring an especially
  significant role in the collective-bargaining process. This entity is a cadre
  of individual lawyers, law firms, and special consultants which have
  descended on the educational establishment like *post-bellum* carpetbaggers
  into the Deep South.

- Contrary to the hopeful expectations of the Legislature and the citizenry, there has been little decline in the number of strikes or work stoppages by public school employees.
- Most practitioners under the new law, namely lawyers and consultants representing both employers and employee organizations, make little distinction between private-sector and public-sector collective bargaining.
- Perhaps most significantly, an unsuspecting public is by design or its own apathy, losing control of its local school districts.

These elements hold the potential for disrupting the entire process of public education in California. Yet, none is so out of control as to warrant fundamental changes in the current law at this point.

When EERA was being debated by the Legislature, it was humorously referred to as the Lawyers Unemployment Act. The Educational Employment Relations Board (EERB) itself, with its procedural rules and regulations added to the already complex statute, initiated the first job opportunities for lawyers. Each of the three board members has two personal legal counsel. This, added to the general counsel's staff of hearing officers, totals 20 lawyers on the 31 member professional staff.

Thus the agency entrusted with the implementation of the new law signaled to the parties appearing before it that its approach would be almost entirely legalistic.

Private law firms are doing a land-office business as a result of the collective bargaining law. Records indicate the law firm of Breon, Galgani and Godino had 63 cases before the EERB in the first full year of the law. In addition to representing school districts at $140 an hour in unit disputes and unfair-labor-practice cases, the law firm also negotiates contracts and handles other legal matters for school districts ranging in size and diversity from Lodi Unified to San Francisco Unified.

The law firm of Paterson and Taggart, which employs perhaps more lawyers and para-legals than the EERB itself, had 58 cases before the EERB. With their fleet of private airplanes they are able to fly from Placerville to Coachella Valley, representing school districts in all aspects of collective bargaining.

There are numerous other law firms and individual lawyers soliciting clients among the 1,172 school districts of the state. The services they provide are by no means of poor quality. The question really is whether these services are necessary and should be subsidized by the general public.

On the other side of the bargaining table sit lawyers hired by the employee organizations. The California Teachers Association and the California School Employees Association, for instance, have staff and contract lawyers representing local chapters in hearings before the EERB throughout the state.

One private firm, VanBourg, Allen, Weinberg and Rogers, was involved in 21 cases before the EERB in the first year of the act. Here, too, the quality of counsel is equal to that of the firms representing school districts. The question again is: *Is it necessary?*

Beyond the emergence of the lawyers as crucial elements in the public-sector collective-bargaining law, there are groups of consultants, advisory firms, publishing companies, and others offering services to either school districts or employee organizations.

These groups—along with the Educational Employment Relations Board itself and other state agencies such as the State Conciliation Service—constitute a third element in what traditionally had been a two-part system involving only employer and employ organizations.

Probably as a result of the overdependence on the legal profession by the parties and the built-in adversary process, the law has not reduced the number of strikes, as was hoped. John Auerback, in a study of the legal profession, cites the main reason why the practice of law itself leads to the type of confrontation resulting in labor strife: "The adversary system, with two small combatants in every ring, is ill equipped to consider the social good beyond the implicit assumption that every fight and any winner is good for society."

From the enactment of the law in 1976 up to the opening of school in 1977, there were 19 strikes. In the previous year there had been only 10 strikes.

Ironically, the largest strike during the first year of the act occurred in the San Juan School District in the legislative district of Sen. Rodda, author of the collective-bargaining law. This prompted the senator to say that teachers, "are violating the intent of the law, that strikes are illegal . . . it also could generate adverse public attitude towards teachers because I don't think the public is in sympathy with the strike."

There is little doubt the public, and most of the press, are opposed to strikes by public employees. Labor leaders have their work cut out if they intend to convince the public that strikes by teachers and civil servants are justified.

As yet, the Legislature and the governor remain unconvinced the teacher collective—bargaining bill, or the new state statute (Dills SB 839) giving similar rights to state employees, grants the right to strike. The existing Labor Code Sec. 923 and subsequent case law hold strikes by public employees to be illegal. The fact is, however, that a strike occurs with or without the sanction of statute or common law whenever enough employees stay off the job.

A real issue here is a political one. Both the employee organizations must surely realize what the public mood is. When a national television audience views striking firemen standing idly by with picket signs as a neighborhood of houses burns to the ground, little sympathy for the strikers' cause is generated. By the same token, management in many instances has expressed a very uncooperative attitude in situations where it almost appeared they hoped a strike would occur so they would win public sympathy.

Management has used other devices, too. There is little doubt that Superintendent Robert Alioto's decision to delay the opening of school in San Francisco last fall was viewed as a management lock-out which co-opted the teachers strike potential. It was a skillful maneuver that often has been used in the private sector.

The third observation about the law is that lawyers, consultants, and some employees of public agencies tend to make little distinction between the private sector and the public sector. This failure comes from the evolution of collective bargaining over the years.

As a result of the early history and development of formal labor-management relations in private industry—years of turmoil, violence and economic strife—a body of behavioral and symbolic myths evolved. These myths persist and may indeed result in behavior, from both sides, that reflects an attitude born of another age.

The players in the private sector are almost pushed into a role they feel they must play. This role is one of suspicion, mistrust and sometimes hostility and contentiousness born of a more violent age.

Unfortunately, these myths and attitudes have found their way into the public sector. With the advent of formal public-sector labor relations structurally similar to the private sector, it is only natural that management and employee organizations would enlist legal counsel, consultants and organizers with backgrounds in collective bargaining, backgrounds almost always acquired in the private sector.

This has had significant effects on the fledgling law in California because public-sector collective-bargaining does not support the transplantation of the attitudes and many behavioral myths brought to it by the more militant private-sector actors. As a result, it seems that both management and employee organizations have failed to distinguish between what is accepted practice in the private sector and what ultimately will be accepted in the public sector.

The most glaring error made by both sides in public-sector relations is the failure to recognize the significant presence, if not role, of the public. There are strategic alternatives in private industry that do not exist in the public sector.

For example, in the private sector management may abandon its position, indeed abandon its very existence. Bankruptcy, termination of the corporation itself, the total rejection of labor's presence in the industry, the right-to-work concept, all are possible alternatives such as transferring the business off-shore to avoid unions.

That is not the case in the public sector. Governmental services established either by statute or the Constitution must be provided to the public until the Legislature or the people themselves wish to repeal those services. There is no way a school district in this state can choose not to offer an education to its citizens.

The Constitution requires it. Schools will not be shut down. Fire Departments will not be eliminated. Public hospitals will not cease to exist.

When labor costs become prohibitive in the private sector, the assembly plant is moved to Taiwan or Hong Kong or Mexico. This is not possible in the public sector, for it is the people who create the need or demand the service that public employees are paid to provide.

Those entrusted with making public-sector collective bargaining work should never fail to recognize this element. A clear distinction must be made between private and public sector labor-management relations.

This leads us to the fourth problem, the fact that an unsuspecting and apathetic public may be losing control of local school districts. In a recent conference on the public's role in teacher-contract negotiations sponsored by the League of Women Voters, Dr. Charles Cheng, an authority in the field of public-sector bargaining, expressed the view that "labor-relations experts are becoming the decision makers in education."

Cheng, an assistant professor of urban education policy and planning at the University of California, Los Angeles, said he "is a strong advocate of collective bargaining for teachers and considers it a progressive step." But he said it should be viewed as a means not the end in itself.

"As more issues are placed on the negotiating table there is a tendency to involve fewer and fewer people in the process," he said.

In an article published in the *Harvard Educational Review,* Cheng warned of the erosion of public interest in education as collective bargaining emerges:

"This process has been accompanied by one other major development: The rise, over the last decade, of a new class of professionals consisting of union staff, board of education negotiators, and neutral third parties (arbitrators and mediators). This new class has used collective bargaining to attain a strategic position in public-education decision-making."

"And, as the scope of bargaining has expanded, community groups have discovered that these new professionals comprise yet another impenetrable layer in the educational power structure. The community, then, is no closer to the educational decision-making process than before."

What Cheng and others are concluding is that in addition to labor experts counseling both sides during the negotiation process, the entrance of third party neutrals as mediators, arbitrators and fact finders in public-sector labor disputes might be harmful, for it places "the final decision-making authority in the hands of persons not accountable to the public interest."

The conclusion is that the process may weaken political democracy in that elected officials have abdicated responsibility either by failure to resolve the dispute locally or by the imposition of higher authority, such as the state, in the resolution of disputes. Cheng suggests several reforms such as "encouraging unions and boards to seek community input during the formation of bargaining demands." He asks that citizens be allowed to view negotiations in open bargaining sessions. This last suggestion is anathema to labor-relations professionals schooled in the ways of private-sector bargaining with its roots in the 19th century where business was conducted behind closed doors.

Sentiment is so strong against the fish-bowl bargaining concept that when the EERB adopted a modest set of rules implementing the public-notice provisions of the Educational Employment Relations Act, the action was severely criticized by employee organizations and management alike. In one publication, an employee organization suggested the rules might sound the doom for collective bargaining.

Opponents of the EERB action complained the rules would allow a complaint to be filed by "any individual who is a resident of the school district involved in the complaint or who is the parent or guardian of a student in the school district or is an adult in the school district." Of course the opponents did not consider that the individual taxpayer could have an interest in the matter.

The rule further declares it is the policy of the board to encourage the parties to comply voluntarily with *Article 8, Public Notice,* and that "these rules and regulations provide for expedited proceedings to protect the right of the public to receive notice, to have full opportunity to express its views to the public-school employer and to know the positions of its elected representatives."

It is amazing to realize that in this post-Watergate period of American history, public employers are fearful of allowing the public, in a modest fashion, to understand what is going on in public-sector collective bargaining.

It should be apparent to public-sector labor-relations participants that a new dawn has come. Groups such as the League of Women Voters, Common Cause, Nader's Raiders, and Public Advocates are, with great success, guaranteeing the public no longer will be kept in the dark about government actions.

The sooner the practitioners in public-sector bargaining realize they are in the 20th century and the old ways may no longer be appropriate, the sooner there may be peaceful solutions to public sector labor disputes.

On the whole, the new law has been a success. EERB records indicate that in the 1,172 school districts in the state there have been 1,800 to 2,000 voluntary recognitions of employee organizations by management, no doubt because of generally good prior relationships between employees and employers. Additionally, 700 to 1,000 contracts have been signed without disruption of the educational process. Importantly, the actual number of strikes during the first 18 months of the EERA is not significant when compared to the number of peaceful settlements.

What is of concern is that in all but one of the strikes the employ organizations failed to exhaust the very administrative remedies for which they lobbied so heavily when the Legislature was considering the measure. Unless the administrative-impasse procedures (mediation and fact finding) are used to the fullest extent by the parties, there may be rough sailing ahead for those seeking to expand collective bargaining in the public sector.

The Controversy Over Bilingual Education Continues: Take the Broader View of Real Benefits to U.S.

The Sacramento Bee, September 10, 1978

F or Chicano educators whether one supports bilingual education or not has become somewhat of a litmus test of one's solidarity with the Chicano movement, just as black leaders are evaluated by whether or not they support school busing. Unfortunately, both the question of bilingual education and busing appear to have more political significance than any real relevance to the fundamental educational needs of children. Supporters of both causes too often rely on the rhetoric of social movements while opponents worry more about fiscal responsibility.

Unfortunately, too, in both the case of busing and bilingual education, the educational establishment is being asked by politicians to solve societal problems caused by a 200-year history of racial isolation, unequal educational opportunities, and prejudice towards new arrivals to this country. More recently, legislative bodies have been required to bite the bullet after such major court decisions as Brown vs. the Board of Education, which ruled that there should be equal educational opportunity across the land, and Lau vs. Nichols which decreed school districts are compelled to provide children who speak little or no English with special language programs which will give them equal opportunity in education.

Laws have now been passed both at the federal and state levels in attempts to comply with court rulings and foster the concept of equal education programs. Forty-three million dollars of state and federal money are spent yearly in

California with the result that both supporters and opponents of bilingual education conclude that the money is not being well spent in a majority of the programs throughout the state.

Various reports such as the recent study issued by the U.S. Office of Education do not give bilingual education very high marks. What is unfortunate about the blanket condemnation by the study is that it fails to consider the politics of the issued and how this affects the success or failure of any such categorical aid program which is funded separately from the rest of the education programs of a given school district.

First, one must consider whether or not the people at the top support or even understand the concept of bilingual education. In California the highest level Chicano educators and most of the Chicano legislators have long felt that State Superintendent of Public Instruction Wilson Riles has never truly been a supporter of bilingual education. They cite his almost yearly change of leadership of the bilingual office at the State Department of Education. In the last three years there have been an equal number of directors of the bilingual office. Critics of the superintendent conclude that such musical chairs approach to leadership can only lead to continued confusion in the field.

Additionally, it is no secret that many county superintendents and school principals are not sympathetic to the program and do little to guarantee any success. Faced with declining enrollments among Anglo students (just the opposite of what is occurring with Hispanics) and pressured by the large teacher organizations such as the California Teachers Association that have never been supporters of bilingual programs, school administrators have put many unqualified and non-bilingual teachers into bilingual programs in order to solve their teacher surplus problems. The result is that politics of a labor relations nature has been more of a factor in the controversy over bilingual education than any real consideration of the true value of bilingualism to American society.

True bilingual education is not supposed to be merely the teaching of English to non-English speaking students, nor is it intended to be solely a maintenance program for the dominant language group. It is supposed to have the result of making the child, ethnic or Anglo, fluent in two languages and familiar with the basic cultural elements of the people who speak both of the languages. True bilingualism is not designed merely so that Spanish and Chinese speaking children can succeed in an English speaking society or so that they can successfully enter the "American mainstream." This so-called "American mainstream" according to the 1970 census had 33.2 million people in it "who speak a language other than English as a native tongue, Spanish, German and Italian being the most dominant in that order."

What many educators and politicians fail to see is the broader picture that bilingual education offers this country. While they haggle over achievement gains or whether the data is accurate in assessing the program, they fail to make any true commitment to the need for bilingual, bicultural individuals in our society.

For while the world is getting smaller and smaller for us, and the Japanese and West Germans prosper after the loss of a world war, and the victor of that war's Yankee dollar continues to plummet, we still wonder why some people view us as ugly Americans. Japan and West Germany were occupied countries after the war. Businessmen, politicians, students were forced to become bilingual to survive. Americans, on the other hand, built isolated colonies for their people living abroad. The Japanese checker working in a PX store on an American military base in Kyoto makes change in English. American residents of the Panama Canal Zone seldom socialize with Panamanians.

Now it all begins to hit home. Bilingualism is not only a good idea for giving Chinese and Chicano children and others an equal opportunity to survive in our public schools. Certainly it makes more sense to allow a child to continue learning in whatever language that he or she can, rather than to wait a few years until fluency allows the student to join the rest of the class. Arithmetic is neither English nor Spanish., but a universal language.

But more important than these obvious educational issues to this country should be the idea that these 33.2 million Americans who have not melted into the "mainstream" have much to offer this country. They have much to offer in the development of a more meaningful and effective foreign policy and foreign trade.

The State Department has just now embarked on a crash program of affirmative action hiring because, among other things, only 173 (1.4 percent) of its 12,467 employees are Latinos. There would be no need for these types of aggressive programs that often irritate the Anglo community and patronize minority groups, if our educators and politicians would take a more practical view of bilingual-bicultural education rather than only quibbling over the economic and racial politics of the issue. No one wants to see money being wasted on a poor program. On the other hand, there has to be a more enlightened commitment to the basic philosophy of bilingualism and a realization that there is a need for it in our ever-shrinking world where a global economy is emerging. There are already 33 million people in our midst who are our greatest resource.

Whose Level Playing Field?
Attack on Affirmative Action

Hispanic Link News Service, **February 1995**

A speaker at the affirmative action workshop at the recent National Council of la Raza conference in Dallas perhaps put it best when referring to affirmative action: "I got into college because of affirmative action, but I also know I didn't get out of college because of affirmative action." The issue continues to surface as it did again recently in California.

As dozens of speakers noted at last weeks University of California Regents' meeting where the issue of race-based admission to its campuses was debated, affirmative action programs have helped the country deal with the diversity that has become so much a part of the American population. But despite the arguments, the Regents voted 14 to 10 to end affirmative action for student admissions and university hiring. The UC system of nine campuses and 162,000 students, one of the country's largest systems, is perhaps the most diverse in the nation, with a student body made up of 52% white, 23% Asian, 12% Hispanic, 4% black, and one percent Native American. This diversity has occurred as a result of affirmative action programs begun in the Sixties when the institution was almost all white. Yet, even with these affirmative action programs now under attack, which have resulted in this diversified student body and faculty, the university still continues to be the premier public university system in the nation.

What particularly offended the nine campus Chancellors, the President of the system and the entire Faculty Senate of the university, who all opposed the Regents' actions, was the fact that Republican Governor Pete Wilson was promoting the end of race-based admissions, not because of academic concerns or fairness issues, but because of his own political agenda. Jesse Jackson, of the Rainbow Coalition, was perhaps the toughest on Wilson's seemingly insensitive quest for the Republican presidential nomination at the Regents' meeting.

Wilson, a bland, unimaginative politician, has succeeded for nearly three decades in gaining election to office by pushing the "hot buttons" during a campaign, without reference to right nor reason. Starting off as mayor of San Diego in the 60s and then as state assemblyman, Wilson always sought to incite the voters. In his 1990 gubernatorial campaign against Diane Feinstein, he ran against the "Big Green" environmental initiative that brought in big dollars for Wilson from farmers, land developers, and oil interests and succeeded in burying Feinstein. In his 1994 re-election bid against Kathleen Brown, Wilson was again the leading spokesperson for the anti-immigrant Proposition 187. Now, he is already running for the U.S. presidency on the back of the "Stop Affirmative Action" proposition which has not yet been given a number for the 1996 presidential election in California.

Wilson's entire political career has been a no-substance, anti-anything, push the hot button strategy. He even supported abortion rights when it was popular and is now back peddling as fast as he can on that issue. He is unruffled by logic or principle. He appears not to be bothered by consistency since in his first term as governor, he signed over a dozen laws that included pro-affirmative action language.

But let us return to the University of California's race-based admission issue. Opponents of affirmative action, led by black Regent, Ward Connally, a Wilson affirmative action appointee, argued that, "affirmative action was polarizing the nation and needed to be curtailed." Supporters of the position argued that by now, the playing field had been leveled and minorities were just as capable of reaching the same entrance test scores and having the necessary grades for admission as white students were.

These Regents, including Governor Wilson, are either naive or ignorant. Even though Wilson proclaimed that, "we can't tolerate policies that trample on individual rights," he, as governor, is ultimately responsible for the failure of elementary and secondary public school systems that have dropped the state from number one to number forty-one in the nation in educational attainment of the state's children. All of this during his watch.

Test scores have plummeted, funding has been reduced to the lowest percentage of any state, and the states' school districts are in a shambles, especially those serving non-white children. As white flight has occurred from the inner cities to the ever more distant suburbs, large inner city school districts such as Los Angeles, San Francisco and Oakland in California, are left with schools unable to cope with the depression and despair that usually follows. Educator Kenneth Clark once noted at another point of crisis in U.S. education that, "ghetto/barrio schools regularly succeed in lowering the IQ's and intellectual curiosity of their pupils." They do so because many of the children who pass through their doors enter already intellectually handicapped as a result of poverty, violence, and neglect in the home and neighborhood environment.

If anyone believes that the educational playing field is level for inner city children, or migrant children, or immigrant children, then they are as foolish as Pete Wilson. The dropout rate is 52% and 46% respectively for black and Hispanic children in Los Angeles Unified. Every other indicator of educational achievement is equally as outrageous. And while we can blame, parents, society, the system, we certainly cannot blame the children.

Uncle-Tomism reached a new level when black Regent Connally offered his end to affirmative action proposal to the Regents of the University of California. It proclaimed that affirmative action caused polarization, when in fact it has been politicians like Wilson who fan the fires of polarization and use tokens like Connally to make it acceptable.

Instead, an integrated and diversified student body and faculty in the nation's most intellectually successful public university system has, in fact, moved the system toward the 21st Century. U.C. President J. W. Peltason put it correctly when he said, "We are a public institution in the most demographically diversified state in the nation . . . Our affirmative action and other diversity programs more than any other single factor, have helped us prepare California for the future . . . ."

But what appears to lie ahead for the state and the nation is another political campaign issue pushed by those presidential candidates who seek to win the middle and right wing votes at the expense of millions of worthy students in this country, students whose test scores ought to be given a handicap because of the conditions under which many of them have had to attend public schools. The equality of educational opportunity at urban, suburban and rural schools should ultimately be the test of equal playing fields. Politicians like Pete Wilson should be seeking to improve opportunity, instead of trying to make political points by pretending to defend individual rights. When we can say that our public schools are equal in giving each student equal opportunity to learn, then we can focus on test scores and other criterion. To abandon these students because of our own inadequacies as a nation in providing equal educational opportunity is the ultimate folly. We should ask ourselves why our playing fields have become the killing fields of our inner city children.

Conclusion

It has been a little more than 30 years since I published the first articles contained in this book. Over the years I have written continuously on political issues, foreign affairs, education topics, and Latino and U.S. cultural issues in general. It is interesting to note that many of those topics that I first dealt with years ago are still with us. The political excesses dealing with lobbyists' influence in the legislative halls of the country continue as a problem today. The Abramoff affair is a good example of the continuing problem. And what can we say about the shenanigans relative to redistricting. The Tom DeLay meddling that resulted in the Republican control of the Congress is a prime example of how broken the system is as we continue to allow the very politicians, the proverbial foxes in the hen-house, continue to control the process.

I wrote early on the emerging political strength of the Latino community in this country. From the days in 1973 when, Richard Alatorre, Joe Montoya, and I joined the only two Latino legislators serving in the California Assembly, forming the original Latino Caucus, to today when 27 Latino members now serve, Latinos have come a long way. The last three Speakers of the Assembly in California have been Latinos and we have the first statewide Constitutional officer in Lt. Governor Cruz Bustamante. Antonio Villarraigosa has also been elected mayor of the second largest city in the country. The future looks bright for Latinos politically, but it is yet to be seen how both national political parties will embrace these new voters.

In terms of the Latino social and cultural issues that I have written about over the years, it is a positive note that labor leader César Chávez, since his death in 1993, has joined the pantheon of American heroes. Schools, libraries, highways, government buildings now proudly carry his name, a far cry from the attacks and abuses he often suffered during his lifetime. Co-founder of the UFW, Dolores

Huerta, is now an honored and sought-after speaker around the country on the significant social issues still facing the nation like immigrant-bashing, hate crimes, the rights of workers and much more. I have also recorded the country's acceptance and even celebration of Cinco de Mayo and Hispanic Heritage Month as relevant to the ongoing rediscovery of our American heritage. I continue to note, however, that much of the media in this country still does not give due recognition to the Latino community as it has emerged as the largest cultural group in the nation, probably now numbering more than 45 million, and growing at a rate that will make them the majority in such states as California by mid-century.

While many of the articles I wrote on foreign affairs, most of them dealing with the turmoil in Latin America during the 1980s are certainly dated, the fact is, that that part of the globe continues to be of great importance to our country. Unfortunately, the present administration, and most administrations of both political parties, have never truly paid attention to this part of the world, a region that we have called "the good neighbors" for more than a century. We seem only to focus on the region when it suits us, or when we feel threatened. The fact that we give more foreign aid to little Israel than we do to the entire continent of South America and Central America, is indicative of what we value in our foreign policy. The tepid relationships we have with most of the countries in Latin America continues to reflect a modicum of arrogance on our part. The issues of immigration from the south, NAFTA and CAFTA, the Cuban embargo, continuous drug proliferation, and a myriad of social issues affecting our relationship with Latin America have not been addressed by our country in any significant manner. Hopefully, future administrations will give this part of the world the attention it deserves.

And, of course, the War with Iraq that I anticipated in an article written just prior to Bush's invasion of that country continues today. More than 23,000 young Americans have been wounded or killed in that conflict that is turning into a civil war rather than our promised model of a new democratic society as an example for the region. Billions of dollars are being spent monthly on this war that has become the quagmire of our own time as Vietnam was a quarter century ago. Instead of using our American tax dollars to do good in the world, to end hunger, disease, illiteracy, we build and send bombs to the middle east for the destruction of the homes of both enemies and friends, and unfortunately, the death of their children.

Finally, as an educator, I wrote about some of the issues of concern over the years that were resulting in the decline of our public school system in this country. Unfortunately, many of those issues are still with us. Our school calendar is impractical. Our children need more time in school, not more time to play video games and run the streets. Our education should be creative, vigorous and effective. Our model for public school education is two centuries old. It is in drastic need of an overhaul. We continue to fall behind the educational systems in most of the industrialized world. Latinos, as a group, have clearly demonstrated that they are very concerned about the education of their children. Natives and immigrants alike fully understand that a sound education is the stepping-stone for leading productive lives in this country. The nation needs to act now, before we lose too many more youngsters to the idleness and danger found on many of our streets.

I hope that with this collection of articles, I have stimulated some thought and opened the door for discussions of many of the important issues still facing this country as we move firmly into the twenty-first century. I continue to believe that if our citizens are unhappy with the direction the county is moving, it is never too late to dissent, dissent, dissent.

Appendix

Ex-lawmaker Opened Doors to Latinos

**By LEONEL MARTINEZ, Bakersfield Californian
contributing columnist**
Posted: Friday February 27th, 2004, 11:10 PM

A telling moment in the life of a political warrior: In the early 1990s, former state Assemblyman Ray Gonzales was in the last weeks of his unsuccessful political race against immensely popular 5th District County Supervisor Mary K. Shell.

Gonzales, who spent most of his life as an educator, had lost some important endorsements and his patience was wearing thin. More and more, he used terms like "hacienda Mexican," to describe the Latinos who opposed him. In a favorite Gonzales parable, he likened the critics to crabs in a bucket who could only drag their colleagues down. The story had some truth to it. It still does.

"A lot of Latinos are walking around bent over all the time," he muttered to me as he looked toward the floor of his worn campaign office at the Padre Hotel downtown. "And they don't even know they're bent over."

As a reporter, I covered that race. It would be Gonzales' last. After losing to Shell, he faded from the Kern County political scene, winding up as a professor at California State University, Monterey Bay. Now 65 years old, Gonzales recently announced his retirement.

But in an age when Latinos are finally ascending to political power throughout the nation, Gonzales' pioneering efforts should be etched in the memory of every Kern County resident.

In 1972, he made history by becoming the first Latino state legislator elected from the Central Valley. It wasn't Cruz Bustamante. It wasn't Dean Florez. It was a fourth-generation Mexican kid who was born in Bakersfield and had the audacity to take on the goliaths of local politics during a time when the good old boy network was closed to Latinos.

It didn't happen right away. Over a dish of huevos rancheros at the Arizona Café on Baker Street, not far from where he had his first campaign office, Gonzales recently reflected on a life of dissent.

In 1965, Gonzales became the first Latino faculty member at Bakersfield College. When he left, he submitted a resolution asking the Academic Senate to demand that 10 minority faculty be hired. They were hired the next year.

Also in the 1960s, he led a picket of the Bakersfield City School Board in an effort that forced the hiring of the first Hispanic principal at Mount Vernon School. Later that decade, he became president of a group that challenged the transfer of FCC licenses at Bakersfield radio and television stations, demanding that women and minorities be included in front of the camera. The effort was largely successful.

But all those were only a prelude to his win at the State Assembly. The times were not welcoming for Hispanics. When Gonzales ran for assemblyman of the 28th District, only 8 percent of his constituents were registered Latino voters. So he cobbled together a broad coalition that included Hispanics, blacks, educators and others, knowing that was his only shot at Sacramento.

"I didn't run as a Chicano," said Gonzales. "I ran as a Ph.D."

His Spartan office off Baker Street had only a pay phone because his campaign couldn't afford the $800 deposit for a private line. Gonzales' whole campaign cost $20,000. Many thought it was highly unlikely for a portly, liberal Latino to win election to the state Assembly. Much less possible, they thought, was Gonzales beating GOP incumbent Kent Stacey.

Others fought to make sure he didn't. One local politician warned that Gonzales and United Farm Workers union President Cesar Chavez were training guerrillas in the hills of Keene. The truth was less sensational. Chavez had offered his endorsement, and Gonzales had turned him down.

"I said, 'Don't endorse me publicly, but I need all your troops,'" recalled Gonzales.

The troops arrived, and Gonzales won, but by only a handful of votes.

As assemblyman, he immediately bucked the system by returning the checks he received after his election to the corporations who sent them. Gonzales also carried campaign reform legislation that created the Fair Political Practices Commission and voted against the death penalty.

Gonzales lost his bid for re-election, but even then, he wouldn't shut up. As chairman of the Kern County Latino Redistricting Coalition Committee, he attempted to design legislative and congressional districts that would have a Latino majority. The state Supreme Court accepted the coalition's recommendations, creating the new districts.

In 1990, Gonzales attempted to carry the banner for the Democratic Party in a Senate race against Don Rogers, but he lost. A couple of years later, he took on Supervisor Shell in a district he had fought to design and lost again.

"In retrospect, it was a very dumb thing to do," Gonzales admitted. "It was going to happen. We just didn't have to do it at that time."

Gonzales' timing may have been wrong, but more than a decade later, everyone can see the results of his redistricting efforts. If the names of the people who represent the districts carved out by his coalition sound familiar, it's because they are:

Supervisor Pete Parra. Assemblywoman Nicole Parra. Senator Dean Florez.

Gonzales helped open the door for each one, and he served in public office decades before them with healthy measures of political savvy and righteous anger at a system that once excluded Latinos.

What he did should not be forgotten.

Leonel Martinez is a former reporter for The Californian. His column appears every other Saturday.

Gonzales Ignores Taboos

By Susan Sward
Associated Press. Oct. 8, 1973

Sacramento *(AP)*—When Raymond Gonzales first arrived in Sacramento last January, the California Legislature struck him as "a convention of used car dealers."

From the start, the 35-year-old, Gonzales set a totally different tone for himself.

The Bakersfield Democrat quickly broke the legislators' unspoken taboo against members speaking publicly about lobbyists and behind-the-scenes legislative dealings.

He talked about the lobbyist gifts he kept—such as wine, fruit and nuts—and the lobbyist money he rejected. An ex-Marine who studied four years for the priesthood, Gonzales even suggested legislators use less profanity.

An avalanche of free tickets and passes were shoved into a desk drawer for use in a huge collage he plans to make at the end of the next legislative session.

Gonzales' behavior makes backroom manipulators shake their heads. He is somewhat like the lovable character James Stewart portrayed in the movie, "Meet John Doe"—a green, well-intentioned fellow who battled corrupt cigar-smoking politicians.

At the movie's climax, the character triumphs over Norton, a powerful king-maker. As a crowd clusters around Stewart, one of his supporters snaps: "That's the people, Norton. Try and beat that."

In the real world, California legislators get big campaign contributions from many of the 625 registered lobbyists, who buy testimonial dinner tickets usually costing from $25 to $250. Gonzales said he's planning to confine his fund-raising primarily to the voters of his district. Recently he held a hot dog feed that raised $1,000.

Not all lobbyists have bankrolls comparable to the thousands spent by some representatives for oil companies and banks, for example. Some struggle along with small budgets trying to help the disabled or welfare recipients.

For the first six months in Sacramento, Gonzales thought "about 10 guys I used to see all the time in halls were senators. You know, distinguished looking characters. One by one, I found out they were lobbyists."

Unhappy with what he saw, he introduced a bill to require lobbyists to specify which legislators they wined and dined and outlawing lobbyists gifts and contributions to legislators. The bill was killed by the Assembly Rules Committee, which passed another less restrictive lobbyists' control measure.

Meanwhile, the lobbyists still come to chat with him in his office (his rule) about legislation, Gonzales says.

As for the free tickets, Gonzales said, "I have a full drawer. I am seeing how many I can collect in my first term. You know, race track tickets, movie passes."

He said the only lobbyist money he has accepted is a $100 check from a source he refused to identify. He said he immediately signed the check over for use in a special election in Los Angeles, but he doesn't remember which election.

"The biggest problem is that legislators develop personal relationships with lobbyists. When you have a personal relationship you reach a point where you no longer know what motivates your action—whether it is based on fact or friendship."

"The most successful lobbyists here never talk legislation. They just do everything for you. You play cards with them, vacation with them. Then they become pals rather than lobbyists anymore."

Gonzales, a former Latin-American studies professor, said he's observed that he is not on the guest list "for obvious reason" when lobbyists take a group of legislators to Mexico.

An example of how lobbyists work, Gonzales said, occurred one night at a Sacramento restaurant.

"It was kind of shocking to go out on my wedding anniversary with my wife to a Sacramento restaurant and have a lobbyist offer to buy my dinner for me. I paid for it. That kind of thing never happened to me when I was a teacher."

Meanwhile, Gonzales' outspoken stance makes some of his colleagues wary about him. "Anytime you talk about members, you are kind of in a way violating the code of the club. I didn't know that when I first got here. I just reacted because things bothered me.

"But some legislators thought I was just headline-hunting. And a lot of people thought I was very naive because I didn't know the press was out to get me. Maybe some press people are. I don't know. Members get upset when the press writes about the kind of cars they lease," Gonzales said.

The Bakersfield Californian

Community Voices
Dr. Jess Nieto Filed: December 8, 1998

In a recent article in *the Californian,* reporter Vic Pollard described some of the activities undertaken by Kern County Latinos over the last two decades to improve political conditions. Pollard showed insight and respect in his article.

But sufficient credit should be give to Dr. Ray Gonzales as one of the individuals who helped lead the wave of changes that have occurred during the last 25 years or so. Gonzales has been a pioneer in providing leadership in political, educational, and civil rights issues in Kern County. In addition to being one of the first Latino educators at Bakersfield College in the mid-1960s, Gonzales was also one of the founding faculty members at Cal State University, Bakersfield in 1970.

In 1972, he astounded political figures in Bakersfield, Kern County, and California when he was elected to the California Legislature, the first Latino from the San Joaquin Valley. Later he served California and our country in a number of prominent positions as a member of the Public Employment Relations Board for California and as a Foreign Service Officer for the U.S. Department of State.

While in Bakersfield in the 1960s and 1970s, Gonzales participated in a number of organizations and efforts, as president of the Kern Council for

Civic Unity, which provided much needed leadership as an advocate for civil and minority rights.

When he returned to Bakersfield in the early 1990s, he again provided tremendous leadership in a number of efforts aimed at leveling the political playing field for Latinos. His leadership was invaluable to the redistricting work done by the Kern County Latino Redistricting Coalition which he established, especially in the design of the 5th District of the Board of Supervisors, and the design of the 20th and 21st Congressional districts as well as the 30th an the 32nd California Assembly districts and the 16th Senatorial District.

Gonzales, on behalf of the KCLRC, resisted efforts by the Mexican American Legal Defense Fund and even the Democratic Central Committee that wanted to take away from the potential gains of Kern County Latinos in favor of a stronger Fresno County Hispanic base. MALDEF, the Mexican American Political Association, and the California Democratic Party felt that it was useless to provide districts drawn to make them more representative of Latinos in Kern County since it was believed a Latino could not win here.

The State Supreme Court in 1992 said that the proposed, "changes by MALDEF (and the Democratic Party leadership) would unnecessarily divide Kern County." The Court also added that the proposed changes would, "risk possible challenge under Section 5 of the Federal Voting Rights Act by reducing the minority percentage of the new district(s) that includes Kings county and would conflict with the position of the Kern County Latino Coalition, which endorses the Masters' plans in this area." The KCLRC proposal, as represented by Gonzales as its chairman at the court hearing, was adopted by the State Supreme Court.

Although Gonzales suffered some political defeats as he attempted to win election to the Board of Supervisors and the 16th Senate District, his victories and contributions in the political arena far outweigh the individual losses he experienced. He has left his imprint with his invaluable contributions to Latinos, women, and civil rights. Bakersfield and Kern County are lucky to have Gonzales as one of their sons.

Author's Bio

R ay Gonzales began his teaching career at Bakersfield College in 1965 and subsequently taught at California State University at Long Beach, Bakersfield and Monterey Bay. Between his teaching years he served in the California Legislature, the first Latino elected from the San Joaquin Valley of California in 1972. He later served in the Jerry Brown Administration in Sacramento. From 1980 to 1989, he was a political officer and labor attaché in the foreign service of the United States, with tours of duty in Guatemala, Barbados, Belgium, and Washington, D.C., where he served as Director of State Department's Latin American Refugee Program. In 1993, he was appointed Director of Minority Recruitment for the U.S. Peace Corps by the Clinton Administration. In 1997 he returned to Cal State, Monterey Bay from where he retired in 2004. He earned his B.A. from San Francisco State, an M.A. from the University of the Americas in Mexico City, and a PH.D. in Latin American Studies from the University of Southern California. He has published more than 200 articles on such topics as U.S. foreign policy, education issues, the history and culture of Latinos in the U.S., and American politics and culture.